ARRESTED JUSTICE

ARRESTED JUSTICE

Black Women, Violence, and

America's Prison Nation

Beth E. Richie

NEW YORK UNIVERSITY PRESS
New York and London

NEW YORK UNIVERSITY PRESS
New York and London
www.nyupress.org

References to Internet websites (URLs) were accurate at the time of writing.
Neither the author nor New York University Press is responsible for URLs
that may have expired or changed since the manuscript was prepared.

Richie, Beth.
Arrested justice : black women, violence, and America's prison nation / Beth E. Richie.
p. cm.
Includes bibliographical references and index.
ISBN 978-0-8147-7622-3 (cl : alk. paper) -- ISBN 978-0-8147-7623-0 (pb : alk. paper) -- ISBN
978-0-8147-2391-3 (ebook) -- ISBN 978-0-8147-0822-4 (ebook)
1. African American women--Abuse of. 2. African American women--Violence against. 3.
African American women--Crimes against. 4. African American women--Social conditions. 5.
Abused women--United States. 6. Victims of crime--United States. 7. Violence--United States.
8. Crime--Sociological aspects. I. Title.
HV6626.2.R57   2012
362.82'9208996073--dc23   2011050459

New York University Press books are printed on acid-free paper,
and their binding materials are chosen for strength and durability.
We strive to use environmentally responsible suppliers and materials
to the greatest extent possible in publishing our books.

Manufactured in the United States of America
c   10 9 8 7 6 5 4 3 2 1
p   10 9 8 7 6 5 4 3 2 1

For my daughter, Ella, and my late mother, Beatrice.
They are my two beloved muses whose spirits open my heart every day.

Contents

Acknowledgments

I realize that almost everyone who ever finishes a book begins to think about the acknowledgements midway through the writing when they realize how long they have been at it, and how much longer it will take to finish. It either occurs to writers then or when they are challenged by long periods of distraction and start to worry that they will never be able to turn their attention back to writing. For me, it was midway through the writing when life circumstances distracted me and I realized that the only way that I could ever finish this book was to accept the generous support I was being offered, and to lean as graciously as possible on others for inspiration. Thankfully, I was given permission to step aside from the demands of daily life; I had the privilege of personal and institutional support; I was able to open myself to the profound twin muses of joy and heartbreak; and I just kept writing. I finished this book because of the generosity of others—the communities who inspired me politically, the friends and family who forgave my absences, those activist allies who lovingly challenged me to finish this project. Ultimately I did finish because of the urgent, courageous stories of Black women trying to survive violence within a prison nation, each of whom demanded that I get this book done. There are a lot of people to acknowledge, and I am very grateful to each of them.

Early in the writing of this book, one of my greatest muses, Ella Carmen Cohen-Richie, was born and came home to help raise my partner,

Cathy J. Cohen, and me to be her parents. Quite literally, Ella brought new life to my world; helping me to renew my commitment to writing about Black women and male violence *while at the same time* deepening my appreciation for the important daily routines of playing, dancing, and singing with those that I love. She has been a wonderfully huge distraction and a mighty motivation for this book. Ella, Cathy, and I are so lucky to share our family routines with a large community. My ability to be a parent while writing a book was only possible because of the cadre of aunties and uncles, cousins, babysitters, and playmates, teachers and wise friends who helped out along the way. Norma Gabb, Fallon Wilson, Luz Perez, LaTosha Traylor, Perla Lopez, and Leigh Richie were particularly dear to Ella, and therefore to me. The Black Girls' Group that Fallon facilitated (which we called Just a Sister Away) provided a steady group of family friends to learn and grow up with. Just down the block were our constant companions, Nate and his parents Jill and Laura, Katie and her parents Lynn and Todd, Nyla and her parents Amanda and Tyrone, Niama and Sage and their parents Shelley and Omar, Malcolm and his parents Garland and Michelle, and our neighbor Stephanie and her mother Doriane, all of whom kept the play-life in our home joyful and interesting. I appreciate the other adults who brought needed distractions during the years that I was writing this book. I am grateful for the meals, the discussions, and the invitations to the parties and events. And I am also grateful that my communities understood when I could not show up. My appreciation for the company and for the understanding goes to Catlin and Sansi Fullwood, Jason, Asha, Peter, and Barbara Ransby-Sporn, Willa Taylor and Mary Morten, Kimberly Smith and Michelle Lawrence, Tracye Matthews, Lynette Jackson, Barbara Phillips and Robert Howard, Jane B. Jacobs and William Ayers and Bernadine Dohrn.

I am grateful for the longevity of my friendships with P. Catlin Fullwood, Suzanne Pharr, Kata Issari, Katherine Acey, Nan Stoops, Dana Ain Davis, Sue Osthoff, and especially Valli Kalei Kanuha. Even though I saw these sister-friends less frequently than I wanted to during the years I was writing, I held tightly to their support as well as their wisdom. You see, this group of friends is much more than that; we share deep political values, strong intellectual commitments, and a history of organizing against violence against women of color. They were able (and willing) to keep me focused, and to help me remember what needed to be said. The book and the process of writing it would have been very different if they had not been alongside me as I wrote. They were my earliest writing group and are my final community of accountability about the history of the anti-violence movement, and the promise of doing more radical work in much better ways than we have. These women make writing a book about growing up in a social justice movement as much about praxis as it is about principle; as much about commitments to social change as it is about building and sustaining community.

Indeed, this loving and loyal group of friends and I grew up as feminists and anti-racist activists with others who populated key organizations that serve as the scaffolding of anti-violence activism during the 30-year time period that this book covers. I appreciate the National Coalition Against Domestic Violence (P. Catlin Fullwood, Valli Kalei Kanuha, Nan Stoops), the Violence Intervention Project (Elsa Rios, Haydee Rosario, Evelyn Garcia, Grace Perez), New York Women Against Rape (Katherine Acey, Sandra Comacho), the Women's Leadership Institute (Susan Schechter, Barbara Hart), the Institute on Domestic Violence in the African American Community (Karma Cottman, Gretta Gardner, Tricia Bent-Goodley, Linner Ward Griffin, Robert L. Hampton, Shelia Hankins, Esther Jenkins, Johnny Rice, Joyce Thomas, Antonia A. Vann, Oliver J. Williams, Kelly Mitchell-Clark, William Oliver, William Riley, Loraine Haley, Marcus Pope, and Lynn Matthews), and the Battered Women's Justice Project (Ellen Pence, Sue Osthoff, Loretta Frederick). These groups, like Sisters of Color Ending Sexual Assault, A Call To Men, Men Stopping Violence, the National Network for Women in Prison, and the grassroots networks of women of color caucuses that work in coalition with larger national anti-violence organizations have created a strong platform for the anti-violence work that I describe in this book.

More recently, I have had the privilege to work with a radical organization, INCITE! Women of Color Against Violence. Born ten years ago out of frustration with the ways that the buildup of America's prison nation was co-opting the anti-violence movement, INCITE! continues to provide a space for radical discussions and organizing against the buildup of a prison nation. I proudly claim my association with INCITE! and I am deeply inspired by the feminist politics and commitment to community justice of my co-founding sisters—Michelle Erai, Mimi Kim, Isabel Kang, Julia Chinyere Oparah, Andrea Smith, Alisa Bierria, Clarissa Rojas, Nan Stoops, Kata Issari, Valli Kalei Kanuha, Andrea Ritchie, Jamie Jimenez, Jamie Lee Evans, Janelle White, and Paula Rojas. I have depended on INCITE!'s steadfast position in the landscape of organizations working to end violence against women, and I wrote this book hoping to contribute in some way to that.

I also leaned heavily on the national prison abolition group, Critical Resistance, which for the past ten years has been working alongside of INCITE! to change how we understand, and what we do about the state's commitment to building a prison nation. I learned a great deal about the importance of political clarity and strategic visioning from working with Critical Resistance; and I am grateful for the inspiration provided by Ruthie Gilmore, Angela Y Davis, Ari Wohlfeiler, Dylan Rodriquez, Rachel Herzing, Rose Braz, and Ellen Barry. They, like the local Chicago crew of Miriame Kaba, Shira Hassan, Erica Meiners, the women of CLAIM, the local INCITERs, and activist-author Jamie Kalven, are among those I thank for the deep inspiration and challenge to not just reform, but end the violence of a prison nation.

INCITE! and Critical Resistance are like the steady group of scholar activists who continue the work to push the limits of institutional constraints. In the academy, I have been fortunate to have friendships based on shared feminist projects and it helped me to be writing about violence and prisons alongside of Kimberlé Crenshaw, Gail Garfield, Valli Kalei Kanuha, Dana-Ain Davis, Kathy Boudin, Dorothy Roberts, Beverly Guy-Sheftall, Alisa Bierria, Aishah Shahidah Simmons, Natalie Sokoloff, Vickie Sides, Ann Russo, and Francesca Royster. These women and their writing on violence inspired mine, just as the movement for social justice education, critical race theory, queer studies, and feminisms of color have helped me ground this book in a kind of intellectual landscape that I can believe in.

At my own institution, the University of Illinois at Chicago, I am very fortunate to share intellectual space with an exceptionally strong group of faculty, administrators, and staff who believe that the mission of an urban public research university is to commit resources (intellectual and other) to social justice scholarship and community engagement. That commitment helped make the task of writing this book seem as important as the other duties for which an academic is typically responsible. For that, I thank my colleagues in the Departments of African American Studies, Criminology, Law, and Justice; and the Program in Gender and Women's Studies, as well as the staff of The Institute for Research on Race and Public Policy, who are among the most dedicated scholar activists that I know. Key among those who work on topics related to this book are Barbara Ransby, Michelle Boyd, Francesca Gaiba, Lynette Jackson, Laurie Schaffner, Lisa Yun Lee, William Ayers, David Stovall, Alice Kim, Kevin Kumashiro, John D'Emilio, Cynthia Blair, Amanda Lewis, Tyrone Forman and Lisa Frohmann. They are the kind of scholars that I want to be, and the kind of friends I want to keep. Some university administrators as well offered support during key moments when the balance between writing, teaching, and being an administrator was challenging: Thank you, Dean Dwight McBride; Dean Michael Pagano; and former Provost Michael Tanner. And, of course, there are my students and the student workers who I have had the benefit of working with: Vickii Coffey, LaDonna Long, Tracy Smith, Yvonne Isom, Fallon Wilson, Aarati Kasturirangan, Meg King, Lisa P. Jones, Ericka Adams, Rhoda Rae Gutierrez, Delaina Washington, and Iliana Figueroa. Anyone who has been around my office for the past five years knows how much I have depended on LaTosha Traylor for research assistance, editing work, computer help, and helping to provide order to my writing life when it was getting out of control. LaTosha improved this book in countless ways, and alongside Delaina Washington, Catlin Fullwood, and Carla Plambeck, I could not have completed it without her assistance. Thank you also to Ilene Kalish, my editor at NYU Press who, for the second time now, believed in my writing and helped me turn my sometimes random ideas into a book. She, along with Aiden Amos, weathered the distractions to my writing with just the right balance of anticipation and understanding; checking in and following up with interest and advice just when I needed them.

One of the most profound events that occurred while working on this book is the passing of my beloved mother, Beatrice Jourdain Richie. As I was writing, I watched her live with and fight back against cancer for almost a year. After she passed away, I felt a deeper sadness than I have ever known. At the same time, I was inspired by my mother's unimaginable strength, reminded of how unusual and important my connection to my family is, and gained a fuller appreciation for the fragility of life; all of which deepened my resolve to write in a dignified way about suffering, resistance, and change. My writing really slowed down, but my heart opened and my life profoundly changed. Faith communities helped and so did extended family and friends, who reached out constantly. But what really got me through the pain and back to writing was my mother herself and lessons from the rest of my family.

I appreciate my father, Winston H. Richie, and what he taught me about commitment to people he loves and to ideas about justice. I am grateful to my brother, Winston H. Richie, Jr., and my sisters, Laurel J. Richie and Anne C. Richie for the ways that each of them is smart in ways that I am not and because we have learned to "keep each other close" even when we are far away and times are hard. My sister-in-law, Charlotte, brother-in-law Louis, nieces Kara, Leigh, and Camille, my nephew Alex, my Aunt Janet and Uncle Doug and the Jourdain cousins have all linked hearts, and we are working together to build a new configuration of our family. The love provided by Charlene, Charles, Jr., Charles, Sr., and Quinters Jean Cohen and the rest of the Cohen family has filled out this configuration. It is both the aspirations of the young people and the grace and wisdom of the older members of my various families that have kept me moving during the past few years of writing this book. For this I am most grateful.

The ultimate family appreciation goes to Cathy J. Cohen. As a partner, she teaches me every day about what it means to be loyal to those you love. As a scholar, there is no better model of dedication and commitment to the highest intellectual standards. As a friend, she gets me laughing at times I thought nothing would ever be funny again. She gives Ella and me what my grandmother used to call "a strong place to start from," and each time I thought I couldn't finish, she helped me, in one way or another, to begin again.

And finally, this book and my appreciation for having the opportunity to write it is about the women—the Black women whose stories are told here and the others whose suffering, degradation, and humiliation are invoked through the telling of those stories. I feel very fortunate to know Mildred Muhammad, Kemba Smith, and Ms. B. well and to have witnessed their personal transformations. They are generous, courageous, and inspiring beyond words. Others I write about I have only met once or briefly, and some I do not know personally at all. But I want each of the women that I name individually, and others that I write about, who are in dangerous positions in a prison nation to know that I take my responsibilities to tell these stories seriously, and that I do so humbly. And even though this book is finally finished, I will keep working until the work is done because I feel outraged by the circumstances of a prison nation that they face on a daily basis, and that wounds their bodies and their spirits. I hate that so little has changed for them and that so many of the strategies that we thought would help have backfired because of conservative state policy and political ideology. I wish we had been able to win some of the battles that we fought against the mainstreaming of the anti-violence movement. The regret is tempered by the inspiration to keep pushing back. That so many Black women not only are surviving but also thriving and fighting back is the greatest inspiration of all for this book. My hope is that this book dignifies that struggle and that these lengthy acknowledgments express my profound appreciations and my deep commitments to love and to justice.

1

Introduction

The year 2010 marked several important anniversaries in my work as a Black feminist scholar and anti-violence activist. More than 25 years earlier, I was one of a group of women of color living in New York City who organized one of the country's first community-based anti-violence programs for women of color. We were working in Harlem, a predominantly Black and Latino community in New York whose renowned history of cultural and political activism led us—perhaps naively—to expect that our community would be open to our feminist analysis of, and responses to, gender-specific problems concerning the community's health and well-being. We were surprised to find ourselves struggling with the community leadership who, at the time, resisted our attempts to intervene in what we considered problematic politics around issues of gender and sexuality.

That same year, I attended a conference sponsored by the National Coalition Against Domestic Violence in Milwaukee, Wisconsin. There, I learned about the dynamic radical feminist activists who were building a grassroots movement in response to the problem of violence against women. Their analysis of gender inequality was powerful; it resonated deeply with the political work that we were doing in Harlem, except that their emerging feminist analysis did not adequately incorporate an understanding of race and class inequality. I was reassured that there was a Woman of Color Institute at the conference where a more intersectional analysis of the problem prevailed—a perspective that was more consistent with our own experiences. I was immediately drawn to nationwide efforts by women of color to challenge white-dominated groups to relinquish their hold on the growing resource base and resultant power, and to challenge patriarchal assumptions in communities of color and the growing body of Black feminist literature that was informing my work. It was an exciting time to be a Black community activist coming into feminist consciousness, and the burgeoning anti-violence movement served as a stimulating environment for my feminist anti-racist praxis.

Our young, energetic, feminist group of women of color had very high expectations for both the anti-violence movement *and* our communities. Our analysis around race, class, gender, and sexuality was solidly embedded in our everyday activism, which was informed by the stories of women among us who were beaten, raped, stalked, kidnapped, harassed, humiliated, and degraded by individuals *as well as* by state-operated systems of domination. We were as spontaneous, and naively optimistic, as we were strategic. We were passionate about our work and profoundly determined to find ways that communities of color and anti-violence programs could join forces to end the systematic abuse of women of color. We thought social and political conditions were ripe for building autonomous Black and Latina feminist organizations, and we expected that people we considered "natural" social justice allies would meet our efforts with enthusiasm. Instead, we found ourselves in a constant struggle with the more mainstream groups around us. The white feminist anti-violence movement was becoming more entrenched in an overly simplistic analysis that argued that gender inequality was the main factor that motivated violence against women—almost to the exclusion of other factors. At the same time, the leadership in male-dominated organizations in communities of color actively rejected the notion that gender inequality had much of an impact on women of color and that feminist analyses had much to contribute to racial justice work.[1]

These political contradictions and dichotomous analytical positions have profoundly shaped my work as a Black feminist activist working against gender violence for the past 25 years. Despite some important intellectual and political progress in advancing a more coherent analysis of the relationship between white supremacy, class exploitation, and gender inequality, I continue to feel a strong tension in political and cultural spaces where theories of race, class, and gender oppression clash, *in particular* in the U.S.-based anti-violence movement.[2] The tension has escalated for me in the past ten years as a new political dynamic has emerged in this country—the buildup of America's prison nation.

The notion of a prison nation reflects the ideological and public policy shifts that have led to the increased criminalization of disenfranchised communities of color, more aggressive law enforcement strategies for norm-violating behavior, and an undermining of civil and human rights of marginalized groups. A prison nation refers to those dimensions of civil society that use the power of law, public policy, and institutional practices in strategic ways to advance hegemonic values and to overpower efforts by individuals and groups that challenge the status quo. The political apparatus that goes into building a prison nation includes (1) practices that increasingly punish or disadvantage norm violations (adolescent pregnancy); (2) institutional regulations designed to intimidate people without power into conforming with dominant cultural expectations (welfare reform); (3) legislation that deliberately narrows opportunities for cultural expansion (English-only laws); (4) and ideological schemes that build consensus around conservative values (the primacy of heterosexual nuclear families). A prison nation depends on the ability of leaders to create fear (of terrorism or health-care reform); to identify scapegoats (like immigrants or feminists); and to reclassify people as enemies of a stable society (such as prisoners, activists, hip-hop artists). Most intellectual and political responses to this buildup look at how these developments disadvantage men, particularly Black men.[3]

what leads to a prison nation

Some aspects of the work to end violence against women have benefited from the ideological shifts associated with the buildup of America's prison nation. These "benefits" include harsher punishments for so-called violent perpetrators, technological advances to monitor threatening and illegal behavior, and a fundamentally conservative public commitment to "law and order" that does not take into account the roles that families play in social stability. To the extent that these changes can be considered advantages at all, it is critical to note that they have benefited groups of women who have power much more than others. Indeed, there is evidence that *some* women are safer in 2012 than they were 25 years ago

counter argument

because of the success of the anti-violence movement in changing policy and because of America's growing prison nation and the concurrent focus on punishment in the United States.[4] At the same time, there is growing concern about women with less power who are in as much danger as ever, precisely because of the ideological and strategic direction the anti-violence movement has taken during the buildup of America's prison nation.

This, the central argument of this book, takes me back to the blatant contradiction that I initially felt between white feminist anti-violence activism and Black community organizing efforts. Still, after 25 years, racism persists in the mainstream anti-violence movement, and some leadership in communities of color continues to refuse to pay sufficient attention to gender inequality. In fact, the politics that led to the buildup of America's prison nation may have actually deepened the divide between mainstream anti-violence work and marginalized Black communities. That growing divide, and the women whose lives are caught in it, compelled me to write this book.

Three specific stories of male violence against Black women that I describe in detail, and the others that I reference throughout the book, inspired me. I learned about them quite by accident, *not* from my involvement with feminist anti-violence agencies or community-based organizations in the Black community. Upon reflection, it is the lack of response from social justice networks that I had worked within that shocked me, almost more than the stories themselves. Investigating them left me with feelings of outrage and despair and confirmed my sense that more than 25 years after my first introduction to the work in New York City and at the National Coalition Against Domestic Violence, Black women in low-income communities are perhaps in greater danger than ever.

A Discovery in the Schoolyard

There was something about the number of police cars, the schoolyard full of reporters instead of children, and the morning sunshine casting a bright light on such a troubling moment that made the discovery so shocking. It amazed me that an otherwise mundane object—a trash dumpster—could be transformed by one simple act of despair into a site of tragic meaning and consequence. At first, the discovery so violated my sensibilities that I couldn't grasp its enormous significance; the scene seemed so fundamentally out of order. It took only a few moments, however, for me to realize that under different circumstances the young woman at the heart of this tragedy very well could have been my niece, my sister, or one of my female students. Indeed, any number of young Black women I have known might have become pregnant at age 15. I could well imagine that one of them might have found herself sitting in a bathroom stall at her high school, desperate and frightened, trying to figure out what to do. I attempted to convince myself that if it *had* been someone I knew, the outcome would have been different, although there was no way to know for sure. But on this spring morning, one particular young woman, who until this point was a stranger to me, decided that she had no better option when she went into labor at school but to deliver the baby herself, put the newborn into her backpack, and then place the backpack in a dumpster behind her south side Chicago high school.

Why? How could anyone feel so desperate? What tragic events could possibly have led to such a heinous act? There seemed to be no good explanation for what I was witnessing. The public discourse that surrounded the event offered no plausible explanations for it. When the young woman's friends learned what had happened, they claimed ignorance of both the pregnancy and the tragic discovery in the dumpster. Her overwhelmed teachers, alienated by their work as public school educators and socially distant from their disadvantaged students, responded with shock. Her parents, distracted by pressures of negotiating a large family's needs with insufficient resources, denied any knowledge of the young woman's impending crisis. Then, in a bizarre and outlandish move, the media spun the story as part of an ongoing labor strike that was crippling trash collection in the city.

In a matter of hours, the wider public was riveted by local news coverage of the discovery of a newborn who died tragically, in a dumpster. The story, buttressed by stereotypical images and accompanied by the quick judgments and constraints of television sound bites, was embellished and spread quickly. A dramatic and troubling narrative emerged that portrayed a ruthless, irresponsible, and brutally uncaring young Black woman whose unconscionable behavior was heroically revealed by reporters covering the labor strike. By nightfall, most audiences accepted this analysis of the infant's death because of the way moral condemnation and institutional disregard for their well-being have shaped the general conception of young women of color's lives in contemporary society.[5,6]

From here I will use the name Tanya to refer to the aggregate version of several similar cases where this racialized formulation of gender and class—sexually promiscuous young girls, turned into irresponsible young pregnant women and then recklessly dangerous Black mothers—can flourish in part because in many cases no one—no friend, family member, or advocate, no official representative from the state, and no reporter—asks about these young women's lives outside of the tragic events. The fact that a dangerous series of abusive episodes could escalate in a young woman's life for years until everything spiraled out of control is astonishing; all the while she could be repeatedly raped by her uncle, under her boyfriend's constant surveillance, and terrified of her family or community's response.

The more I learned about the similarities between the cases, the more I became convinced that young women's marginalized status in their communities, coupled with their isolation, had a great deal to do with both the harm caused to the infants in these cases and the resulting furor. Like most vulnerable young women of color, these young women did not turn to formal systems as a remedy for their victimization because of the strong distrust of the criminal legal system in their disadvantaged communities. There was no official documentation of their victimization and no references in public records to the broader context of their lives. No one responsible for investigating the cases seemed to have the insight or the inclination to delve deeper into the situations to uncover the difficult circumstances they were in. And no one from their communities spoke out to support them or offer more information. There was no counter-narrative of how the combination of childhood sexual abuse, adolescent intimate-partner violence, racial stigmatizing, and social marginalization could turn lethal; resulting in young women's desperate feelings of hopelessness. The absence of such a counter-narrative combined with community silence and the passivity of anti-violence advocacy groups around cases like these is deeply disappointing.

As a result, highly sensationalized, oversimplified versions of these stories prevail. The institutions that should have protected young women are not held accountable for their failure to intervene. The adults who should look out for their well-being are absolved of any responsibility as they claim shock and horror. Members of the advocacy community distance themselves from these cases. Because of the profound stigma associated with such events and young women's social vulnerability, the tragic circumstances that culminated in pregnancies and the outcomes were ignored.

The aggregate version of several cases is emblematic of hundreds of other Black women in low-income communities where disadvantages are concentrated, and who experience male violence during an era in which public policy has virtually locked them into desperate and often dangerous situations. This public policy environment is the prison nation I referred to earlier, where conservative state forces have gradually but systematically eroded the rights, privileges, and opportunities afforded disadvantaged groups. In cases like Tanya's, the political dynamics of a prison nation interact with racial and other stigmas in such a way that women of color are more likely to be treated as criminals than as victims when they are abused. Indeed, the victimization of some Black women seems to invoke a set of institutional reactions that lead to further vilification, rather than protection or support. In the face of ongoing abuse, these young women acted out of desperation to shield themselves from further harm, largely because of the early lessons learned as poor, young, Black women trapped in dangerous interpersonal relationships. The media's portrayal of these events typically furthered the criminalization of their experience. Because young Black women in these circumstances are depicted *not* as frightened, pregnant adolescents who are raped and abused by men in their families, but as criminal defendants charged with neonaticide, it is virtually impossible for the mainstream public, their communities, or their potential advocates to understand their vulnerability or to respond accordingly. Instead, these women became known as "perpetrators" of one of the most unthinkable crimes a woman could commit; the "ultimate other," immoral and beyond redemption in the eyes of a society that is increasingly committed to unconditional punishment.

Arrested Justice: Black Women, Violence, and America's Prison Nation[7] is about how the prevailing analysis and the dominant rhetoric about violence, race, class, gender, and sexuality conspire to limit comprehension of the experience of male violence for Black women like Tanya. The conventional analysis of crime and victimization, and the public policy that it reflects, makes it impossible to fathom that a young Black woman's options could be so limited that she would feel compelled to place her newborn in a backpack and leave the bundle in the school trash. As such, these situations became a criminal matter for the police.

The Brutality in Public Housing

Three weeks after a young Black woman was arrested for murder of her infant, just nine blocks south of her high school, Ms. B was watching television in her small apartment when she heard a loud knock at the door. When she opened it hesitantly, she was violently pushed back and thrown against the wall of her narrow hallway. The lightbulb had burned out, which prevented her from seeing their faces, but Ms. B was sure that the intruders were the five undercover Chicago police officers who had been harassing her for three months. She was terrified that they had come back to make good on their ongoing threat to "never let her forget who she is."[8]

This intrusion, the latest in a series of violent attacks, could be traced back to an evening two months earlier when the same police officers stopped Ms. B outside her apartment building in the large public housing complex where she had lived for 27 years, which had recently been targeted for demolition by the city's Department of Housing.[9] Paradoxically called "The Plan for Transformation," the city's decision to tear down the building represented a complex set of public policy decisions that included temporarily suspending public services in the area, increasing police surveillance of residents during the transition, and advancing a public relations campaign to convince homeowners in neighboring communities that the widespread destruction of this disadvantaged community would ultimately benefit them.[10]

The initial attack on Ms. B was facilitated by the barrenness of the landscape; approximately 75 percent of the units were empty at the time. Former residents had been forced to leave their homes for unfamiliar neighborhoods in outlying areas where the housing was even less secure than the tenuous—but familiar—environment they were accustomed to as residents of deteriorating public housing in the city. The arbitrary and chaotic nature of the human dispersion meant that the remaining residents, mostly Black women and their children, did not know which apartments were occupied and by whom. Women like Ms. B were left to fend for themselves, making their way through a once lively but increasingly desolate neighborhood. Now her daily life—trips to the grocery store or the laundromat, visits to members of her family, and other activities—were fraught with the risks that characterize abandoned and isolated streets. Ms. B did *not* expect that the police would pose the greatest danger to her life.

On the evening of the first attack, the five undercover officers, three with guns drawn, accosted Ms. B outside of her building and demanded that she give them her apartment keys. The officers then forced Ms. B into the one working elevator and, when the door opened on her floor, pushed her inside the apartment. They then proceeded to ransack her home, throwing her belongings around and breaking precious objects (like a picture of a brown-skinned Jesus) while they cursed and threatened her, referring to her in sexually and racially demeaning terms like "nigger-cunt-bitch." Three of the officers broke down the door to her 19-year-old son's bedroom and ordered him and a visiting friend to lie face down on the floor while they handcuffed them. Three officers took turns punching and kicking them for more than 30 minutes before taking them forcibly out of the apartment. In response to Ms. B's pleas for mercy for the young men, the two police officers who remained in the apartment led her to the bathroom, ordered her to remove all of her clothing, to lie down on the floor, to spread her legs, and to effectively do an internal cavity search on herself while they stood over her and watched.

During the vicious attack, the police officers made constant demands that Ms. B give them the drugs that they were *allegedly* searching for, threatening to "put some stuff on her" if she did not produce some illegal substances. The officers never found any drugs. They did, at one point in the ordeal, find approximately $100 in cash, which one of the police officers pocketed. By the time the police officers left the ransacked apartment, Ms. B was physically battered, naked, emotionally traumatized, and terrified about where and how her son and his friend were. The police officers, who work on a special unit of the Chicago Police Department, never identified themselves as such. They did not produce a search warrant, explain the reason for the "search," or read Ms. B her constitutional rights as required by law. They left as abruptly as they came, leaving a trail of violence, fear, humiliation, and degrading destruction in their wake.

That occurred on April 13, 2003. Over the next three months, this same group of rogue police officers (all white, all men, and all young) assaulted Ms. B six times. The brutality included physical beatings, sexual harassment and stalking, destruction of her personal property, and threats to members of her family who were particularly vulnerable because they were on parole or probation (and subsequently at risk of re-arrest at the whim of the police). During most of these assaults, the police officers had their weapons drawn. In three of the instances, the officers placed drugs on her person and forced her to perform sexual acts in order to avoid false accusations and subsequent arrests. Ms. B called these experiences "dry rapes."

Regrettably, it was easy for Ms. B to make an analogy between her experiences with the police and being sexually assaulted. She had been gang-raped twice, both times by acquaintances. Her tense neighborhood in transition served as an ideal backdrop to the violence she was experiencing. Community members were resentful of the potential displacement that they faced and misdirected anger toward other vulnerable residents, like Ms. B.[11] The presence of aggressive demolition crews and other city workers was a constant reminder of the general vulnerability that she faced. Ms. B learned that it was futile to rely on state authorities for protection. Her attempts to get help from two rape crisis centers were futile. On no fewer than three occasions, she filed complaints with both the Chicago Housing Authority and the Chicago Police Department's Office of Professional Standards, to no avail. Eventually, Ms. B began staying home, avoiding interactions with others, and refraining from seeking any personal or institutional support. In doing so, she left herself at even greater risk because she was so isolated and attempting to cope alone.

Although it was never clear why these police officers targeted Ms. B, it is possible that it stemmed from her activities years earlier as a member of several local community organizations, particularly one that was beginning to organize in resistance to the city's plan to demolish public housing. Ms. B had no criminal background, she had been an active member of her church, and she had raised three sons in the once-thriving community of Stateway Gardens.[12] As the city divested its resources from the neighborhood in order to "transform" the community, she became a target for horrific abuse, from which there was virtually no protection. Even after her case was taken up by a progressive university-based legal clinic and eventually resulted in an out-of-court settlement from the Chicago Police Department, she was still living in isolation and in fear. She still has a hard time believing what happened to her because, as she says, even after all that she lived through, never in her wildest imagination did Ms. B anticipate that at age 50 she would be targeted for such brutality by the police, and that her case would become emblematic of the state's complicity in gender violence and the impunity of white men who work for it.

As with Tanya's case, I listened to Ms. B's story in horrified disbelief. How could I have been living in the same city, not very far from where these incidents happened, and not have known about them? How is it that the representations found in the local or national campaigns against police brutality seldom depict *women* as victims? Where were the local anti-violence programs when Ms. B needed them? And what political and ideological shifts associated with the buildup of America's prison nation linked Ms. B's situation with those of women like Tanya?

The Trial Injustice in the Courtroom and the Streets

Both women live in disadvantaged African American communities. Their neighborhoods are typical of low-income urban areas in the United States where public policy decisions made principally between 1996 and 2006 have created the dynamics that I am calling a prison nation. These include the passing of legislation that created a set of economic conditions that has seriously limited opportunity and essentially destroyed the possibility that individuals can ever become self-sufficient.[13] In these communities, the generally accepted measures of economic and social well-being—income, homeownership, high school graduation rates— predict ongoing disadvantages and persistent poverty, which profoundly shaped women's experiences of abuse.

This link is critical, but it is important to understand that the male violence that Black women experience stems not only from neighborhood conditions or poverty. As the analysis in later chapters will show, other factors are equally important, including issues related to how racial ideologies interact with hegemonic ideas of proper gender roles, and how cultural and political shifts over ideas about crime and punishment reflect growing conservatism in the United States. These factors were readily visible in a very different kind of neighborhood, halfway across the country, where four young African American women found themselves in trouble.[14]

Early one summer evening in 2006, Venice, Terrain, Patreese, Renata and three of their friends were walking through the streets of Greenwich Village in New York City, an urban neighborhood with a liberal reputation earned through activism and resistance by members of the Black gay, lesbian, bisexual, and transgender community in the late 1960s.[15] Today, Greenwich Village is associated with ideals of tolerance and openness, and these proudly lesbian-identified, young women (aged 19–24) were enjoying the rare public space where being openly gay was acceptable—or so they thought. As they walked past a young man selling DVDs from a card table on the sidewalk, he sexually propositioned them in insulting ways by hurling degrading proclamations at them like "I will fuck you straight" while grabbing his genitals. Angry and embarrassed, the young women hurried to cross the busy street. A security camera from a nearby store shows the young man following them and escalating his defaming remarks. He continued harassing them as they moved down the street, until they finally stopped and confronted the harasser, which led to a heated argument. When the aggressor spat in the face of one of the young women and threw a lighted cigarette at another, a physical fight ensued.

Eyewitnesses have verified what happened next.[16] The young man pulled out patches of hair from one of the young women and choked a second one. Eventually, one of the other women pulled out a small kitchen knife and threatened to stab the man if he did not stop the violent assault. Two men who had been watching intervened to help the women. At some point, the young man who began the assault was stabbed in the abdomen; he later required surgery for a lacerated liver. He initially reported to the police that he was stabbed by one of the men who had intervened, *not* by any of the women.

Indeed, there is no forensic evidence linking the woman's knife to the injury because investigators did not deem forensic testing necessary. Eyewitnesses confirm that the young women acted in self-defense against a blatant anti-gay sexual attack, and that the fight became physical only after the young man's violence escalated. Witnesses further reported that the men who intervened were, in fact, significantly more aggressive than the women who were defending themselves.

The two young men who intervened are both white; the police never interviewed them. The aggressor, who was never charged with a crime, is an African American man reported to be a part-time student at an elite university in Greenwich Village. All seven of the young African American women, the victims of the attack, were arrested and charged with crimes such as "gang assault." Three of the women took plea agreements. The other four went to trial and were found guilty. Terrain Dandridge spent two years in prison, after which her conviction was overturned. Renata Hill and Vernice Brown served more than two years and then were released on bail after a re-trial. Patreese Johnson, initially sentenced to 11 years, has had her sentence reduced to 8 years and continues to be held in a New York State Prison. At the time of this writing, Patreese remains in prison, where she has gotten her GED and is planning to attend college. The jury that convicted them was comprised mostly of white women. Despite the widespread media coverage of the case, mainstream gay rights organizations and groups concerned with violence against women did not attend the trials. Also absent was the established African American community leadership known for their engagement both with high-profile trials of African American people arrested in New York City and vicious hate crimes—especially those against Black men. There is now a powerful, grassroots advocacy network led by mostly queer young women of color and transgendered people who are supporting the women. Updates on their case, as well as information regarding a documentary film that is being made about them called *The Fire Within* can be found at www.freenj4.wordpress.com. *The Fire Within*

By most accounts, these sentences are extreme, given the nature of the case. Those who worked on the defense attribute the long sentences to several factors. First, the media accounts of the incident inflamed growing anti-gay, anti-youth sentiment in New York City, where tourism and gentrification are hallmarks of the city's new, more conservative image of itself. In addition, consistent with various themes about the motivations and actions involved in gentrification in urban areas, there is a strong lobby of wealthy real estate developers in New York City advocating for the "law and order" agenda that local politicians have advanced since the tragedy at the World Trade Center on September 11, 2001.[17] This agenda has included increased surveillance of young people and the enforcement of curfews and other "anti-loitering" ordinances in the historically tolerant but now gentrified neighborhoods. Second, and most important, the racist and homophobic atmosphere that the prosecution created at the trial essentially convicted the assaulted women before the jury reached its verdict. The women's names were seldom used and when they were, they were mispronounced. There was constant reference to their non-normative gender appearance and how it threatened public safety in New York City. The case resulted in intense media scrutiny and the creation of numerous derogatory titles to describe the women, including "lesbian wolf pack" and "fawl brawl," and the vast majority of media outlets referred to the assailant as the victim. The *New York Times* reported that Justice Edward J. McLaughlin used his sentencing speech to comment on the importance of prosecuting "criminals" so that New York City can welcome tourists. In this book, I will refer to the women as the "New Jersey 4," as they have come to be known.

It is obvious that the young Black self-identified lesbians, visiting the city from a working-class neighborhood in New Jersey, were *not* the tourists with whom the judge, the mayor, or the wealthy developers were concerned with. The male violence they experienced was *not* considered a serious blemish on the city's reputation by those conservative forces attempting to redeem it. On the contrary, the convictions and the long sentences are important lessons about increased intolerance for perceived gender transgressions and open displays of nonhegemonic sexuality in the now much-less-tolerant Greenwich Village.

There are a number of factors that comprise the larger backdrop to this story, including how the erosion of hate crime legislation by the U.S. Supreme Court increased anti-gay violence in urban areas,[18] affected the ways that sexual assaults are complicated by issues related to sexuality,[19] and, most important, affected how the prison nation's criminalization of young women of color clearly makes their experience of male violence worse.

Violence against Black Women Inside America's Prison Nation: The Links between the Stories

I was deeply moved by the stories of abandoned newborn babies, troubled by the portrayal of the New Jersey 4 and the outcome of their trials, and outraged by the silence that surrounded the police brutality Ms. B experienced. Together, they represented the new level of disdain for Black women who are young, poor, queer, or living in vulnerable circumstances during the buildup of America's prison nation—groups that mainstream anti-violence programs typically ignore. Indeed, a large part of my strong reaction to the stories resulted from the lack of formal or organized response by *either* the feminist-based anti-violence movement or groups working on racial justice issues. This silence raised old questions for me as a Black feminist scholar and as an anti-violence activist. I was amazed that once the stories broke, anti-violence programs did not respond aggressively to the homophobic violence, the unchecked police brutality, or the complicated situations that women like Tanya find themselves in. It profoundly disappointed me that in each instance the impact of the male violence these women experienced was complicated by policies related to the buildup of a prison nation and that this was not the subject of a rallying call for action.

The links between the cases are as compelling as they are clear. The stories of the New Jersey 4, Ms. B, and women like Tanya become generalizable to other Black women who experience male violence to the extent that they illustrate the perils inherent in relying on intervention strategies that emerge from conservative public policies that focus on punishment rather than on prevention of violence and that ignore the broader need for redistribution of social power along gender and racial lines. These six women represent thousands of Black women, who are similarly situated—in dangerous households, in disadvantaged communities, in neighborhoods in transition, and on contested streets. The abuse they experienced takes many forms and happens in many contexts. It is likely to be physical, sexual, and emotional; it will happen across their lifespan; it will originate from different sources. The more stigmatized their social position, the easier it is to victimize them. The further a woman's sexuality, age, class, criminal background, and race are from hegemonic norms, the more likely it is that they will be harmed—and the more likely that their harm will not be taken seriously by their community, by anti-violence programs, or by the general public. Black women similar to those whose stories I have recounted will be left to cope without formal institutional support. And for that, they will be punished. The punishment—the isolation, further stigmatization, or long prison sentences—is made possible by the social climate that constitutes the prison nation.

The general conditions that link these stories will be familiar to Black women and other women of color who have been activists in the anti-violence movement for the past 25 years. We have been confronting our communities about their complacency on the issue of gender violence and mainstream anti-violence organizations who do not adequately address the concerns of women of color for years. What feels new and different to me as I consider these stories is the pernicious relationship between the mainstream anti-violence programs and the Black community's lack of response *and* the contemporary buildup of America's prison nation.

On a very pragmatic and deeply personal level, the urgency represented by and the links between these stories of violence against Black women led me to write this book. They provided a way for me to frame difficult questions about the relevance of the feminist-based intervention programs that have been created over the past 25 years, and about the outcomes of the social change movement that has dedicated itself to ending violence against women in this country. Indeed, I read the stories as illustrations of how profoundly inadequate some of these efforts have been, particularly the over-reliance on law enforcement. More subtly, perhaps, Black women like Tanya, Ms. B, and the New Jersey 4's experiences show the tremendous cost that resulted from the anti-violence movement's deployment of a rhetorical strategy aimed at bringing legitimacy to the issue of gender violence and the ensuing refusal to acknowledge state violence by, and because of, the public policies associated with the climate of a prison nation.

Put more simply, the cases and the ways they were handled call attention to what happens when the work to end violence against women becomes more focused on establishing credibility with elite power holders than on challenging state institutions or creating social change. These

[handwritten marginalia: gender cannot address w/o state violence violence/build up of prison system]

women's experiences demonstrate the need for attention to issues of social marginalization and community disempowerment; they highlight the dangers of relying on mainstream state institutions to solve complex social problems, in particular those embedded in race, class, gender, and arrangements regarding sexuality in contemporary society. The three cases raise fundamental questions about what happens to Black women who experience male violence in a climate that gives way to the buildup of a prison nation—a climate where the broader social agenda is shaped by mean-spirited public policies designed to create intolerance of difference, to erode public services, and to increase social inequality. It bears repeating that in this book, I use the notion of a prison nation because it points directly to the conditions that have made violence against Black women worse in recent years. The term connotes the set of conditions that surround the abuse; externally imposed state policies that control marginalized communities and limit access to services, resources, and power. A prison nation depends on tactics such as the development of new laws and aggressive enforcement of social norms; tactics that are reinforced by ideology that suggests that deviations from normative behavior or violations from conservative expectations should be punished by the state. Instead of benefiting from law enforcement and punishment, this book argues that women of color from marginalized communities who experience violence are made more vulnerable by the operation of a prison nation.

I begin the discussion here because it is important to notice how the buildup of America's prison nation has an impact on how Black women like the New Jersey 4, Ms. B, and Tanya are treated when they are in crisis, *including* the silence of the anti-violence movement that surrounds them. In addition, a consideration of the prison nation framework allows for a critical examination of the progress of the feminist-based anti-violence movement and the ways it has been derailed because of pressure to legitimize itself in the eyes of powerful elites, and resorted to some of the same tactics that characterize a prison nation. Indeed, the climate associated with a prison nation is characterized by a web of ideological and material constraints that leaves Black women in low-income communities—young, pregnant women like Tanya, women displaced from public housing like Ms. B, and women who dare to transgress geographic and sexual boundaries like the New Jersey 4—in serious trouble. These women's stories demand a reconsideration of the development and design of a social movement in which conservative state forces associated with a prison nation have disrupted its transformative potential and momentum for change. At the very least, thinking about the New Jersey 4's trial, choices that women like Tanya are forced to make, and Ms. B's experiences of state violence, offers us a way to broaden our understanding of violence against women of color and to problematize the evolution of anti-violence work in the United States. That is the goal of *Arrested Justice: Black Women, Violence, and America's Prison Nation.*

The Book

This book is an attempt to provide a context for understanding women like Tanya, Ms. B, and the New Jersey 4 and, ultimately, the thousands of other Black women who find themselves socially marginalized and invisible in very dangerous circumstances. It is a book about women who are disadvantaged by structural racism, economic exploitation, political disenfranchisement, the ideology that informs conservative public policy *and* who experience gender violence. It is *not* a book about all women, all Black women, or all survivors of violence, but rather those who are the most stigmatized, the least protected, and therefore in greater danger. By reviewing the history of the anti-violence movement and then locating the work within the larger public policy shifts associated with buildup of America's prison nation, this contextualization allows us to look at how the disadvantaged position of some women renders the multiple forms of abuse they experience invisible, and thus allows for a more accurate depiction of how gender violence is seriously complicated. It will show how their experiences with sexual violence, physical aggression, and psychological abuse are made more dangerous by communities that tolerate or dismiss the degradation that Black women experience. Furthering this effect are state institutions built on racist stereotypes that profoundly misunderstand and misrepresent Black women's experience of male violence, and public policies characteristic of a prison nation that create a hostile social environment for many poor Black women. The cumulative effect is a vicious cycle of danger, discrimination, and despair.

As part of this effort, *Arrested Justice: Black Women, Violence, and America's Prison Nation* traces the history of the contemporary anti-violence movement in this country between 1960 and 2010 to show how questions of race and class got lost in the battle to win mainstream support and resources for victim services, and how the movement's strategic approaches converged with conservative public policies that are consistent with a prison nation. This is an account of how, in the process of moving toward legitimacy, anti-violence activists have grown (perhaps unwittingly) complacent about repressive shifts associated with the prison nation and the deployment of conservative law-and-order rhetoric. I am challenging the anti-violence movement's uncritical positioning around state policy and punitive interventions, which I argue have contributed to the ongoing escalation of male violence against Black women. So while I wrote this book most immediately because of how the specific women's stories made me think back on 25 years of activism, I hope it will also serve as a way to reflect more broadly on the history of the anti-violence movement and the heightened stakes that I feel characterize anti-violence work against the backdrop of the U.S. policy of criminalization, punishment of the poor, disenfranchisement, and mass incarceration.

In chapter 2, I present the empirical data and a review of the theoretical literature concerning the problem of violence against Black women. The first part of the chapter presents the findings from quantitative and qualitative research that firmly establishes the pattern of physical and emotional abuse, sexual and economic exploitation, and social degradation that Black women experience as a result of male violence. The second part of the chapter reviews the analyses of causes and consequences of abuse, providing a theoretical framework for understanding the social and political context of the stories told at the beginning of the chapter.

Chapter 3 provides the historical backdrop to the data by presenting a chronology of the anti-violence movement in the United States that coincided with the buildup of America's prison nation, which is described in chapter 4. Specifically, I focus on the various critical junctures when ideological, political, and economic decisions won mainstream support for reformists' strategies to end male violence against women while reflecting a decreased commitment to some of the more radical tenets of the work. I argue that the success of the anti-violence movement, measured by factors such as public and private funding for services, academic credibility, and legislative changes, has brought with it unintended negative consequences for women whose experience of male violence does not fit within the dominant paradigm with which the anti-violence movement established its credibility. In particular, I show how the dominant analysis failed women like Tanya, the New Jersey 4, and Ms. B because it relies on a sense of generalized vulnerability based on gender oppression but does not incorporate other manifestations of power imbalances and abuse (most notably issues of race, sexuality, and class). In the end, I argue that despite the important victories for the mainstream movement that I describe in chapter 3, many Black women from low-income communities continue to encounter unsupportive services from anti-violence programs and hostile public policies that leave them in great danger.

Chapter 4 takes up the issues of America's prison nation that have recently surrounded the activities of the anti-violence movement. Here I explore the social, political, economic, and ideological mechanisms that have created a climate of social conservatism with a particular intolerance for poor women of color. I describe in further detail the buildup of the punishment industry in the United States, the subsequent mass incarceration of women from low-income communities who break laws in order to survive abusive relationships, and the so-called deviant behavior that women engage in to cope with the devastation that they face, for which they are ultimately punished. I also present evidence of the negative consequences of the buildup of America's prison nation that complicated the abuse that women like Tanya, Ms. B, and the New Jersey 4 faced. This includes the increased poverty of women who can no longer rely on public assistance for support; the dilemmas women face as they navigate the narrowing options related to their reproductive health, parenting choices, and sexuality; and the sanctioning of women because their economic position or social status leads them into contact with the punitive child welfare system. Readers will note in chapter 4 that I am also using the notion of a prison nation metaphorically to represent the ways that public policy leads to punitive state intervention that targets Black women in ways that leave them vulnerable to male violence.

I make the case in chapter 4 that the buildup of a prison nation is relevant to the discussion of Black women and male violence for two reasons.

First, we cannot understand the experience of violence against women who are socially disadvantaged without an understanding of the broader context of their lives within this prison nation. Secondly, the buildup of the prison nation that surrounded them, the erosion of public support, the mean-spirited public policies, the disenfranchisement facing their communities, and the conservative anti-violence movement are clearly linked in ways that, for them, are deadly. After defining what a prison nation is, I document how its construction is motivated by goals that are far apart from the stated goals of advancing social stability, increasing individual responsibility, protecting vulnerable women, or controlling crime. Instead, criminalization of violence through mass incarceration and other manifestations of the prison nation are linked to goals of maintaining inequality, scapegoating marginalized groups, and promoting economic benefit for social, political, and corporate elites—goals that seem glaringly antithetical to the initial radical work of the anti-violence movement. I explain how the mainstreaming of the anti-violence movement I described in chapter 3 led to the over-reliance on criminal legal responses to male violence, which contributed to the co-optation of once-radical anti-violence work by the conservative mechanisms associated with the buildup of America's prison nation.

In chapter 5, I present an alternative analytical framework, one that provides a much more useful way to understand stories like Tanya's, Ms. B's experience, and what happened to the New Jersey 4 in Greenwich Village and the courtroom. Here, I rely on Black feminist theory to show how Black women are abused and imperiled by the collusion of mainstream feminist dogma and conservative social policy. I argue that conservative rhetoric, punishment ideology, and crime policies have skewed the framework used to understand the violence against Black women in low-income communities, making it virtually invisible to mainstream policymakers, service providers, and the media. This invisibility has positioned Black women's experiences as marginal to anti-violence groups and community-based organizations which, in turn, have failed to address violence against women as a social or political priority. In the end, Black women in vulnerable positions within disadvantaged communities fall so far from the gaze that is now sympathetic to some women who experience violence that they have virtually no right to safety, protections, or redress when they are victimized. At best, they are relegated to the status of undeserving. More often, those Black women with the least privilege, who live in the most dangerous situations, are criminalized instead of being protected or supported. Black feminist analyses can problematize and explain this.

The discussion in chapter 5 concludes with examples of resistance—Black women's anti-violence activism. In many ways, this chapter could be a book unto itself, so powerful is the evidence of Black women's resistance to the degradation of male violence and the destructive power of America's prison nation. Instead, I merely highlight some of the key events, major organizations, and influential theorists who are challenging the anti-violence movement and the process of prison buildup, hoping to thereby reveal possibilities for change. I believe that it is through everyday acts of resistance—the micro-activities that are based on Black feminist politics and the slow but consistent erosion of white supremacy and male power that characterize this work—that the foundation for change will be set. Chapter 6, the concluding chapter, sets out this foundation.

Throughout the book, I ground my analysis of how America's prison nation contributes to and complicates the violence that Black women experience by sharing stories of that abuse. I do so because, as a Black feminist activist scholar, I know that the best way to change how society understands this problem is through sharing the reality of women's lives. It is also the case, however, that by doing so, readers may take the stories out of context, they may assume that Black women are a monolithic category or that I may inadvertently reinforce stereotypes of Black women. Not all Black women live in disadvantaged communities, for example, and the women who do are surely more than victims of abuse. So while *Arrested Justice* focuses on those segments of the Black community who face the most serious social, political, and economic challenges within America's prison nation, readers are advised to understand the stories and the facts that surround them as prototypes of a particular dynamic that is related to the intersection of race, class, gender, sexuality, and political and social ideology, rather than a generalized statement about Black life in America.

2

The Problem of Male Violence
against Black Women

Readers unfamiliar with the problem of violence against Black women may dismiss stories like Tanya's, the brutal police violence that Ms. B experienced, or the sexual aggression in Greenwich Village as a strange mix of extreme or bizarre events that have little similarity to what we commonly consider a "typical case" of gender abuse. Indeed, it may be difficult to comprehend the traumatic effects of ongoing abuse and the extent to which it shapes the choices that adolescent girls make. Similarly, because it is beyond what most individuals or agencies consider when discussing sexual abuse, it is very unlikely that official estimates of sexual violence would include the public aggression directed toward the four young queer Black women. And because few scholars or activists respond to incidents of police brutality as the gender violence that it sometimes is, the experiences of Black women in public housing where police uses of excessive force seldom appear in estimates of violence against women.

The consequences of not attending to these types of violence against Black women in marginalized positions are multifarious. In the most basic sense, the extent of the problem is underestimated and the corresponding public policy and interventions that have been designed to respond to the problems are inadequate. The tremendous unmet needs of women who fall outside of the common understanding of violence against women should trouble scholars and activists alike. Moreover, when the nature and extent of male violence is obliterated by narrow conceptual definitions of the problem, a dangerous schism is created between "deserving victims" (whose experience is easily understood by mainstream society) and the women whose experience is turned against them. Such women are blamed, stigmatized or, worse, criminalized because of their abuse.

The dismissal of these horrific cases as "statistical outliers" or "exceptional situations" is made possible by a number of factors, including the mainstream media characterization of violence against women; the messages about intimate partner violence, rape, stalking, and sexual violence and harassment that anti-violence programs' educational materials provide; and the notion of "innocence" put forward by victim-service programs that typically do not evoke an appreciation of the complex nature of gender violence.[1] Public sympathy has been organized around a fairly narrow set of images of female victims, and a relatively small range of the actual situations that women face in dangerous circumstances or abusive relationships. The conventional analysis critically omits the ways that racial stigma complicates male violence toward Black women, rendering it nearly impossible to convince even more informed readers—such as women who have had personal experience with abuse, professionals who focus on issues of victimization, and feminists whose political commitment to gender equality has led them to anti-violence activism—that there is much about Tanya's, Ms. B's, or the New Jersey 4's cases that is within the parameters of their work as anti-violence activists.

There are two ways to explain the origins of these narrow images and simplistic understandings and how marginalized Black women like Ms. B, Tanya, and the New Jersey 4 are, in effect, conceptually written out of the dominant male violence paradigm. First, it helps to understand the chronology of the anti-violence movement that over time aligned itself with more conservative ideological strategies, which I review in chapter 3. The broader context that surrounded that chronology, one of growing conservatism in the neoliberal state, also influenced the processes that created a narrow, simplistic understanding of violence against women such that many Black women are not included in the definition. My aim in this chapter is to present data to challenge the theoretical, professional, and political reluctance to accept cases like Tanya's as tragically common, Ms. B's case as critically urgent, and hate violence toward Black women who identify as lesbians as not simply *relevant* to the work to end violence against women, but *essential* to the theoretical analysis and political commitments to social justice that the work should inspire.

I begin this chapter with a review of the literature on Black women's experience of intimate personal violence. Next, I present data on community violence toward Black women, and then I focus on incidence rates and the prevalence of state-sanctioned and structured violence in the lives of Black women. I include the more subtle—but nevertheless threatening—ways that Black women are made vulnerable to male violence by punitive social services, degrading public policy, and rigid institutional regulations. The chapter concludes with a review of the more theoretical literature that shows how the mistreatment of Black women in the public sphere, and their disadvantaged position in it, extends the negative consequences of physical and sexual violence they experience in the private sphere. These analyses also demonstrate how institutional arrangements and social forces allow some Black women's experience of male violence to be framed as evidence of their own individual pathology, their social deviance, and their community disloyalty *rather than* abuses of patriarchal power by those who have authority over them. While the qualitative data are presented as if they fit neatly into categories (e.g., physical violence, sexual abuse, etc.), the discussion will show that women actually experience various forms of violence as layers of degradation that have a cumulative negative effect on their lives, resulting in systematic subordination.

Direct Physical Assaults by Intimate Partners

Intimate partner violence clearly is a significant and persistent social problem that has serious consequences for individual women, their families, and society as a whole.[2] The Bureau of Justice Statistics suggests that 1.5 million women in the United States are physically assaulted by an intimate partner each year,[3] while other studies provide much higher estimates than this. For example, the Department of Justice estimates that 5.3 million incidents of violence against a current or former spouse, boyfriend, or girlfriend occur annually. The National Violence Against Women Survey estimates that approximately 22 percent of all adult women have experienced a domestic assault,[4] while 52 percent of surveyed women have been physically assaulted at some time in their lives.[5] In another national study, 56 percent of all Americans report that someone close to them has been involved in an abusive relationship, and 30 percent of Americans say they know a woman who has been physically abused by her husband in the past year.[6]

Fifty percent of women who file police reports were injured by intimate partners during an assault,[7] and 37 percent of all women who sought care in hospital emergency rooms in 1994 were victims of domestic violence; of these cases, 28 percent required admission and another 13 percent required major medical treatment.[8] According to the Family Violence Prevention Fund, about half of all female victims of intimate violence report an injury of some type, and about 20 percent of them seek medical assistance. In 2008, women accounted for 85 percent of the victims of intimate partner violence.[9] Women are far more likely than men to be killed by a spouse or partner.[10] In 2007, women were 70 percent of all victims of the 2,340 murders committed by intimate partners;[11] other studies report slightly different rates. Overall, it is clear that women are killed by an intimate partner at a higher rate than men.[12]

According to most national studies, African American women are disproportionately represented in the aforementioned data on physical violence against intimate partners. In the Violence Against Women Survey, 25 percent of Black women had experienced abuse from their intimate partner, including "physical violence, sexual violence, threats of violence, economic exploitation, confinement and isolation from social activities, stalking, property destruction, burglary, theft and homicide."[13] Rates of severe battering help to spotlight the disproportionate impact of direct physical assaults on Black women by an intimate partner: homicide by an intimate partner is the second leading cause of death for Black women between the ages of 15 and 25.[14] Black women are killed by a spouse at a rate twice that of white women. However, when the intimate partner is a boyfriend or girlfriend, this statistic increases to four times the rate of their white counterparts.[15]

Over time, research has expanded the notion of intimate partner to include "dating or courtship relationships."[16] The studies that attempt to document this problem conclude that among Black youth dating other Black youth, physical and emotional abuse are common, which distinguishes African American women from their peer groups. Thirty percent of Black college students were victims or perpetrators of physical aggression, and nearly half of African American high school students have experienced aggression from a dating partner.[17] Moreover, Black women who are young, who do not live with their intimate partner, who reside in a low-income urban area, and who rely on governmental assistance are particularly vulnerable to both physical and emotional abuse.[18]

Although the data suggest that male and female adolescents are equally likely to experience these acts of aggression, women feel the injury and other negative consequences disproportionately.[19] Black adolescent girls appear to be especially vulnerable to premarital abuse.[20] The nature and prevalence of dating violence toward young Black women has particular salience for this discussion, given the overcriminalization of Black youth and the increased racial and gender stigma that young Black women experience. Other groups found to be particularly vulnerable include incarcerated Black women, 68 percent of whom report having experienced intimate partner violence; women who have a substance abuse problem; and women who are HIV positive.[21]

The data on physical abuse toward adult women by members of their household and the literature that attempts to explain it focus primarily on violence perpetrated by husbands or live-in boyfriends where there is a presumption of marriage-like arrangements. This presumptive conceptualization is based on a limited definition of both the concept of "household" and of what constitutes a "relationship" and, as such, misses a considerable amount of violence that women experience. That Black women fall further from the hegemonic norms of womanhood results in a disproportionate number of them not fitting into the narrowly accepted definition of who a battered woman is or who her domestic partner abuses. Take the case of Sara Kruzan.[22]

Having run away from a dangerous home at the age of 16, where she experienced severe and chronic abuse from her mother and adult male relatives who were living with them while selling drugs, Sara Kruzan found herself in a dangerous relationship with an older man, George Howard, who later became her pimp. Initially drawn in by his benevolent albeit condescending behavior toward her, Sara came to rely on Howard for both emotional and material support. They met while she was living on the streets of Riverside, California, and within a week he took her in and provided a home, food, compliments, and, initially, safety by telling her where she could and could not go. To Sara Kruzan, this felt like a "real family" and because she had so little exposure to care and affection in the house where she grew up, Sara accepted Howard's sexual advances as an uncomfortable but necessary condition to having a place to live.

As is common in situations where adult men prey on vulnerable younger women, the "care" became control and Sara Kruzan began to experience George Howard's sexual advances as evidence of her lack of worthiness, supporting his argument that she was "nothing more than a whore." From there, the descent from a mutually beneficial relationship into abusive prostitution was rapid. Howard became her pimp and she became one of the several young women whom he controlled emotionally, economically, and sexually through his physical violence. He isolated Sara by locking her in their apartment every day and only let her leave to work the streets. He physically assaulted her on a regular basis, especially if she did not bring home enough money while prostituting on any given evening. He threatened to turn her in to the police if she tried to leave. He literally starved her and denied her medical treatment when Sara Kruzan was hurt by one of her customers. Howard created an abusive domestic relationship of forced prostitution that took advantage of Sara's vulnerability and her precarious legal status that trapped her in mental and physical anguish.

The abuse escalated and Sara Kruzan did manage to get away, but only as far as another pimp's house, who let her stay on the condition that she return and steal money from Howard. There was also physical violence in this household, and having lost a sense of any possibility of escape, Sara Kruzan surrendered to her new pimp's demands. Early one evening she used a pistol to hit Howard in the back of the neck and took $1,500 from him. George Howard died from the injury and Sara Kruzan was sentenced to serve life without parole in a California prison. She was not tried as a juvenile and, despite having no criminal background, despite the remorse that she expressed, despite the domestic abuse that she experienced both as a child and later as an adolescent, and despite the fact that she was a victim of human trafficking, she was denied an appeal. Indeed, because of these conditions, her experience of physical abuse by an intimate partner falls outside of the conventional understanding of the problem. In 2011, her sentence was commuted to 25 years to life with possibility of parole. Sara has served 16 years so far and her case has become an important rallying call to end trafficking of children.[23]

The research has not only established a higher *incidence rate* of intimate partner violence for Black women when measured statistically, but qualitative research has suggested that variables such as socioeconomic status, cultural background, and age may influence the *impact* of domestic violence on different groups of women.[24] Factors such as the limited availability of crisis intervention programs, the greater likelihood that a weapon will be used against a Black woman during an assault, and a lack of trust of law enforcement agencies may heighten some women's vulnerability to intimate partner violence.[25]

There is also solid, if less well-documented, evidence to suggest that the incidence and type of intimate partner violence in same-sex relationships are comparable to those in heterosexual relationships.[26] Studies indicate that 25–30 percent of lesbian, gay, bisexual, and transgendered persons are abused by their intimate partners, and that social discrimination and marginalization may complicate their efforts to seek help and therefore increase the risk of serious abuse.[27] The U.S. National Coalition of Anti-violence Programs (NCAVP), which collects statistics from programs that provide services specifically for LGBTQ communities, reported 6,253 LGBT domestic violence incidents in 2003. Of these cases, 3,344 (44%) were men, 2,357 (33%) were women, 161 (2%) identified as male-to-female transgender, and 31 were female-to-male transgender. Of the victims for whom race or ethnicity was known, 44 percent were white, 25 percent were Latino, 15 percent were of African descent, 5 percent were Asian/Pacific Islander, and 4 percent were multiracial.[28] In their most recent report, despite the persistance of under-reporting, the National Coalition of Anti-violence Programs indicates that violence toward LGBTQ communities is increasing.[29] The report clearly links intimate partner violence to patterns of societal discrimination.

[handwritten margin note: reintegration challenges]

Sexual Assault and Aggression toward
Black Women by Their Intimate Partners

A second body of research establishes occurrences of sexual aggression toward women by people who live in or occupy emotional space in their intimate sphere. In the most basic sense, this category of experiences includes what is commonly understood to be marital rape—sexual encounters by intimate or domestic partners that involve the use of coercion, threats, or force.[30] In some national samples, 36 percent of Black women reported sexual abuse by an intimate partner. A broader understanding of this category would help account for the ways that women are forced into prostitution by members of their households, through the controlling behavior associated with forced use of, or denial of, contraception, and the ways that women are demeaned when they feel obligated or are coerced by their intimate partners to use their sexuality in ways they consider distasteful. As in the case of physical abuse by intimate partners, when the perpetrators of sexual abuse are intimate partners or others who have constant access to their victims, the consequences can be physically harmful, degrading, even lethal. Take the case of Tiffany Wright.[31]

Tiffany Wright was 15 years old and eight months pregnant when she was shot and killed in front of a bus stop on her way to school in Charlotte, North Carolina. The person named in the murder was her 36-year-old foster-brother, Mitchell, who had been given temporary custody of Tiffany when their mother died a year earlier. Both of the children were adopted, which is relevant because of the involvement of the child welfare agency that had denied Mitchell a permanent license to keep Tiffany, but did not intervene actively to protect her from his sexual abuse. Despite the fact that social workers reported that they "suspected" that Mitchell was sexually abusing Tiffany, he was not prohibited from seeing her, which provided him with unobstructed opportunity to harass, intimidate, and threaten her. Tiffany ultimately disclosed to social workers and police that she and Mitchell had sex, which constituted statutory rape because of her age and dependent status, and which may have been the motive for the murder. Mitchell was arrested, but the charges in this case were later dropped. The failure of the system to protect Tiffany was complicated by the family's loyalty to Mitchell and the community's sensitivity to Mitchell's vulnerability to the criminal legal system as an African American man who had a prior record (he did receive a two-and-a-half-year sentence for violating his federal probation).[32]

Beyond the physical consequences, the psychological consequences of these kinds of sexual assaults by intimate partners also can be very serious. Thirty-one percent of all rape victims develop rape-related post-traumatic stress disorder[33] and are three times more likely than nonvictims to experience a major depressive episode in their lives, and they attempt suicide at a rate 13 times higher than nonvictims. Women who have been raped by a member of their household are ten times more likely to abuse illegal substances or alcohol. Black women experience the trauma of sexual abuse and aggression from their intimate partners in particular ways, as discussed in studies conducted by Banyard and Graham-Bermann, West, and others.[34] It is also important to note the extent to which Black women are exposed to or coerced into participating in sexually exploitative intimate relationships with older men and men who violate commitments of fidelity by having multiple sexual partners. Far from infrequent or benign, these experiences serve to socialize young women into relationships characterized by unequal power, and they normalize subservient gender roles for women.[35]

Although direct physical assaults and sexual abuse are often studied separately, evidence suggests a strong connection between these two forms of violence against women in the context of intimate relationships. For example, between 57 percent and 63 percent of rapes involve a person the victim knew well and saw frequently in the course of her daily life.[36] In earlier research Bachman and Saltzman established the relational nature of sexual abuse. According to their research, 82 percent of women raped or sexually assaulted between 1992 and 1993 by a lone offender were victimized by a spouse, ex-spouse, partner, friend, acquaintance, or relative, and 26 percent of all rapes and sexual assaults against women were perpetrated by an intimate partner.[37] Several studies have shown that marital rape is often more violent and frequent than other rape and is less commonly reported.[38] The aggregate picture of these two forms of violence against Black women by members of their households presents a compelling call to action for researchers, policymakers, and practitioners alike.

Emotional Manipulation of Black Women and the Creation of a Hostile Social Environment by Their Intimate Partners

Intimate partners also control Black women by creating a hostile social environment in the shared intimate sphere of their lives. Understanding this form of violence is predicated on the recognition that when domestic relations are characterized by power exercised by one person's extreme and persistent tension, dominance of their needs over others, chronic irritability, and irrational agitation that escalates over time, then a pattern is set that is abusive and controlling. The relationship becomes shaped by a cruel dynamic whereby the controlling partner can deploy a set of psychological, emotional, and/or verbal tactics that result in fear, anxiety, or at the very least confusion as a response. Take the case of Lanie.

Lanie worked as a supervisor at a homeless shelter and food bank in the same low-income community where she and her husband lived with their 3-year-old child, her 12-year-old nephew, and her husband's 63-year-old aunt. Her household was a busy one, where the extended family gathered for meals, where neighborhood children played, and where an occasional bible study meeting was held. Despite the very limited material resources, which were strained by the chronic medical problems of the aunt who did not have health insurance, the family appeared to be positioned well relative to their neighbors. Or so it seemed. Lanie, who dedicated herself to "the care of others," was battling a serious threat in her household in the form of her husband's emotional manipulation and psychological abuse. Each morning, Lanie awoke to his demand for sex, after which he criticized her using degrading language. His monitoring of her clothing was accompanied by negative comments about her body and his constant proclamations of attraction to other women. The food she prepared was never good enough, the house was "too noisy" or "too messy," despite the fact that it was often at his initiation that they had visitors, in front of whom he belittled her. She had almost total responsibility for taking care of their child, her nephew, and his aunt, although she never did so to his satisfaction. He ridiculed her work and he made it difficult for her to maintain her friendships by making her friends feel unwelcome and out of place when they visited. His moods were unpredictable, his insults were constant, and his verbal assaults were cruel and degrading.

To the outside world, however, her husband was a charming man who was a good father and a solid member of the low-income community. That it was difficult for him to keep a job was understood as a manifestation of the failed economy and the disappearance of work for unskilled Black men. Lanie helped perpetuate that image of her husband because it "made her look good to have a man like that." Even those who witnessed the abuse expressed envy for Lanie's "stable" household. It was only when she lost her job because of the impact of profound depression on her performance that she was able to admit to her alcohol abuse and self harm. She had spent six long years trying to manage the ways that her husband had created a hostile social world in their household by tip-toeing around his aggression, only to emerge emotionally exhausted, angry at herself, and without support from the community she worked so hard to nourish.

Cases like Lanie's show how the creation of a hostile social environment is effective in disorienting and disadvantaging women in abusive intimate relationships because of the socially constructed expectation that one's domestic space should—at best—be characterized by the absence of persistent negative interactions. When there is no sense of safety, when conditions are chronically tense, and when conflicts build to the point of regular verbal altercations (unless one person disengages), then the conditions are ripe for the creation of a hostile social environment. It is important to emphasize the two distinguishing features of this form of abuse. First, the negative environmental condition is chronic instead of episodic, and the hostility and tension that arise are beyond what is considered normal in domestic relationships. Second, the dominant partner intentionally uses the behaviors that create a hostile social environment to disorient, terrify, or otherwise disadvantage the less powerful partner. A key dimension of how a hostile social environment works is that it goes against hegemonic expectations of domestic life. That is, there is not only a direct emotional effect (feelings of fear and humiliation) but also an indirect effect (feelings that one is "outside of the norm" or "in a crazy relationship"). The conditions of a hostile social environment and their negative consequences significantly worsen the impact of physical and sexual abuse by deeply threatening an abused woman's sense of self, her ability to delineate who is right and what is wrong, and her ability to emotionally resist the impact of further physical and sexual aggression.

effects of emotional abuse can impact incarcerated women [handwritten marginalia]

 While most of the research on intimate partner violence focuses on either physical abuse or sexual aggression, evidence suggests that emotional abuse in a hostile social environment also has serious psychological consequences for female victims of male violence.[39] Women who experience physical assaults and/or sexual abuse by an intimate partner are four to five times more likely to require psychiatric treatment than nonbattered women, and they are five times more likely to attempt suicide. Other psychological consequences include anxiety disorders associated with hypervigilance, diminished affect, disassociation, and the inability to engage with one's feelings as a result of living in constant fear.[40] Research also establishes a range of depressive symptoms that accompany the sense of betrayal of trust caused by violence from an intimate partner and the generalized sense of worthlessness that results from constant insults and disrespect.

These affective states are neither trivial nor uncommon. Additional studies show how profoundly impaired women become when their everyday living conditions are characterized by fear, shame, regret, and dread. Even when direct physical assaults are infrequent and sexual aggression is only suggestive, the prolonged deprivation of rest, comfort, and intimacy associated with a hostile social environment completes a tightly woven web of control that violent intimate partners have over the women they abuse.

One of the most common manifestations of emotionally controlling tactics is minimizing or denying the abuse and its consequences. Perpetrators attempt to shift blame for the physical assaults and sexual abuse onto the victim, and make excuses that are intended to engender compassion *from* the victim *toward* the person harming her. In many cases, the physical assaults and sexual abuse of Black women are punctuated with verbal insults and degrading comments both during an abusive incident and afterward. Sometimes these comments are made in public, in order to remind the victim of the assault and to mark the abuser's power in a social context. There is evidence to suggest that use of arguing as an escalation technique and the use of threats and intimidation can be as injurious as a physical or sexual assault.

Emotional abuse extends beyond the psychological sphere and into the social domain. When children are hurt and families are involved, the impact of physical assaults and sexual abuse is multiplied and constitutes a form of emotional abuse as well.[41] Abusers create a hostile public environment as well as a private one in which women are threatened and degraded in the presence of others, which places restrictions on their daily functioning. Emotional manipulations typically include being shamed in front of, or forcibly isolated from, one's family, having constraints placed on employment and educational opportunities, being denied control over household finances, and facing unreasonable domestic demands. Abuse in this context also includes denial of medication or health care after an assault, coercion to use drugs or alcohol to manage physical or emotional pain, stalking, excessive criticism, and constant surveillance or monitoring by an intimate partner.

It is important to emphasize in this discussion that the type of abuse being described is far beyond the level of the tension associated with domestic disagreements, the occasional use of disrespectful language, or attempts to manipulate a situation to one's advantage. These types of behavior arguably occur in many intimate relationships, even healthy ones. Rather, the situation described by the research on this form of violence against women reveals a pattern of controlling emotional and social behavior that reinforces the terrifying consequences of physical assaults and routine sexual abuse. These behaviors are harmful in and of themselves, but their dangerousness lies in how it layers on to physical injury and sexual trauma, creating a hostile social context of shame and terror within which intimate physical and sexual violence occurs. The case of Mildred Muhammad clearly illustrates this situation.[42]

Mildred Muhammad was abused by a man who never laid his hands on her. His ability to terrorize her didn't require it; he was an expert sharp shooter, a master fighter, and a keen strategist, which had been proven when he was in the military where he worked as a demolitions expert. She knew that he had the ability and the commitment to "destroy her life," but she was surprised by the extent to which he would go to do so. After all, who would ever imagine that when he said he would "bring a city to its knees with terrorism," that he meant it literally.

Ms. Muhammad remembers clearly when she realized that her estranged husband of 12 years was the so-called DC Sniper. She had been hiding from him for years; living in battered women's shelters and with family members, taking out restraining orders, fighting for custody of her children whom he had kidnapped. Despite how scared she was of him, she never lost focus of her goal of keeping her children safe despite his irrational volatility. In retrospect, she understood that his reign of terror, in which ten people died and three others were injured, was actually a horrific cover so that when he murdered her, it would be understood to be part of the pattern of a serial murderer, not a result of her husband's deep aggression toward her.

In her book, *Scared Silent: The Mildred Muhammad Story*, Ms. Muhammad shares in vivid detail the ways that a man like her estranged husband can create a hostile social environment that is permeated with danger if he so chooses. He can remind a woman of his physical strength by destroying property, he can control her movement by having people stalk her, he can isolate a woman by turning family and friends against her through false allegations of infidelity, poor parenting, or mental illness. And he can threaten to hurt her and dozens of others, as Muhammad ultimately did.[43]

Today, Ms. Muhammad is a devoted mother of adult children who are faring very well. As founding director of After the Fall, Inc., she is an inspiring motivational speaker and moving author. Seeing Ms. Muhammad today, it would be hard to imagine that she was so terrified given the tenacious manner she presents and the humor she brings to the telling of her story of male violence. She is also very clear; that violence against Black women does not always involve physical assaults and, as we have learned, the consequences can be just as lethal.

This form of abuse is harmful to any person who experiences it, but the emotional manipulation and social abuse of Black women takes particular forms. Understanding requires attention to broader cultural patterns and social arrangements in the public sphere that influence private-sphere lives. In 1985, I described this problem as "the trap of loyalty"[44] in an article that conceptualized a racialized and gendered loyalty—a set of cultural mandates that exploit women's emotional commitment to their intimate relationships and to members of their households. The notion of a trap of loyalty includes (1) the obligation that Black women feel to buffer their families from the impact of racism in the public sphere; (2) the pressure to live up to the expectation that they, as Black women, will be able to withstand abuse and mistreatment more than other members of their households; and (3) an acceptance of the community rhetoric that argues that Black women are in a more privileged position than are African American men (including those who abuse them). This manipulation of cultural attachment can operate for Black women at an unspoken, self-imposed level, and it is rewarded socially and politically in some parts of Black communities.[45]

Women, like Lanie and Mildred Muhammad, who show unconditional support for Black men, are rewarded with elevated status as "race women." These women go to great lengths to show solidarity with men, even when it means denying their pain and compromising their safety. For example, the trap of loyalty leads some Black women to conceal the abuse they experience, to avoid enlisting support or intervention when they are in danger, and to turn their backs on other vulnerable Black women and children, even their own. The trap of loyalty also enables the systematic rejection of a feminist analysis of patriarchy described earlier and renders gender oppression irrelevant in the Black community. Beyond abuse that women experience in the intimate sphere of their lives, Black women also face risks in their neighborhood and the community context.

[handwritten margin note: specific to women]

Direct Physical Assaults by Community Members

Eleven Black women were found at the home of accused serial killer Anthony Sowell on Imperial Avenue in a low-income community in Cleveland, Ohio.[46] Sowell had a history of sexual violence toward women and allegedly was under police surveillance during the time that he committed the murders. The gruesome discovery of the bodies hidden in interior walls, buried in the backyard, and decomposing in the basement was ironically a huge relief to women in the surrounding communities, who had been living in fear for months because of the violence that seemed to be directly targeted toward marginalized Black women—a group that society let "simply disappear."

Clevelanders are still debating who, in addition to Sowell, is to blame for the delay in interrupting the reign of terror that women in low-income Black communities felt. That it took so long to apprehend him is surely due, in part, to the profile of Sowell's victims. Families were dissuaded from reporting the women as missing by lax law enforcement officials who cited the women's history of substance abuse and prostitution as reasons that they were "gone." City officials pointed to detectives and parole officers who failed to take seriously reports that women had been seen fleeing Sowell's house. Victims' advocates were slower to respond to these cases than others because the women came from communities where few make use of rape crisis and other victims' services. The convergence of this heinous series of crimes that only affected low-income communities, along with Black women's stigmatized position within those communities, and uneven and seemingly reckless law enforcement strategies, resulted in the death of 11 Black women and harm caused to at least another three.

Arising from the myriad of conditions in disadvantaged neighborhoods, the case of the serial killer in Cleveland captures the effect of direct physical assaults of one member of a community by another. Various groups collect incidence data concerning physical assaults, and depending on the measurement, we can draw a range of conclusions. According to the Bureau of Justice Statistics (BJS), Black women have a greater chance of being physically assaulted in their lifetime by people in their neighborhood who are not intimate partners.[47] While these data do not identify the precise relationship between the victim and the alleged assailant, an analysis of the research suggests the following three patterns of direct physical assault of Black women by community members, patterns that are important to the discussion of Black women and male violence.

First, Black women with lower social status are more likely to be victimized and their cases less rigorously investigated than their white counterparts. In general, most assaults are intra-racial, and women are more likely to be physically assaulted by someone familiar or known to them than by a stranger.[48] Attacks are not only *less* likely to be random but also are targeted toward particular women because of their perceived vulnerability, or to achieve an instrumental goal such as "settling" a disagreement or acquiring money or property, as in the case of a robbery. A particularly troubling dimension of this pattern is the extent to which women are assaulted as an extension of antagonisms between men, as in the case where when a woman is beaten because of ongoing trouble between her brother, her male partner, or her son and another man.

A second feature of the pattern of direct physical assaults of Black women at the neighborhood level is that they are more likely to occur close to home than in a different neighborhood.[49] This is true for most crime victims, but in the case of Black women, there are important implications of this pattern. First, many women in low-income communities only infrequently venture far from their neighborhoods. It is a peculiar social fact regarding race and class segregation in this country that many people who live in large urban areas tend to be confined to relatively small geographic areas. They tend not to cross the invisible—but nevertheless clear—boundaries that separate neighborhood groupings, and they do not engage equally in the life of a city.[50] The impact of this behavior is paradoxical: in some instances this insularity can lead to a type of familiarity and emotional proximity that potentially breeds strong community ties.[51] This limited mobility can also lead to isolation, and in the case of women who experience both intimate personal violence and violence from community members, it can exacerbate the trap of loyalty I described in the previous section. That is, reluctance to use public services (especially law enforcement agencies) as a remedy to abuse is confounded by the sense that "everyone knows everyone else" and there is little privacy or anonymity when personal trouble occurs.

A third dimension of the context within which community violence toward Black women exists is the extent to which they are at risk of experiencing harm as "innocent bystanders," witnesses to community violence, or assaulted randomly because of attitudes or perceptions of people around them. Esther Jenkins, in her work describing these patterns of witnesses, has identified the emotional and physical harm that women are particularly vulnerable to in communities where there is a high rate of violence.[52] Jenkins and others argue that, based on an understanding of the "gendered use of space," women who live in neighborhoods where there is a high rate of community violence experience a risk of being hurt by it, even in those instances where the violence is not directed toward them.[53] This literature also notes the long-term consequences of witnessing community violence, with particular attention to the ways that it desensitizes one to the other forms of violence, including intimate personal violence and denigration in the domain of social policy.[54] The experience of a resident of an infamous public housing complex in Miami, Florida illustrates this case.

Rape, Sexual Harassment, and Sexual Aggression toward Black Women from Their Community

The research on non-intimate sexual assault indicates that Black women are overrepresented in the statistics on sexual oppression, rape, harassment, coercion, and other sexual violations in their communities.

Dunbar Village is a public housing project in West Palm Beach, Florida, located blocks from wealthy private residences that line the Intracoastal Waterway. The apartments are one- or two-story barrack style units, where mostly Black or other people of color live. It is a poor community that is plagued by the typical markers of urban blight. According to research conducted by the Associated Press for a July 10, 2007 article, close to 60 percent of the residents lived with incomes that put them below the poverty level in 2000.[55] Despite an aggressive police presence, crimes against property and people organize daily life for the residents. Early one evening, a woman who was the resident in Unit 2 of building 1943 answered a knock on her door and was lured outside by a young man who claimed that she had a flat tire on her car. Once outside, nine other young men, who were armed with guns, demanded money and then forced her back into the apartment, where they proceeded to rape her repeatedly. Following the multiple sexual assaults, the woman was then forced to perform oral sex on her 12-year-old son.

The sexual assault and physical violence were atrocious. It went on for over three hours and involved at least nine attackers. Importantly, the victim of the assault was a Haitian immigrant who had come to the United States in search of a better life for herself and her family. She, like many of the residents of Dunbar Village, had experienced other violations over the years, but none as violent or degrading. What complicated it for her was that none of her neighbors responded. It is a cruel irony that once the case became public, the general sentiment was to support the attackers, all of whom were young Black men under the age of 21. Local community organizations called for compassion and leniency, legal groups called for their defense, and, equally telling, national civil rights organizations moved in to portray the young men as victims, without attention given to the woman who was raped, or her son. Indeed, there is some evidence that the young men had had troubled lives and were impacted by the same social and economic conditions that the residents of Dunbar Village had experienced. That their experiences of degradation and their subsequent need for community support superseded that of the victim and her son is an atrocity.

In another brutal sexual assault case that characterizes the experiences of Black women who live in precarious situations, the issues commonly associated with child rape are complicated by adult culpability and community disregard. In this case, Trenton, New Jersey was the site where a seven-year-old girl was gang-raped by two adult men and three under-aged boys while attending a party with her 15-year-old stepsister. Worried about her safety (with good reason, given the violence that loomed in the social network that the older girl circulated in), the young girl had tagged along to a gathering in Rowan Towers, an apartment complex that was known for violent crime. Once there, the seven-year-old was held against her will and sexually assaulted, while the older girl witnessed the assault. Some accounts of the incident position the older girl as more directly culpable, accusing her of "selling" the younger child to the accused assailants. There were witnesses to the assault and it seems that there was widespread knowledge of the sequence of events that surrounded it. However, residents have been hesitant to come forward with information for fear of retaliation, worries about the safety of the older girl, and a sense that the seven-year-old should have "not been at the party in the first place." The community's response—the lack of coordinated efforts to challenge the various dynamics that lead to the horrific assault—are emblematic of the complex nature of sexual violence in low-income African American communities.

Exposure to unwanted sexual contact like this—be it physical or verbal, direct or suggested, by strangers or acquaintances—causes serious harm to victims.[56] It creates fear and apprehension, limits women's mobility, threatens women's sense of control over their environment, and leads to physical and emotional injury.[57]

The research uses a broad definition of sexual aggression: "sex without consent, rape, sexual control of reproductive rights, and all forms of sexual manipulation carried out by the perpetrator with the intention or perceived intention to cause emotional, sexual, and physical degradation to another person."[58] Using that definition, according to the Crime

Victims Research and Treatment Center of the National Victims Center, 700,000 women are sexually assaulted every year in the United States, which has the highest rate of sexual assault of any industrialized nation in the world.[59] In a report of the National Violence Against Women Survey conducted by the National Institute of Justice and the Centers for Disease Control, 17 percent of all women over the age of 18 had been raped; almost 19 percent of those women are Black.[60] Younger women seem to be at heightened risk; 32 percent of rapes occur when the victim is between the ages of 12 and 17, and women between the ages of 16 and 24 were three times more likely to be raped than women in other cohorts.[61] Twenty-two percent of rapes occur when women are between the ages of 18 and 24.[62]

When race is considered as a variable, in some community samples, 7–30 percent of all Black women report having been raped as adults, and 14 percent report sexual abuse during their childhood. This unusually wide range results from differences in definitions and sampling methods. However, as is true in most research on sexual victimization, it is widely accepted that self-reported data are underreported and that Black women tend to underutilize crisis intervention and other supportive services that collect data.[63] Even though Black women from all segments of the African American community experience sexual violence, the pattern of vulnerability to rape and sexual assault mirrors that of direct physical assaults by intimate partners: Black women from low-income communities like Dunbar Village and Trenton, NJ, with known substance abuse problems or mental health concerns, and those in otherwise compromised social positions are most vulnerable to sexual violence.[64]

In addition to direct sexual assaults, Black women experience a disproportionate number of unwanted comments, uninvited physical advances, and undesired exposure to pornography at an alarming rate in their communities. Almost 75 percent of Black women sampled report some form of sexual harassment in their lifetime, including being forced to live in, work in, attend school in, and even worship in degrading, dangerous, and hostile environments where the threat of rape, embarrassment, and public humiliation is a defining aspect of their social environment.[65]

For some women, this sexual harassment escalates into rape. According to the National Violence Against Women Survey, the rate of non-intimate partner rape is higher for Black women, a rate higher than for most other groups.[66] Not only is the incidence of rape higher, but a review of the qualitative research on Black women's experiences of rape suggests that Black women are assaulted in more brutal and degrading ways than other women.[67] Weapons or objects are more often used, so Black women's injuries are worse than those of other groups of women. Black women are more likely to be raped repeatedly and to experience assaults that involve multiple perpetrators.[68]

Exacerbating these devastating forms of sexual aggression are community norms and values that degrade Black women. These values, which reflect broader narratives about race and gender, are expressed through frequent name-calling, teasing, verbal taunts, and positioning Black women as sexual objects that are public property. Considerable research has examined how the music, media images, and pornography that members of African American communities consume degrade Black women and reinforce their vulnerability to victimization.[69] While clearly linked to broader patriarchal and capitalist interests, this form of sexual degradation reinforces the shame and stigma of the community sexual abuse and aggression that Black women with limited economic resources experience. Because of their over-representation in disadvantaged social positions, Black women are more likely to have low-paying jobs, live in unsafe public housing, be forced to travel on inefficient public transportation, and otherwise be left in harm's way because of their class status; they are more vulnerable to all forms of abuse, and it is more likely that community-level aggression toward them will be minimized or ignored.[70]

Emotional Manipulation of Black Women and the Creation of a Hostile Social Environment in Their Communities

A sixth form of violence documented in the research attempts to encapsulate the ways that women are degraded by or emotionally manipulated by members of their community and the injurious consequences of these experiences. This form of violence includes harm caused by relationships, conditions, and experiences that result in women being taken advantage of, misunderstood by, and exploited by members of their communities in a pattern consistent with other forms of male violence. The harm that results from the experiences and conditions includes decreased sense of self-efficacy, inability to garner resources for remediation in cases of injury, and isolation from potential sources of support. These are serious consequences in and of themselves, but when combined with the other consequences of the physical abuse and sexual aggression that Black women experience, the effects are significantly enhanced.

It is important to return to the notion of "the trap of loyalty." The rhetoric of racial solidarity that can be used to manipulate Black women's commitment to individuals, their families, and their peer groups to fully understand the harm created by social isolation and hostility. Historians and social scientists who study the gender dynamics of race have pointed to the ways that Black women's roles in their communities have been organized around notions of allegiance to family, dedication to collective advancement, and respectability.[71] This literature describes the sense that Black women are uniquely responsible for "racial uplift" because of their particular positioning in relationship to Black men and the larger social world. In comparison to Black men, Black women are assumed by some to be less vulnerable to attack by social critics and legislators and therefore better positioned in the social world. Evidence used to support this claim includes the higher rate of incarceration of Black men, the higher employment rate of Black women, and the attacks on Black men by targeted policies such as the establishment of paternity.

The experience of Karrine Steffans provides a vivid example of how the Black community's response to the physical and sexual abuse creates hostile social environments that contribute to violence against Black women. As a high-profile performer in the music industry, Ms. Steffans (also known as "Superhead") surprised fans of rap music when she wrote openly about her physical abuse by rap stars in *VIBE* magazine.[72] This widely read magazine, which is not known for its feminist coverage of issues related to Black women, was a strategic and courageous place to raise the issue of domestic violence; the promise of mass education to an audience who is not the target of mainstream anti-violence messages was impressive. By disclosing how she was "choked, whipped with belts," "raped and disregarded as a human being" and in her description of the "vicious cycle of abuse that she was trapped in," Steffans brought to light in very personal terms the terror and humiliation that physical and sexual abuse brings, erasing all of the benefits and glories of fame. Steffans' experience was met with surprise by many fans. That a talented, success-ful young Black woman who seemed to reflect the community's images of vibrancy and beauty (albeit a problematic image) could be in such danger of physical abuse, sexual exploitation, and emotional degradation, may have shocked some readers and listeners.

That Steffans had no place to turn should have been even more shocking. In the *VIBE* story, she describes friends saying, "what did you do to him" or, "don't tell anyone because you'll only make yourself look bad." Indeed, judging from the majority of responses these predic-tions may have been right; in blogs, editorials, television commentar-ies, and other popular venues, there are accounts that show how Black women who disclose their abuse—especially abuse from high-profile Black men—will be met with a series of insulting and degrading charges.

Two other cases illustrate the ways that physical violence toward suc-cessful Black women by non-intimates is complicated by the combined dynamics of racism and gender oppression. Commonly known as "The Cracker Barrel Assault," a man dressed in fatigues beat a highly regarded Army reservist when she politely asked him to be careful when he roughly pushed a revolving door when entering a Cracker Barrel restau-rant.[73] Worried about her seven- year-old daughter who was also in the revolving door, the woman asked that the man "be more careful" which prompted him to yell racist slurs and beat the woman by kicking her and punching her in the head. Witnesses to the assault in Marrow, Georgia did not intervene.

Few responded either when a man in Orange, Texas dragged 26-year-old Theresa Adell Ardoin to her death behind his pickup truck after beating her in the head with a hammer.[74] While these assaults could eas-ily meet the standard definition of a hate crime, the ways that they were presented to the public by the media left lingering doubt with regard to the women's culpability in the abuse they experienced. Was Ardoin with the man preparing to use drugs? Did the Army reservist really shout or push the man who beat her in front of her daughter? Was Karrine Steffans looking to advance her own career?

The pattern of discrediting Black women furthers the impact that vio-lence has both on the victims themselves and the communities that they come from. It emerges from the Black community's hesitation to take the

violence seriously, lest it discredit Black men. Contemporary race scholars and Black feminist activists have linked this hesitation to the popular
notion that Black women face significant advantages when compared to
Black men. This skewed analysis emerges from the trap of loyalty which
results in Black women having their needs denied, their contributions
discounted, and their victimization ignored. Indeed, in this problematic formulation, Black women are expected to sacrifice their claims to
resources and power because of the disadvantages and risks that Black
men face.[75] In the case of male violence, this means that Black women's
experiences must be subsumed to the needs of Black men. At a very concrete level, if a woman involves the criminal legal system following an
abusive episode or assault, it can be viewed as turning a Black man over
to the police.

In addition to the racial uplift discourse that leads to the trap of
loyalty, contemporary media images contribute to the emotional
manipulation of Black women, and the creation of a hostile social
environment in their communities. One need only look at the portrayal of Black women in cultural venues like music videos, movies,
and novels.[76] The primary culprit is surely the mainstream entertainment industry controlled by capitalist markets that are by and large
owned by white men. However, there is a subgroup of Black produc-
ers, artists, and profiteers who control negative images of women that
Black communities consume. To be sure, there are complications to
this analysis: the ways that women participate in these portrayals, the
counter-images that are very positive, and so on. In this discussion
however, it is important to make connections between those images
that are advanced by and controlled by the Black community and the
creation of a hostile social environment that harms Black women. And
there are many.

When you combine racial uplift rhetoric and the community-level
expectations associated with it, the profoundly negative media images
that are more contemporary, and the ways that Black community leaders
have responded to male violence, the impact of the experiences becomes
clearer. On the one hand, Black women experience tremendous pressure
associated with bearing a disproportionate burden for caring for "the
community." When they cannot (or choose not to) perform the roles that

responsibility demands, the consequences are considerable. One need only look at the recent criticism of Black women by community leaders for problems such as Black fertility rates, child development, crime, *and* violence. Despite limited resources, opportunities, and support, Black women are still blamed for problems in the Black community, *including* those that result from their lack of power and subsequent victimization.

In sum, Black women's experiences of emotional manipulation and social disregard at the community level parallel the trap of loyalty noted in the discussion of intimate personal violence. In addition, Black women encounter unequal demands for performance of the duties required to maintain social life and community responsibilities, and then they are blamed for the failings in Black neighborhoods. At a minimum, Black women are disenfranchised in terms of community decision making, and the forms of abuse they experience are trivialized. It is not an overstatement to suggest that in the same ways that women are denied power in the relational and domestic spheres, the community embraces a set of dynamics that conspire to foster an environment where individual men can use physical and sexual violence against Black women with few real or long-term consequences. Black community members tolerate direct physical assaults, sexual abuse and aggression, emotional manipulation, and social alienation of Black women.[77] This betrayal is furthered by the absence of gender analysis in the rhetoric of race and power, the discrediting of Black feminist leadership, and the disregard for the needs of Black women. The forms of abuse Black women experience in the community context—including assaults by neighbors, sexual aggression in the community, and the social disadvantages inflicted by neighborhood structures and processes—only intensify their vulnerability.

Direct Physical Assault of Black Women by State Agencies

A more complicated understanding of violence against Black women necessitates attention to the research on direct physical assault on Black women by state agencies and the physical consequences of public policy decisions that disempower them.

The convergence of conditions that leave Black women vulnerable to abuse from state agencies and actors can be illustrated in the death of

Aiyana Jones, who was killed while sleeping on a couch at home where she lived with her grandmother and several other relatives.[78] The incident happened early one morning in a low-income community on the east side of Detroit, when police raided the home by first launching a flash-bang grenade, and moved in with guns drawn. They were allegedly searching for a person suspected of homicide who reportedly lived in the house. One of the officers entered the house firing his gun and shot Aiyana.

The officer's account claims that the gun discharged following a physical altercation between one of the officers and the victim's grandmother, Mertilla Jones. While the details of the circumstances that led to the murder of Aiyana are disputed, it is clear that aggressive police action left the child and her family at risk. The alleged suspect was apprehended at a different location and the family is currently involved in a lawsuit against the Detroit Police Department both for the murder and for initiating a "cover-up" in the circumstances surrounding Aiyana's death.

There are many other illustrative cases of police brutality against Black women. Six bullets killed Kathryn Johnston, a 92-year-old grandmother, when police stormed her house in Atlanta, Georgia looking for illegal drugs. Shelia Stevenson was riding her bicycle on the sidewalk (a crime in the city of Philadelphia) and was punched repeatedly by a police officer, and Carolyn Sue Botticher died after police in North Carolina fired 22 rounds at a car she was in when she refused to stop at a police checkpoint.[79]

Despite the number of similar cases, most of the conceptual and empirical analyses of male violence pay little attention to the overt physical assaults that authority figures, who have official roles in state institutions, inflict on Black women. Examples of this form of male violence include excessive use of force by police officers toward women during an arrest, physical abuse while in the custody of state agencies, and battering by public employees upon whom women depend for protection and resources, including child welfare workers, employees in public assistance offices, and drug treatment counselors. While accounts of these forms of direct physical assaults are not uncommon to those who interact with women who rely on public services, a review of the literature on overt use of state violence reveals a paucity of published data that establish national rates of these problems.[80] There are only a few national studies that measure physical assault of clients by employees of state-run institutions and governmental agencies, but they do indicate that direct physical assault of detained women is a serious problem that is primarily documented through informal discussions. There are, however, national organizations, including Human Rights Watch, and a few smaller local groups that collect qualitative data on the mistreatment of clients, consumers, or citizens who are in some form of state custody.[81]

A less overt aspect of direct physical assaults of Black women by state agencies is how the state's lack of response to acts of male violence leaves women vulnerable to prolonged dangerous abuse. More a public policy issue, this includes instances where police have not responded to battered women who reach out for assistance in an emergency, women who have been retraumatized by insensitive medical examinations, and cases in which authorities have failed to intervene or interrupt an assault on a woman in state custody.[82] While indirect, this neglect by state agencies mandated to protect women is a contributing factor to the disproportionate rate of male violence against Black women, who are more likely than other groups to depend on public services.[83]

In addition, there is a broader web of public policies that, contrary to their stated intention, harm Black women by limiting the opportunities in their lives. Those women with the least amount of social privilege are the most vulnerable to these harms. Here I am referring to the ways that state economic policies limit women's access to basic resources, how the removal of decision-making rights constrains their health choices, and how regulations regarding family and households sanction women who make choices that are considered non-normative. In some cases, these policies directly harm women. Reproductive health policy leads to harm when it denies women access to safe, legal abortions or effective contraception. Being forced to endure unwanted and sometimes high-risk pregnancies can, of course, cause physical harm.

Sexual Exploitation and Aggression toward Black Women Who Are in State Custody

The physical harm caused by assaults (or the risk of harm) is further complicated by sexual exploitation and aggression. Angel thought she understood how the system worked—"you follow the rules, despite how arbitrary you think they are, you find your crew and protect them like you want to be protected, and you never show your pain." These strategies had gotten her through three previous incarcerations. When she walked into her housing unit at Rikers Island Correctional Facility, she made a commitment to do what she knew would work to keep her relatively safe, hoping that this would be a short stay since she was charged only with violating the conditions of her parole. Angel's expectation was that when the judge heard the situation—that she had missed her appointment with her parole officer because her mother was in the hospital—she would be released. She hoped to only have to survive for a few days.

On her way to her medical exam, she passed a sign on the wall that said "No talking, no standing still, and no co-mingling." The sign indicated that violations of these rules would result in punishment in solitary confinement. Angel had not seen that sign before and found it curious, because correctional officers *regularly* asked women walking in the halls to "stand still"; co-mingling was unavoidable in a place like Rikers Island given the number of women who came through the Rose M. Singer Center, and she knew very well that she had to talk when spoken to for her own safety. Even more troubling was the statement that was hand-written at the bottom of the sign—"no holding hands and no wearing of men's underwear." Angel knew that these two additional rules were aimed at controlling women's sexuality; one directed toward those who form intimate relationships with other women and the other giving blatant authority to correctional officers to examine the women's underwear and to deem it acceptable or not. The fact that women were given clothing from the clothing bin (typically articles that have been donated) and were not free to choose the type of underwear they wore was not important. It was not clear what threat to safety or security one kind of underwear had over another, or why such an infraction would require solitary confinement. What was most significant to Angel was that those who wrote the sign had the right and even the responsibility to look at her underwear at any point in time. As Angel continued down the hall to her medical examination, she realized that things had changed in the jail since her last arrest and the risks to her safety were expanding beyond what her commonsense survival strategies could offer. Indeed, the sense of sexual vulnerability that is created through pat searches, open showers, and public sexual harassment had increased significantly.

Sexual aggression toward Black women from employees in state agencies is one of the most pernicious forms of male violence. In many instances, this abuse is used to create shame and fear, and to further compromise women's sense of self-worth and their entitlement to services. The sexual abuse of women in state custody or in other dependent positions is enabled by the stereotypical images of Black women's sexuality; it exploits one of the most vulnerable aspects of women's lives in a way that parallels sexual abuse by an intimate partner and rape perpetrated by community members and acquaintances. There is a profound impact when women are sexually assaulted and exploited by state institutions that are theoretically designed to protect or support them—or at least not harm them.[84]

Take, for example, the sexual abuse of women in prison by correctional officers, estimated to be a significant and complicated problem in many penal institutions. When women are forced into sexual contact with those who are "guarding" them, they have very limited recourse because the "guard" is authorized by the state (and rewarded by the institution) to confine and control women in its custody. So, because pat searches and body cavity examinations are routine "security procedures" in most jails and prisons, women are exposed to potential legitimate sexual exploitation. Indeed, while most casual observers would be able to distinguish a "security procedure" from an act of sexual aggression, most of these encounters are not, in fact, monitored by impartial outside observers. Female inmates have reported that the use of highly sexualized cell extractions and searches, performed in the presence of male officers, is commonplace.[85] It is not uncommon, therefore, for women to complain about a guard groping rather than "pat searching," forcefully inserting foreign objects in them as a way to conduct a "cavity search," or "taunting them in sexually explicit terms" while observing them during bathing and dressing routines. Most women confined to correctional institutions report overt sexual misconduct by those with authority over them, and they claim to feel very limited protection and few opportunities for recourse from "the system."[86]

A 1996 survey of incarcerated women conducted by Human Rights Watch found that at least half of all female prisoners have experienced some form of sexual abuse prior to incarceration and that 60 percent of women in state prisons were physically or sexually abused in the past.[87] In terms of governmental research, in those states that collect such data, women have filed charges against prison guards, police officers, probation officers, or other "supervising authorities" for sexual abuse in 41 percent of state and federal prisons and jails operated by the government as well as in private institutions.[88] Because incarcerated women are the victims and are in a compromised relationship with the state authority figure, the extent to which these forms of male violence go unreported, uninvestigated, or dismissed is significant.

Researchers affiliated with national advocacy groups provide very moving accounts of the sexual abuse of women (overwhelmingly Black women) who are under the control of state institutions, including prisons, psychiatric facilities, welfare offices, and others.[89] While even less well documented, sexual harassment and stalking are also serious, common, and threatening experiences for women that carry grave physical, emotional, and social consequences.[90] Even in cases where women report consensual sexual relationships with people who have tremendous decision-making power over them, it is logical to suggest that engaging in a sexual relationship with a person who has arrest power, who can limit one's phone calls, who can deny access to food or water, or who can restrict movement in a confined facility is far from a "free choice." I am not suggesting that women do not have the capacity (and the right) to decide who they will be sexual with and under what circumstances. However, in this analysis of male violence against Black women, it is important to question what "free choice" would even look like. When a woman's "best option" is to engage in a sexual relationship to ensure that her rights are protected, that she is not arrested without cause, that her welfare benefits are not terminated, that she is not denied a visit from her family, or that she is provided with food, medical care, counseling, or education in a prison, is that decision "free"?

Sexual assault is not limited to incarcerated women or those inhabiting low-income neighborhoods. Black women who have chosen to pursue careers in the military have reported instances of sexual victimization both on active duty and in the reserves.[91] The U.S. Government's Accountability Office reported that 113 military personnel reported sexual assault in 2008.[92] Other evidence of institutional disregard for Black women's vulnerability can be found in the data regarding the lack of protection of Black women faculty members in predominantly white institutions of higher education and Black women executives in large corporations.[93]

In addition to sexual assaults and harassment, social policies result in the sexual manipulation and harmful control of Black women's lives through policies concerning sexuality and reproduction.[94] It is clear that these policies are targeted toward Black women with less privilege, although it is impossible to estimate the number of women who are affected. For example, policies embedded in some welfare regulations require women to limit their number of children by using specific methods of birth control, including Depo-Provera and Norplant, which are known to pose risks to women's health. These population control policies are linked to larger state initiatives concerned with control of poor women's bodies and families. Research indicates that these policies are targeted and serve the interests of profit-motivated corporations.[95] Another example is the 1996 law, signed by President George W. Bush, called the Unborn Victims of Violence Act, which established criminal penalties for anyone who injures a fetus in the commission of another federal offense. This could include men who abuse their pregnant wives, pregnant women who use drugs, and women who choose to end their pregnancy with an abortion. The list of draconian applications of policies aimed at controlling the reproductive lives of women is extensive, including the denial of contraception or information about HIV prevention, and the threats to abortions, the arrest of prostitutes on sex-offense charges, and the anti-lesbian agenda that permeates most social, health, and educational policies in the United States.

Emotional Manipulation and the Creation of a Social Environment that Is Hostile to Black Women

The rate of physical abuse and sexual aggression toward Black women confirms that at the most basic level, institutional protections are unequally available to Black women who live in low-income communities and face disproportionate levels of male violence. The understanding is deepened by including the vulnerability created by ongoing social practices and public policies that constitute a form of structural abuse of Black women in compromised social positions which result from their economic status, their legal troubles, their sexual orientation, or other markers of a stigmatized social identity.

In the most basic sense, this case points to the circumstances that poor Black women victims of male violence face that leave them uniquely disadvantaged by the state, because they have fewer support services to help them care for their families, fewer opportunities to get a meaningful job or pursue an education, limited access to safe housing, and very little protection from agencies when they experience bodily harm. Secondarily, a definition that includes structural violence provides a more complex analysis of the ways the state abuses its authority through discriminatory public policy that systematically disadvantages Black women who experience male violence. Three examples of this violence are (1) the role of mainstream media in creating stigmatized images of Black women, (2) the public policy decisions surrounding child custody issues for women who experience male violence, and (3) the ways that welfare policies have created a hostile social environment that has disadvantaged Black women who experienced male violence.

The larger framework here is the claim that social institutions have the same power to denigrate vulnerable Black women who depend on them for services or protection as household and community members do. Those who are in the most destitute situations—for example, incarcerated women—experience this profoundly; their basic needs are routinely denied as a form of punishment, and they face inhumane sensory deprivation, objectification, overmedication, and other forms of abuse that parallel the ways that intimate partners abuse women.[96] The direct physical assaults and/or sexual abuse of women perpetrated by state institutions or people with institutional power lead to a hostile social environment, which results in fear and humiliation. This condition reinforces a negative social perception and puts women at risk of male violence in other contexts.

In addition to the ways that the state neglects its responsibility to Black women by not protecting them when they are in danger, other aspects of the social environment leave women vulnerable to degrading social circumstances that have emotional and material consequences. For example, mainstream corporate-controlled media colludes with the more overt forms of abuse of Black women by promoting images that degrade them.[97] These images position women outside of the protective assumptions of state agencies.

On January 7, 2011, Jamie and Gladys Scott were released from the Central Mississippi Correctional Facility just outside of Jackson, Mississippi after being incarcerated there for more than 16 years. They are now living in the Florida Panhandle, where they have been reunited with their large extended family while Jamie, 36, awaits a kidney transplant from her 38-year-old sister, Gladys. The sisters were released from prison on the condition that Gladys provide a kidney for her sister—a deal that would save the state of Mississippi $200,000 a year, which covered Jamie's dialysis, according to Governor Haley Barbour, who suspended their sentences.[98]

While the women's release is to be celebrated, the background to this case casts a long shadow on the extent to which the move could be considered an act of justice or not. Gladys and Jamie, two African American women, were sentenced to double life sentences for a crime where they were allegedly accomplices to an armed robbery that involved $11. The men who actually committed the crime served two years of an eight-year sentence. The women had no previous criminal record. The excessive sentences separated them from their children and other family members, and may have contributed to Jamie's deteriorating health. Persistent pressure from civil rights groups and the legal advocacy community was not powerful enough to influence their release; but money that would be spent on the transplant was, which has raised questions from ethicists who think about issues of medical coercion and transplants.

Some argue that granting freedom in exchange for a transplant is tantamount to "paying" a donor for their organ. Others point to issues of coercion; the women were poor, they had exhausted their appeals, and they were clearly vulnerable to the state's ability to manipulate their willingness to comply with its demands so that they could be released. Some liken this unprecedented mandate to paying a fee for release—much like practices associated with debtors' prisons which are being reinstated through policies like having incarcerated people pay for court fines, electronic monitoring devices, drug tests, or rehabilitation classes.

The system of imprisonment in the United States is pernicious in deploying strategies that control vulnerable populations, including Black women who are dependent on them for their survival. The Scott sisters represent one example of coercive control. There are other examples where state agents are authorized or at least not deterred from using insults, discriminatory practices, and subtle forms of harassment to control vulnerable women's lives.

Take, for example, Duanna Johnson, a Black transgender woman who was harassed by police (called "he-she" and "faggot") while she was being beaten in police custody in a Memphis jail,[99] or the case of a Black lesbian arrested for "disruptive behavior" and told by a Boston police officer that had restrained her, "you want to act like a man, I will treat you like a man." These examples of the ways that women who do not subscribe to traditional gender roles are vulnerable illustrate the circumstances that create conditions where male violence can be furthered.

The mainstream media rarely covers these kinds of stories as examples of abuse, manipulation, or maltreatment, and if they do, they present the women in unsympathetic terms. The lack of political response of media reinforces the sense that Black women's experience and how it is related to victimization is not serious; that maltreatment is somehow deserved, and that it is not an important commentary on community or social life. Claire Renzetti, an influential social scientist whose work focuses on gender violence, sums it up well: "They (Black women in this case) are depicted by politicians and others as promiscuous, lazy and undeserving."[100] Such a sentiment, fueled by the media representation I previously described, leads to concrete dilemmas associated with how poor Black women who are abused are treated by victim's services and public agencies.

A key dimension of the hostile social world created for Black women is stringent regulation by public policies that constrain their opportunity to lead healthy, safe, full, and self-determined lives. Two areas directly linked to male violence are welfare policies that have substantially limited support for low-income women and child welfare policies that apply harsh sanctions against women who have difficulties performing typical tasks associated with their duties as mothers. It is ironic that while some women have benefited from 30 years of advances in working conditions, family life, and health status because of feminist organizing, others have faced increased surveillance and punishment, a disparity that has seemingly gone unnoticed by those who have reaped the most benefits. In fact, the disadvantages of social policy changes are concentrated in the subgroup of Black women who have been demonized by the new welfare legislation and are most likely to lose custody of their children to agencies designated for child protective services.[101] They are also the women who are most vulnerable to intimate partner violence, assaults in their neighborhoods, and violence through state-run institutions.

The child protective system has a long and well-documented history of targeting families with children in which parents have limited resources.[102] In recent years, researchers have paid considerable attention to women who experience male violence at the hands of the Child Protective Service system. The authors of "Understanding Families with Multiple Barriers to Self Sufficiency"[103] noted that state employees viewed long-term welfare recipients as having few marketable job skills and thus reduced the level of service to this population. These policy changes are directed with noteworthy vigor toward women who have a complicated relationship with the law, women who are involved in non-normative sexual relationships, and young women (the overwhelming majority of whom are Black). Dorothy Roberts, a well-known feminist legal scholar, makes the compelling case in *Shattered Bonds*[104] and *Killing the Black Body*[105] that the state and conservative ideology have assumed a very aggressive position toward Black women and their families. This position contributes to violence within and destruction of Black families that is virtually wiping out communities.[106]

In 1996, the public welfare system was restructured. What was previously called Aid to Families with Dependent Children (ADC) is now called Temporary Assistance to Needy Families (TANF), part of the Personal Responsibility and Work Opportunity Reconciliation Act. This reform was initiated, in part, for ideological reasons documented in many analyses of welfare reform.[107] The subsequent process for the distribution of services is organized to the disadvantage of Black women who experience male violence. This, coupled with the lack of protection and opportunity, is as effective in creating a hostile social world as actual direct physical abuse and sexual assault because women may internalize the potential harm and change their behavior as a way to avoid it.[108]

The Broader Context of Violence against Black Women: Theoretical Review of the Literature

The data presents a compelling case about the persistence and seriousness of the violence that Black women face by pointing to the range of forms it takes and the various contexts within which it is experienced. However, the full impact of what happens to Black women, like Tanya, Ms. B, and the New Jersey 4 is best understood by adding a more theoretical analysis of Black women's subordination that occurs because of the dynamics associated with the buildup of a prison nation. In this, the concluding section of this chapter, that theoretical literature is reviewed. It is organized according to a logic that is similar to the framing I used in the first part of this chapter. There are distinct themes that describe the layering on of circumstances that disadvantage Black women and that these disadvantages cut across different spheres of social life. The overall conclusion that can be drawn from this review is that the patterns of subordination in households, neighborhoods, and society, and persistent disadvantage caused by physical, sexual, and social abuse, constitute a profound form of structural violence against Black women.

This review starts from the perspective that quantitative conclusions that rely on statistical analyses do not fully capture the impact of violence in the lives of Black women. Sociologist Kathleen Ferraro is among the anti-violence scholars who study social problems from a feminist perspective and who identify the various shortcomings of using statistics to study violence against women of color; including the lack of historical context, an inability to consider the social and political context in which the violence occurs, and the ways that statistics reify race as an objective fact as opposed to an ideologically based system of domination.[109] The shortcomings in the quantitative literature reflect broader criticism of social research that feminist scholars make—that simply describing racial difference is inadequate to the task of explaining persistent racial disadvantage and how it is correlated with the concentration of social problems and institutionalized racism.[110] In particular, simply providing a statistical picture of racial disproportion leaves open the possibility that "conservative politicians and racial realists may employ these data to reinforce the individualistic interpretations of behavior that emphasize the pathology of families of color."[111]

The rich body of literature that has therefore emerged to complement quantitative analyses could be considered a subfield in the area of violence against women. It focuses on the ways that race/ethnicity, class, sexuality, age, disability, compromised legal status, and other conditions and marginalized identities complicated the experience of violence against women.[112] The work calls attention to the particularities of the suffering that Black women and other women of color experience and the failure of conventional remedies to respond to the physical, sexual, and social abuse from household members, neighbors, or structural conditions that affect Black women's lives.

In one of the first comprehensive edited volumes, domestic violence scholar Natalie Sokoloff gives voice to scholars and activists who have advanced the position that violence against women must be understood from within the context of race, class, *and* gender.[113] This collection of readings firmly establishes the relevancy of social context, in that women's social position profoundly complicates their experience of violence. Like the more recent *Incite! Anthology*, it deeply enriches how violence against women of color is understood as part of a larger pattern of abuses and the broad changes that need to be made to stop it.[114]

A considerable amount of this theoretical literature relies on discussions of negative cultural images and how vulnerability to violence and other social disadvantages become naturalized through the process of their stigmatizing identities. Building on the work of scholars like Janette Taylor[115] and Evelyn White,[116] Shondrah Tarrezz Nash brings an interest in Black women's methods of coping to this work. She argues that focusing on how Black women's experience of physical and sexual violence is affected by a range of culturally constructed identities that take shape from living under conditions of social inequality.[117] She illuminates how Black women's gender roles and relationships are at the center of their vulnerability to all forms of male violence. This analysis points to the association between racist stereotypes and how women are victimized in their households, communities, and institutional settings, and explores the dynamics that create sympathy for Black men's positioning within the racial hierarchy. This combination makes it easy for those in power to misinterpret Black women's responses to being victimized, including their resorting to violence as a means of self-defense and other involvement in behavior that is considered illegal.[118] While much of this work focuses on adult women, criminologists Meda Chesney-Lind and Jody Miller make similar arguments about Black and other girls of color and the ways that their position in the world, and in their communities, disadvantages them and leaves them vulnerable to violence.[119] This work draws attention to the connection between abuse, delinquency, and gender.[120] Some of this literature draws direct connection between racialized and sexist images to gender violence, (as in Miller-Young's work on Black women's involvement in pornography), while others draw on broader theoretical work in fields like psychology to look at questions of self-esteem, sexuality vulnerability, and stigma.[121]

The impact of stereotypes, stigma, and marginalized identities extends far beyond the realm of creating an emotional and social circumstance for Black women that leaves them vulnerable to male violence. There is a growing body of literature that links institutionalized racism to violence against women, and Black women's particular vulnerability to it. Several key studies have linked structural conditions to increased violence. Robert Hampton, William Oliver, and Lucia Magarian are social scientists whose influential work on violence in the Black Community has provided a theoretical explanation of macro-level vulnerability to male violence that hinges on looking at structural, cultural, and situational neighborhood and institutional contexts and how they create subordinated masculinity. They argue that loyalty to Black men emerges from these contexts and the need for Black women to be "strong in the face of racism in society" leads to increased violence within their communities.[122] This argument builds on a broader body of work that looks both at how perceptions of racism lead to violence,[123] as well as how racism *is* violence in and of itself.[124] The issue of social context and victimization is also raised in work by Jennifer Wesley who, like La Donna M. Long and colleagues, looks at experiences of subordination across the lifespan in their household, community, and society to see how they influence women's experience of physical, sexual, and social violence. Her work on how women negotiate power inequality and violence as well as structural issues like homelessness points to the relationship between micro-level issues and macro-level problems.[125]

When specific institutions are considered, a clear and persistent pattern that links institutionalized racism to violence against women can be identified. Janette Taylor focuses on how discriminatory practices in domestic violence services can be understood as a form of cultural violence insofar as it leaves Black women disproportionately vulnerable to abuse.[126] Bryant-Davis, Chung, and Tillman consider the relationship between racism and violence by looking at the societal trauma and distress for Black women who experience sexual assault that results in problems associated with substance abuse, low self-esteem, and inaccessible mental health services.[127] In similar work, Tricia Bent-Goodley and Michael Rodriquez look at the health-care delivery system and ways that health and mental health disparities are linked to structural racism and violence against women.[128] This work builds on voluminous research on domestic violence and health, but is distinguished in its focus on how the co-occurrence of health problems must include a discussion of racism and cultural discrimination as factors in physical, sexual, and social abuse of Black women.

Shannon Monnat applies the analysis to the welfare system in a 2010 article that looks at how racial ideology, images of women, and the policies associated with the U.S. welfare system contribute to Black women's social and political marginalization as well as their economic vulnerability.[129] While Monnat does not focus on violence against women, her analysis is relevant to how women are left vulnerable by public policy and are therefore vulnerable to various forms of violence in several contexts. Dana Ain Davis relates welfare policy specifically to violence against women.[130] Complementary analyses can be found in the work of Tester, who looks at sexual harassment and public housing, and Holzman and colleagues, who explore how gender, race, and housing leave women vulnerable to structural violence.[131]

Prisons and penal institutions are the subject of Thompson's and Struckman-Johnson's work that firmly establishes the vulnerability of women to institutional practices that discriminate both in terms of gender and race and leave Black women vulnerable to violence.[132] Sudbury also makes this connection directly in her work on Black women, violence, and incarceration.[133] Two final examples of the emerging literature that links violence against Black women and racism is the work of Carol Stabile in her book *White Victims, Black Villains: Gender, Race and Crime News in US Culture,* and Hillary Potter's work on Black women who have experienced violence and their use of religious services.[134]

Of particular relevance to this discussion of *Arrested Justice: Black Women, Violence, and America's Prison Nation* is the theoretical literature that looks at the relationship between violence against women and their coerced involvement in crime. This body of work extends the discussion of the statistical overrepresentation of women of color in the criminal legal system to a focus on how the criminal legal system, that should be responsible for protecting women, is fundamentally organized according to the ideology and politics of systematic racism to the disadvantage of Black people, poor people, women, and other marginalized groups.[135] This assumption was the starting point of my interviews at Rikers Island with African American battered women who were forced or coerced into participating in illegal activities, which built on the work of feminist scholar-activists Angela Browne and Susan Osthoff and was later taken up by Cathy McDaniels-Wilson and Joanne Belknap, and Dana D. Dehart.[136] The central argument is that there are some aspects of the criminal legal system which, like other institutions, don't protect Black women who have experienced violence and, instead, criminalizes them.

Conclusion

The review of the data and theoretical literature on male violence I have presented in this chapter is an attempt to explain Black women's experience with multiple forms of abuse from their households, communities, and from society, and a wide range of consequences to it. By delineating the various forms of the abuse and describing the contexts in which they occur, I provide a way of systematically understanding the enormity of the problem of male violence that Black women face. Indeed, experiencing any form of abuse has serious physical, emotional, and social consequences for women. Just to name a few individual effects, physical assaults cause serious injuries and result in chronic disabilities; emotional and psychological abuse leads to mental health and substance abuse problems; and community violence isolates and limits Black women's ability to contribute to their extended families.

The broader point of the theoretical review of the literature is to show that Black women experience multiple forms of male violence simultaneously over the course of a lifetime—in many contexts—it's not just the experience of an isolated event. As a result, they are seriously disadvantaged. The effect of this disadvantage is powerful, pulling Black women who experience the worst aspects of it into the path of the buildup of a prison nation, the topic of chapter 4. First, in chapter 3, I explain how the anti-violence movement failed to protect them from this pull.

3

How We Won the Mainstream
but Lost the Movement

Around the time that I began collecting stories of women like Tanya, Ms. B was assaulted, and when the New Jersey 4 were convicted, there was a national celebration of the decennial anniversary of the Violence Against Women Act, which had passed with bipartisan support. Former Attorney General John Ashcroft was one of the featured speakers.[1] Ashcroft is a conservative Republican, appointed by President George W. Bush as a strategic and symbolic representation of his conservative agenda, including harsh criminal justice approaches to persistent social problems. Ashcroft's appearance at a conference on violence against women was paradoxical and profound. To many activists in the audience, it spoke volumes about the ways in which the anti-violence movement in this country had become institutionalized. That the anti-violence movement had achieved sufficient social validation that John Ashcroft would be invited to speak at this critical event (and that he would accept the invitation) demonstrated that the anti-violence movement had won mainstream legitimization. This validation was a result of key decisions that softened the radical politics of the work and ultimately betrayed the visions of the early grassroots feminist, anti-racist activism.

As I discussed in chapter 2, the problem of violence against Black women is pernicious and the causes are systematic. The chapter showed that the staggering rates of physical abuse, the harrowing emotional torture, and the degrading sexual assaults occur in all spheres of life for some women. The further marginalized their status is, the more devastating the impact, such that Black women in the most marginalized communities are not safe in their homes or in their neighborhoods, and the institutions that should assist and protect them do not. Additionally, public policies are hostile to poor, Black women, already stigmatized, which furthers the impact of male violence. The data shows how the brutal attacks injured their bodies and their psyches and that the emotional scars are often permanent, creating internal trauma and persistent climates of fear and feelings of worthlessness. The consequences for individuals, their families, and communities are far reaching, profoundly shaping the social, emotional, and political experiences of the vulnerable population of Black women who are the focus of this book.

This chapter is the first of two chapters that lay out the social and ideological conditions that surround the male violence that Black women experience. Here I describe the evolution of the social response to violence against women; beginning with the first organized programs in the early 1960s, through the establishment of a formalized governmental response with the passage of the Violence Against Women Act in 1994, to the critical juncture that the anti-violence movement finds itself in today; facing challenges associated with institutionalization, co-optation, and declining influence which leaves some women in as much danger as ever. This chapter will describe the key events that led us to this point as well as the shifts in public consciousness and political ideology that characterized eight distinct stages of the anti-violence movement's history. By reviewing the various pressures and influences on the work over time, readers will come to understand how and why we won the mainstream, but lost aspects of the work that characterized it as a social change movement. In chapter 4, I describe the broader social and ideological changes that were occurring at the same time that the anti-violence movement was evolving—the conservative wave that lead to the buildup of America's prison nation.

How We Won the Mainstream but Lost the Movement: From Grassroots Activism to Institutionalization

It is important to begin this discussion by defining the conceptualization I am using of the "anti-violence movement." When I use that phrase in this book, I am referring to the work that is done by individuals, groups, and organizations to end male violence against women by looking at the root causes of the problems. This work has as its goal taking steps toward making systemic changes in how society is organized so that women are not in positions that are vulnerable to male power. The anti-violence movement is a loosely organized collectivity that challenges individual behaviors, cultural values, accepted norms, public policies, and laws that lead to abuse of women. In contrast to agencies that are more focused on providing services and support to individual women who have been harmed, the work that I am referring to when I use the term "anti-violence movement" includes those groups of social actors that are making demands on the existing social order to be different; more oriented toward social justice than social services.[2]

As is true with other social movement formulations in the United States, the anti-violence movement can be hard to identify in precise ways. There are times and places where the internal coherence is less strong and charismatic leaders are difficult to identify. Still, participant observers and scholars who study social movement would agree that, historically, a major dimension of the work to end violence against women in the United States can be understood to be the work of a social movement on many critical measures.[3] For example, the anti-violence movement began much like other contemporary organizing efforts designed to create social change in this country—those who were most affected by the problem declared that they had "had enough" abuse.[4] Male violence was previously understood to be a "private issue" or a "personal problem," but public perceptions changed when women began to speak out about their abuse. Building on the examples of the Black civil rights and Black Power movements and the social unrest that led students and other leftist groups to organize in the 1960s, women in abusive interpersonal relationships began to speak out in an effort to externalize the experiences of terror and humiliation that they experienced in their own households. They demanded public attention to the causes and consequences of the male violence they were experiencing and institutional accountability for it.[5] They named gender inequality and the subordination of women in both the public and private spheres as the root cause of rape, battering, stalking, and harassment and called for an end to sexist oppression as the only acceptable solution to the problems. The transformation from understanding violence against women as a personal problem to one that is rooted in the politics of patriarchy began with grassroots activism.[6]

Stage One: Grassroots Activism and Self-Help

In a world of celebrity-driven reality TV confessions, it may be hard to believe that there was once a time when the private was truly private. Prior to 1960, few women publicly shared stories of the abuse they experienced in the private sphere of their lives. Although solid evidence indicates that violence against women by intimate partners was not a new problem at that time, a review of the literature reveals a sense that the full extent of male violence was uncovered in the mid-1960s, when women began to describe the extreme nature and extent of the violence they experienced both at the hands of someone they knew and by strangers. The very first public accounts of the private terror came from ordinary women who, buttressed by an increasingly influential women's liberation movement, disclosed the horrific pattern of intimate partner abuse, sexual assault, and assaults by strangers who were most often men.[7]

Woman by woman, stories of male violence emerged, and in communities all around the country, women responded by offering each other a safe place to live, economic and emotional support, and perhaps most important, a way to frame an analysis of their individual experience that had not been understood before. That is, a *social* understanding of one's private life emerged. Social movement theorists have identified this process of external recognition as the pivotal moment when groups were able to link individual experiences of degradation to the social conditions that surrounded them. A collective exclamation of "I am not alone" could almost be heard. It was at this moment that activism surrounding violence against women was recognized as the building of a social movement, insofar as the work focused on structural change.[8] The problems were coming to be understood as a widespread pattern of oppression that women in different circumstances shared—one that had social, rather than personal, roots. The early analysis stressed the perspective that male violence had little to do with women's behavior, clothing, or location, and everything to do with the abuse of male privilege in all spheres of society.

Importantly, the first published accounts that identified the public dimensions of the private terror lack any reference to variations in social identities.[9] They described women's experiences as strikingly similar across racial, ethnic, and class lines, and even noted that male violence did not stop at national borders—women recognized their shared fate with regard to violence whatever their nationality.[10] These early-published accounts argued that money, region, age, and race were irrelevant: when male violence was left unchecked, it would escalate into a very dangerous situation for *any* woman. Because the early activism resulted so directly in the development of a political analysis around gender as a static, unifying identity, the self-help strategies that emerged appeared to be universally appropriate and necessary for all women, everywhere.

Subsequently, the origins of the contemporary U.S.-based anti-violence movement were profoundly simple. In daycare centers, around kitchen tables, and in other everyday gathering places, women began to talk about their experiences of abuse in their homes, and because there were no other options available, they began to help one another. Consciousness-raising groups formed spontaneously, and from them, networks of support emerged. Consistent with the notion of grassroots organizing, survivors of male violence and their feminist allies began to build a social change movement to end violence against women, one important encounter at a time.

Stage Two: Shelters and Services

From these grassroots community-based discussions about gender subordination and the resulting violence that women experienced, more formal groupings emerged. According to the National Center for Victims of Crime and early activists, the country's first shelters for battered women opened in 1972.[11] That same year, the first two rape crisis centers opened—Seattle Rape Relief and the DC Rape Crisis Center. There is some disagreement about which shelter for battered women opened first, in part because the organizations were so informal and the evolution into more formal organizations was so gradual. By the mid-1970s, a range of formal services existed where previously there had been none. These early anti-violence programs reflect their social movement origins;

they were informally organized and relied almost exclusively on volunteer labor. The typical shelters were modest single-family homes that had been transformed into multiple-family residences with common living areas and a shared kitchen, and multiple families occupying small bedrooms. Rape crisis centers were operated out of community centers, apartment buildings, or small women's counseling programs. While shelter workers and rape crisis center counselors were preoccupied with responding to the crisis nature of male violence and women's needs for immediate protection, medical care, and emotional support, they were also advancing an analysis of male violence as a political problem related to the more general oppression of women. In addition to offering abused women a temporary safe place to stay with their children (in the case of shelters), or 24-hour advocacy (in the case of rape crisis counselors), these early intervention programs provided support-group counseling led by peers, as well as legal advice, informal referrals for employment and educational services, and opportunities for long-term life planning.

As they responded to these immediate needs for social, legal, and emotional assistance, shelter workers and rape crisis counselors remained committed to social activism around a broad set of issues related to gender equality. In this early period of the anti-violence movement, many shelters and rape crisis centers engaged in direct action and other forms of social protest alongside the women they were assisting.[12] The activism served both as an outreach strategy, whereby women in crisis learned about the assistance available to them, and as a way to raise public consciousness about the nature and extent of intimate partner abuse and rape. An important symmetry existed between activism and direct service work during this era. Support groups were aimed at consciousness-raising around gender inequality, peer counseling models were used to offer individual support instead of relying on more professional or clinical paradigms. The range of services offered to women extended beyond the need for emergency intervention to include attention to the long-term health, economic, and housing needs of women and their children.

It was not uncommon for shelters and rape crisis centers to be staffed by women who had experienced violence themselves. Anti-violence programs were often governed by non-hierarchical collective decision-making structures, they were supported by small grassroots fund-raising efforts, and they operated independently from state resources or control. While the focus of the work was clearly on intimate partner violence and sexual assault by strangers (as opposed to the other forms of violence described in chapter 2), this grassroots approach did allow for some attention to other risks that women faced, such as disproportionate poverty, employment discrimination, and sexual health problems related to patriarchal medical practices.[13] As such, the early work in battered women's shelters and rape crisis centers reflected an analysis of male violence that understood the multifaceted nature of the harm that women faced. Class-based oppression, racial discrimination, and exploitation based on sexuality were targets in the work against the root causes of male violence, even though challenging gender inequality dominated as the undisputed primary political goal.

Stage Three: Systems Advocacy

As awareness grew about the root causes of male violence, anti-violence activists began to articulate the "unfairness" of the system's response to women's victimization. Accounts from women who sought assistance were imbued with critiques of social institutions, and subsequent discussion about the collective experiences of individual suffering expanded to include bureaucracies' and public servants' indifference to the violence that women experience.[14] For example, women reported that they were ridiculed by emergency room staff when they were raped, questioned by police about what they did to "provoke" an attack by their husband, or advised to change either their behavior or their attitude by social work or mental health practitioners as a way to prevent or interrupt abusive interactions.[15] These micro responses, repeated over and over, formed the typical pattern of how social institutions not only failed to help women in danger, but in effect contributed to the escalation of abuse of women by not taking it seriously.[16] The system, therefore, became complicit in its non-responsive or blaming posture. For Black women in low-income communities, this situation was made worse by their already tenuous relationship with social institutions.[17]

As awareness of the state's inability and/or unwillingness to protect women from repeated abuse grew, a sense of moral outrage took over, and grassroots anti-violence activists began to make demands of the state and its institutions to respond more effectively to women who were victimized. It is important to note that much of the rhetoric at the time relied on the language of "women's equal right to protection" or notions of "women's citizenship" as a way to demand state intervention in the problem of intimate partner violence and sexual assault. The gender essentialism inherent in this formulation of the problem of the system's failure overshadowed the race- and class-specific dimensions of the institutional failure, heavily influencing what happened years later when Black women in marginalized social positions experienced male violence.

Here it is important to note that the shift in focus to systems advocacy that the anti-violence movement assumed is consistent with the theoretical analyses of other social movements. When a civil society understands a problem to have its origin in the social rather than the private domain, it will call for attention to shift from a singular focus on individual suffering to include a focus on so-called helping agencies. When governmental agencies or other state structures fail to meet their designated social responsibility, citizens become motivated to demand the reform of institutions and agencies so that "deserving citizens" are served or protected. In the case of violence against women, these citizen watchdogs pounced on many examples of institutional failures. For example, activists criticized the police for failing to respond to women's calls for help and called attention to emergency room personnel who trivialized women's experiences of violence. Feminists faulted religious leaders for using scriptures to blame women for the violence they experienced, and challenged mental health professionals on their tendency to label women "masochistic" when they were assaulted or "codependent" when they didn't leave abusive relationships.

Survivors of male violence and their advocates began to challenge hostile and neglectful social institutions aggressively, demanding a more accurate understanding of the causes of the problems, more institutional assistance in times of crisis, and more respectful treatment of women who exercised their right to protection as full and equal citizens. This was a very important strategic move because the focus on changing systemic responses to women who experienced male violence and holding agencies accountable for providing services gave additional strength to the expanded vision of the movement's initial goals. That is to say, systems advocacy included both work to reject the cultural notions of gender that position women as subordinate to men and challenges to the institutional practices that disenfranchise women in a more general sense, practices that leave women vulnerable to male violence *and* in other precarious social and political situations. In this amplified formulation of the need for systems advocacy, violence against women came to be understood as an issue of gender domination in a patriarchal society, where most, if not all, social institutions function to subordinate women.

Still, by the mid-1980s, anti-violence activists came to recognize institutional practices that deprived women of rights and protections as a critical target for reform in much the same way that they *already* recognized male-dominated families and neighborhoods. They broadened the framework for political mobilization to include action that would change those systems and institutional processes that forces women to remain in abusive relationships or to endure sexual abuse, and to replace them with different social structures. Scholars of protest movements have identified this shift as a significant evolutionary moment, when activists move back and forth between an oppositional relationship to state bureaucracies and attempts to work inside institutions to change them.[18]

Stage Four: Coalition-Building

From this interrogation of the discriminatory practices of bureaucratic social institutions and attempts to hold them accountable for more humane and effective responses came an even broader understanding of male violence against women. The problem of abuse became understood as emblematic of a myriad of experiences that put women at a disadvantage in society. These experiences were linked to a general lack of political representation, employment discrimination, systematic disregard for women's contributions in the domestic sphere, as well as associated problems like lack of publicly funded child care, health disparities based on gender, constant threats to reproductive health services, and stereotypical media and cultural representations. While these broader issues did not initially motivate grassroots anti-violence activism, deep feminist analyses revealed the extent to which violence against women was embedded in larger structural conditions that disadvantage women. By the late 1980s, anti-violence activists who accepted this deeper analysis began to reshape their response to the occurrences of rape, battering, sexual harassment, and emotional abuse to include organizing around the broader social conditions that have a disproportionate negative impact on women.

A review of the anti-violence movement's literature at the time (including early transcripts of women's testimony, descriptions of the problem in brochures that provide an analysis of violence against women, and flyers that advertised anti-violence programs) shows how the movement strategists linked the problem of violence to other manifestations of gender subordination. Prominent among these issues were the need for economic self-sufficiency, access to health care, fair legal representation, and alternative cultural images. There were explicit discussions in some communities about women staying in abusive relationships because of limited housing options, about the prevailing model of health-care delivery that pathologized or patronized women (particularly rape survivors), and about the need to form intentional networks of feminist activists to address broader concerns about gender equality within which they could nest responses to the problem of violence against women.

An influential sector of the anti-violence movement's leadership at the time suggested that the solutions to gender-based abuse had to include building coalitions for broad-based social change, in some cases as opposed to individual change. Importantly, it was the analysis behind the coalition-building that first challenged feminist activists to move explicitly beyond the singular gender analysis and to incorporate attention to race and class politics into their work. It became clear, for example, that merely providing short-term shelter for three months would not ensure long-term safety for a homeless battered woman who might feel compelled to return to a violent partner in an effort to avoid the dangers of the streets. Thus, for a while anti-violence work included campaigns to reform housing policy that limited access to safe and affordable options. Similarly, rape crisis programs extended the focus of their work to include attention to matters of workplace safety, sexual justice, and girls' involvement in athletics. The analysis behind this expanded thinking was that a more positive sense of women's bodies would not only help prevent sexual assault but would reframe women's sexuality as a source of power rather than vulnerability. This critically important analytical work brought about a new anti-violence praxis, one that focused on challenging the conservative social movements that were beginning to gain political power in the early 1990s.

A considerable body of literature has emerged that documents the changing political, social, economic, and ideological landscape during these years when anti-violence work was embedded in more coalitional politics. With the election of Ronald Reagan as president and the Republican control of the legislative process, there were definitive shifts in the positioning of issues, groups, and institutions. These shifts will be taken up in chapter 4. They are introduced here because this is the point at which the evolution of the anti-violence movement was most dramatically altered by the broader conservative national landscape. This was a critical point in the political organizing during which a seminal set of schisms in the U.S.-based anti-violence movement occurred.

The challenges that emerged for the anti-violence movement because of the broader political changes became key sources of tension between distinct groups of anti-violence activists during this era. One group remained committed to a broader analysis of the systemic causes of violence against women, arguing as strongly as ever for the need for radical social change work based on an understanding of the role that systems advocacy and coalition politics could play in that. For this group, the problem of persistent gender inequality, *as a structural problem*, remained at the center of the analytical paradigm that activists remained committed to. Another group coalesced around a different formation. Compelled to respond to conservative state tendencies regarding families, gender, and sexuality, they pursued a safer, less antagonistic strategy that they expected would be more acceptable to the new conservative national, legislative, and local leadership. This group distanced itself from the former activist-oriented agenda aimed at social change and developed a more professional identity as "specialists" who worked with women who experienced male violence. Believing that politically they would be better positioned to compete for public support, the feminist activists in this latter group became counselors, community organizers became project administrators, and advocates became apologists for the system.

Evidence of the tension between these two approaches in the anti-violence movement echoed broader feminist debates at the time about social change versus social work and the ideological positions that framed each approach.[19] Radical, anti-racist feminists argued that power was at the heart of male violence against women and that only through liberation of women would the problem of male violence end. Liberal feminists took a more moderate approach, arguing for expanding political and civil rights rather than creating structural change. This strategic and analytical divergence became one of the first obvious sources of tension between women of color and radical grassroots activists, and the more affluent mainstream white women who occupied leadership positions at the time.

By the mid-1990s, those who embraced a liberal ideology prevailed in great part because they were less threatening and more tolerable to conservative legislators, foundations, bureaucratic administration, and community leaders who were becoming more powerful. The grassroots feminist collectives that once provided emergency shelter and crisis intervention, who engaged in systems advocacy, and who worked in coalitions were gradually replaced by more formal organizations that advocated institutional reform rather than fundamental shifts in power relations. A growing mainstream leadership pressured anti-violence programs to adopt more hierarchical and authoritarian organizational structures in order to be more consistent with, and acceptable to, traditional social service delivery systems. Questions emerged about working with and on behalf of men who were hurt by intimate partners, despite the fact that the majority of female violence against males is understood to be self-defense.[20] Pressure mounted to use professional counselors with academic degrees rather than volunteers to provide services, and debates about the language became salient, as in the usage of the terms "wife abuse" or "domestic violence" rather than "gender or male violence."

Frances Fox Piven and Richard Andrew Cloward and other social movement theorists offer important insight into this shift that allows for an understanding of the change from a radical social movement to a social reform movement.[21] This literature argues that when the goal changes from structural transformation to accessing resources, establishing bureaucracy, or policy reform, the potential for lasting change is threatened. In particular, when social change movements depend on third parties for financial support, the potential for changing social arrangements is diluted, resulting in factions, co-optation, and backlash. Furthermore, work that does not change ideological positions and unequal institutional relationships will not lead to structural change. In the end, social movements that do not remain outside of established political mainstream organizations, that do not seek to change society but rather seek assistance from the state in creating a more sympathetic moral version of the current society, become static.[22] This analysis is key to explaining how the desire for mainstream credibility on the part of the anti-violence movements' leadership came at the expense of radical social change; a significant part of the movement collapsed on itself and fell into the trap of attempting to become a legitimate player in the fundamentally flawed system of white patriarchal power. It also explains how attention to race and class got lost to a more simplistic set of arguments about gender inequality.

Stage Five: Legal and Legislative Changes

Most successful movements for social change have relied in part on legal and legislative initiatives, through which laws are changed and public policies are reformed with the goal of bringing the legislative power of the state to force change.[23] From some perspectives, it seemed logical that as the anti-violence movement focused on gender oppression it would follow the example of other social movements—like the civil rights movement and the more broadly focused feminist movement—and demand that the government use its authority to remedy social inequality, to punish those who use violence, to compel state bureaucracies to act to protect those who are hurt, and to support intervention programs through the allocation of public resources for services. Initially, these efforts stood side-by-side with activist-oriented activities designed to radically change the society and its institutions. However, by the mid-1990s, following years of tension between social change work and institutional reform work, the focus became more on legal and legislative changes and the procurement of government funding than on challenging patriarchal power at the individual or state levels. An important body of legal and feminist scholarship emerges in the 1990s that describes the problems associated with traditional legal responses to male violence against women and the need for legislative reform. Prior to this, cases of sexual assault were seldom brought to the attention of law enforcement and when they were, they were seldom adjudicated, in part because the standard of proof was so high and the treatment of those bringing the charges was so bad.[24] When it comes to violence by intimates, these cases were considered a civil matter and the small percentage of them ever brought to the attention of authorities were handled in the family court system or its equivalent.[25] Arguing for a new legal paradigm, this scholarship called for the creation of new laws and heightened penalties associated with the use of male violence against women that would treat these crimes as seriously as assaults by non-relatives or strangers.[26] By many accounts, legal and legislative reform work was highly successful. Many states and local jurisdictions fundamentally changed how the problem of violence against women was treated; transforming it from a "personal or even social problem" into a crime (I will return to this point in chapter 4, where evidence will be presented regarding the ways these changes were facilitated by a larger set of legal and political shifts associated with the buildup of America's prison nation). Here, it is important to detail some of the legal changes and how they initially were understood to benefit battered women and sexual assault survivors.

Statutory rape laws, outlawing sexual activity between two people when it would otherwise be legal if not for their age, is one example of a legal reform advanced by feminist activists and legal scholars. Another is a category of laws called "primary aggressor policies" designed to combat the problem of dual arrests by obligating police officers called to domestic violence crime scenes to identify and arrest the person who posed the most serious threat in a dispute. Other new legal concepts were introduced to expand the legal response to violence against women. It is important to emphasize that the target of these legal and legislative reforms was the direct physical assault or sexual abuse and stalking, *not* the forms of violence that are more closely linked to other fundamental aspects of patriarchal power abuse, such as forced sterilization or police brutality.

In addition to changing laws regarding offenses, legal and legislative changes regarding male violence against women also resulted in changes in judicial protocols in the nation's courtrooms. Four particular examples illustrate the breadth of these changes: the development of rape shield laws, the use of the so-called battered women's defense, the establishment of specialized domestic violence courts, and mandatory arrest policies. In each instance, the seemingly progressive changes that during another era might have brought benefit, instead brought unanticipated negative consequences because, as the following discussion in chapter 4 will show, they were embedded in conservative legislative reform efforts rather than processes designed to transform society in such a way that all women would have more options.

The use of what have come to be known as rape shield laws became common in the 1980s.[27] Conceived by feminist attorneys and rape victims' advocates, these laws were actually a set of judicial policies that barred defense attorneys from raising certain aspects of a victim's behavior while attempting to build a defense case on behalf of an alleged perpetrator of sexual violence. Later the laws were extended to include limiting the disclosure of an alleged victim's name or any information about her that would identify her as a victim of sexual assault in the media or any other public representation of the case. The policies grew out of the strong position that anti-violence advocates took in asserting that there is so much negative stigma associated with rape, and it is such a widely misunderstood crime, that attorneys must be legally mandated to avoid the possibility of adversely influencing a judge or jury with what was understood to be irrelevant evidence about a woman's life circumstances that might be used to excuse or justify her being raped. Such evidence included information about a woman's past sexual behavior, descriptions of the woman's clothing at the time of the assault, any accusations the woman made against other men, the woman's current disposition, and other information that might be used to blame a woman for her attack. In effect, the rape shield laws created a level of protection in the judicial process that is not afforded any other crime victim who is pursuing legal redress, which set male violence apart from other violent crimes.

A related legal development was the creation of a set of defense strategies loosely termed the "battered women's defense."[28] These defenses rely on a set of assumptions about the long-term psychological impact of intimate partner violence, a complex referred to in the literature as battered women's syndrome. Psychologist Lenore Walker and other scholars whose work advances this paradigm suggest that women who are abused in the intimate sphere of their lives suffer from a range of psychological problems related to their victimization. These issues of pathology range from what is commonly referred to as women's codependence on their partners, which leads to women's involvement in abusive relationships in the first place, to notions of learned helplessness, which is used to explain why women stay in abusive relationships, to the extreme diagnosis of masochistic personality disorder, which describes the abusive relationships as somehow desirable to women who are in them.[29] In contrast to rape shield laws that *prevented* prosecutors from raising certain issues in the courtroom or in the media, the battered women's defense strategies were aimed at enabling defense attorneys (and in some cases prosecutors) to introduce information about a woman's psychological makeup as a way to explain her current behavior, including criminal behavior, as in the case of a woman who kills her abusive partner even after the relationship has ended.[30] Many of these psychologically oriented defense strategies rely on legal notions of self-defense, which include the right to protect oneself against violence or threatened violence with whatever force or means are reasonably necessary. Others use the concept of duress to explain why a woman in a long-term abusive relationship would involve herself in circumstances that do not serve her well and use what might otherwise be considered an aggressive or unusually violent response to her abusive partner.[31]

It is important to note that these psychological problems, upon which the use of the battered women's defense strategies are based, and the labels used to describe them, are highly gendered; that is, they are often explained as "problems that women have in relating to men," a perspective that locates the problem of violence not with the abuse of power, but with maladaptive gender behavior. Further complicating this is the reified gendered notion of womanhood; a notion that is exclusive rather than inclusive of women from a range of racial, cultural, or class backgrounds.[32] And while a considerable amount of work has been done to dismiss the validity of these notions and the epistemological assumptions on which they are based, the battered women's defense is still employed as a defense strategy in courtrooms around the country where women are charged with crimes as a result of being harmed by their partners, despite the considerable critique of its conservative tendencies.[33]

A third group of legal changes that emerged during the late 1990s involved the development of specialized courts to hear cases related to intimate partner violence. Following a broader trend in judicial reform, relocating the court procedures to discrete facilities and altering their actual structure and process significantly changed the way lawyers and judges handled cases of male violence against women. The operation of domestic violence courts signaled (a) that domestic violence and other forms of intimate partner violence had particular dynamics that warranted special considerations; (b) that issues related to women's safety could be handled more effectively in protective settings, thereby eliminating the risk of what is known as "post-separation violence,"[34] when, for example, an abusive partner encounters a woman outside of the courthouse; and (c) that specialized personnel trained on the issues of violence against women could administer more effective judicial services and also monitor repeat offenders more carefully. Like the rape shield laws and the use of battered women's defenses, domestic violence courts have become an acceptable way to focus judicial attention on the particular dynamics involved when a woman experiences intimate partner violence and/or rape.

The evaluation research conducted to measure the effectiveness of these reforms has noted the important advances in legal practice and, more important, in some women's safety. At the same time, the emphasis on legal, legislative, and judicial reform has created a dilemma for those anti-violence activists whose focus on broader systemic problems (like institutionalized racism) and negative experiences with the criminal legal system, has led to mistrust of its effectiveness. One dimension of the critique was that the legal and legislative changes created new laws or a special category of processes for women who experience violence. From this perspective, instead of creating a "special class" of victims or "special approaches" to those who were victimized by male violence, more radical activists have attempted to shift the focus toward a social justice approach that would allow *all* victims and *every* defendant to receive fair treatment by the state agencies and apparatus, including the legal system.

A fourth example of how the tension associated with legal changes that characterized this era of anti-violence movement work can be found

in the debates surrounding law enforcement protocols, including mandatory arrest policies. It bears repeating that prior to the dawning of the
anti-violence movement in the United States, law enforcement virtually
ignored instances of male violence against women.[35] Most early feminist
anti-violence advocates recall horror stories of women calling the police
for help and the police either failing to arrive at the crime scene, or if
they did respond, literally laughing at the caller or otherwise denying the
seriousness of her risk. The typical response included requiring the abusive partner to "take a walk around the block," encouraging the woman
to change her behavior, and taking a report that either left out information or was biased.[36] Far from being isolated anecdotal accounts of police
misconduct, the reports from women who turned to law enforcement in
cases of intimate partner violence and rape reveal a clear pattern of institutional mistreatment. In response, feminist legal activists filed a series of
lawsuits against police departments on behalf of women who were killed
by their abusive partners because the police failed to respond.[37] These
lawsuits resulted in the development of best protocols and practices that
were assumed to ensure women's safety.

A key element of these initiatives was the long-held consensus among
advocates that law enforcement agencies—as state agencies—were not
likely to change of their own accord; only new law enforcement policies
and judicial procedures, when coupled with police training, could protect
women in crises.[38] Subsequently, the anti-violence movement immersed
itself in the development of strategies such as mandatory arrest policies
designed to *force* police officers to take intimate partner violence seriously. Among other things, these policies resulted in an erosion of police
discretion in a very profound way, and initially led to an increase in arrest
rates for domestic violence crimes across the country. The extent to
which they were accepted by law enforcement agencies is influenced—in
no small part—by the broader changes in law enforcement that expanded
authority through legislative reform. This broader context will be discussed further in chapter 4.

A closer look at the impact of these particular legal and legislative
changes, however, reveals mixed results.[39] On the one hand, more people are arrested today on charges of intimate partner violence, largely
because of these changes in public policy.[40] It could be inferred, there-

fore, that some women are safer, at least temporarily, because man-datory arrest laws require that police remove alleged assailants from the household or community and detain them in police custody for a period of time if they are suspected to be violent toward women. On the other hand, questions remain about the benefits and the possible unintended negative consequences of such enhanced law enforcement policies like mandatory arrest protocols.[41] There is no solid longitudinal research on the relationship between specialized new laws, legal proce-dures, or mandatory protocols and changes in rates of violence against women in more disadvantaged communities. Second, advocates have raised concerns about the extent to which these changes may inad-vertently result in increased stigma—or worse, criminal charges being brought against women. In particular, the extent to which advocates in communities of color have speculated that, since there are differen-tial impacts of arrest on marginalized communities, some women who experience male violence may not call upon the police if they know they can expect an enhanced response from law enforcement and the judicial system. Third, the concern about disproportionate representa-tion of men of color in the arrest statistics raises questions about the fair application of these laws given racial profiling and stereotyping var-ious groups of defendants.[42]

Instead of giving serious consideration to these concerns about dispro-portionate and distributive justice as they were being raised, or attempt-ing an exploration of unintended consequences of these legal changes for women who have a more marginalized social status, the mainstream anti-violence movement put a considerable amount of time and energy into modifying (but ultimately supporting) legislative and legal changes such as law enforcement policies that encourage, if not mandate, arrests. Despite notable objections that were raised in isolated forums, legal and legislative reform work went forward largely unchallenged.[43] The subse-quent over-reliance on the criminal legal system and law enforcement strategies, and on legal and legislative reform more broadly, as the solu-tions to the problem of violence against women, solidified ultimately into one of the most important dimensions of the anti-violence movement's work, second only to providing crisis intervention services. Again, as the discussion of the buildup of America's prison nation in the next chapter will show, this unitary approach, which did *not* take into account race or class difference, emerged simultaneously with other policy changes regulating crime and punishment, family and household composition, and sexuality that have elevated current concern about intimate partner violence and sexual assault.

The issue of legislative changes around child custody in cases of intimate partner violence is another example of policy shifts that have had unintended consequences. There is good evidence to suggest that in many communities around the country, the child welfare system is challenged beyond its capacity to offer protection to children who need it.[44] In fact, some child advocates and public policymakers have gone so far as to suggest that the child welfare system in this country is in a state of crisis, and that in some communities, children are faring much worse than in previous eras. Still, amidst the generalized chaos, anti-violence advocates joined with advocates for children to establish a set of child custody laws that would remove children from homes in which they witnessed abuse, citing the argument that children who witness intimate partner violence in their household suffer damage akin to being abused themselves and hence should be removed from this dangerous situation.[45]

On the one hand, these initiatives had an internal consistency and were very important in sending a message to family advocates, courts, social service agencies, and others about the collateral consequences for children of violence against women. On the other hand, this policy reform in effect entrusted the chaotic child protective system with the authority to consider an additional category of risk to children while assessing the fitness of parents, one that has caused women to lose custody of their children if they do not leave an abusive relationship. Today, many states have policies that criminalize women's inability to protect their children from witnessing abuse, even when in fact they cannot even protect themselves. The unintended consequence of the consolidation of power and authority in the already overloaded and under-resourced child protective services system has a profound effect on Black women experiencing violence.

Perhaps the area of legislative change concerning the social response to male violence against women that has had the farthest-reaching effect is the authorization of public funding at both the state and federal levels that supports intervention programs. Beginning with funding for legal assistance through block grants, advocates pressured state legislators to routinely introduce bills and other mechanisms to support the growing anti-violence movement. One of the most creative strategies was the marriage license surtax. This state tax, which all citizens who applied for a marriage license were required to pay, was based on the premise that since 25 percent of all married women will be abused by their husbands, heterosexual couples entering into these relationships legally should, in effect, pay for the services they might use in the future if the marriage becomes abusive. Through creative maneuvering and sophisticated lobbying efforts, this tax was passed in several states, resulting in funding for shelters and other crisis intervention programs. A parallel strategy of "taxation for services that are likely to be required" exists in universities that charge student fees to pay for campus rape awareness programs.

There are other examples of legislative or institutional policies that generate public funds to pay for services for victims of intimate partner violence and rape. While it is not clear that these strategies actually reallocated resources to a significant extent, they did create an important set of rhetorical arguments about who should be responsible for funding programs for women who have been victimized. Again, against the backdrop of systems advocacy, these important strategic debates broadened the participation of policymakers and lobbyists in the work to end violence against women.

The pinnacle legislative effort to secure funding for shelters, rape crisis centers, and other institutions designed to respond to the problem was the federal legislation that contained the Violence Against Women Act, passed by the U.S. Congress in 1994. VAWA, as it has come to be known, is a comprehensive legislative package that focuses mostly on the goal of improving criminal justice responses to violence against women and, secondarily, on funding services for victims of domestic violence, sexual assault, and stalking.[46] It included a focus on developing coordinated community responses and support for tough new penalties to prosecute offenders. VAWA was reauthorized in 2000 and modified again in 2005 to specifically focus on judicial training, children who witness abuse, and "culturally specific programs."[47] VAWA also created the Office on Violence Against Women, a permanent part of the U.S. Department of Justice that administers financial and technical assistance to communities around the country working to end violence against women. Passing and re-authorizing the Violence Against Women Act and the creation of the Office on Violence Against Women was seen as a critical victory, and those who have worked on it credit not only legislative skill and organized feminist legal community, but also the shifts in social norms and beliefs about violence that occurred since the anti-violence movement began 30 years prior to the organized federal response. In this way, VAWA is understood as a pinnacle success of the legal and legislative efforts to end violence against women.[48]

It is important to note, however, that VAWA was part of a larger, more controversial Violent Crime Control and Law Enforcement Act of 1994, one of the most comprehensive, far-reaching crime bills in the history of the United States. This larger bill included some of the most draconian provisions that had a very serious impact on disenfranchised people. For example, it overturned a law that had allowed inmates to receive funding for education while incarcerated; it created 60 new death penalty offenses, and provided for huge increases in law enforcement budgets and prison construction. It is very significant to note that what could be understood as legislative success with the passing of the VAWA came with a cost—a set of harsh laws that disadvantaged some of the same communities that the population of women who are most vulnerable to male violence come from.

Stage Six: Research and Public Awareness

Far from being neutral or objective, the "scientific" process that is used to explain a social problem and analyze the effectiveness of responses to it is shaped by a dynamic interaction among social researchers, politics, and dominant ideology. Understanding the particular elements of this dynamic provides key insights into the evolution of the anti-violence movement, including the particular factors that have influenced what we know about male violence and how society responds to Black women who experience it. In this section, I will discuss how research and public awareness have been influenced by the grassroots organizing, development of services, systems advocacy, and coalition-building I described above, and how they in turn were shaped by ideology, politics, and rhetoric to create a distinctively racialized response to the problem of male violence against Black women.

By the year 2000, the national research agenda to end violence against women had become impressively broad.[49] It encompassed rigorous scientific research projects, evaluations of model intervention programs, and studies designed to assess the key elements to fostering collaborations between partners interested in a range of public policy changes. The growth in empirical data that has shaped the analysis of the problem presented in chapter 2 is due in no small part to a surge in private and public support through grants to researchers and contracts to universities, to the cultivation of an enthusiastic scientific audience, and, most important, to a desire on the part of practitioners in grassroots programs to understand and respond more effectively to the problems of rape, intimate partner abuse, and the other forms of aggression toward women. The subsequent expansion of knowledge regarding the nature, extent, and consequences of some aspects of gender violence is impressive, particularly given the relative newness of the field.

It is important to reiterate that prior to the 1980s very little empirical data existed on the incidence or prevalence of violence against women. There was no exploratory research on its causes and no experiments designed to test intervention strategies. Importantly, there was also very little theoretical or analytical work that explicitly documented the link between violence and the broader questions of social inequality and power abuse, despite the fact that this was such a critical dimension of the analysis that shaped the work in the early era of the anti-violence movement. The gap was filled in two short decades. A body of scholarship has been produced that now shapes public understanding, frames academic debate, and influences how activists do their work. It is noteworthy that this formal scholarly productivity is solidly built on the work produced by the community of grassroots activists who, without calling it "research," developed the initial explanatory models and identified the first key concepts and patterns associated with male violence. For example, it was activists who advanced the understanding that there was a link between men's power in the world and their power in intimate relationships. The experiences of survivors, once documented, showed that children were affected when their mothers were hurt. Volunteers who worked in rape crisis centers knew that sexual assault had very little to do with sexual desire, that living in constant fear has long-term consequences, and that a person who uses power and control to dominate another person's life may not give up until the subordinate person is dead. These understandings that emerged from the sharing of everyday knowledge and challenging social institutions now constitute major themes in the dominant social science literature on male violence against women. The existence of active academic research centers, validated instruments to measure gender violence, funding streams to support long-term research projects, a body of literature, and a community of researchers, are all evidence of the impact of feminist political and intellectual activism that emerged through the evolution of the anti-violence movement, from grassroots, activist-oriented knowledge to the current state of the field.

It is also the case that the increased formal scholarly attention to male violence emerged within the context of growing social conservatism that characterized the 1980s and 1990s. The growth and transition from grassroots, activist-oriented knowledge that focused on the link between violence and other forms of social oppression to less radical and more simplistic explorations into the causes and consequences of violence against women is noteworthy in a review of the literature. Academic research followed funding streams, which emerged from legislative reforms that were less interested in social justice than social services, law enforcement, and explaining individual behavior. The emphasis was on creating generalized conclusions which, at best, focused on gender as a unifying category, but did not very effectively account for race, class, age, or other differences.[50] From this conservative academic perspective, poor women who are raped, lesbians who are harassed, and battered women who break the law are understood as "troubling cases" or "isolated incidences" rather than social phenomena related to forms of structural inequality that extend beyond gender. A great deal of the academic work produced during this era reflects this epistemological bias, which explains why much of the recent literature, (except for the subfield reviewed in chapter 2) is devoid of a critical racial or sexual politic. Indeed, a review of the most recent literature will show a trend to de-link violence from questions of gender, power, racial discrepancies, or other social disadvantages, in part because the funding streams that define research agendas and the academic researchers who carry them out are increasingly conservative.[51]

Issues of power—as in male power, institutional power, or state power—that characterized the grassroots, activist-oriented analyses essentially dropped away from the scholarship that dominant research advanced. This gap is more than an empirical gap. These limitations are both methodological and conceptual; they reflect general epistemological issues with the overall approach to research on victimization, which avoids attention to most of the forms of abuse and the spheres within which they occur, as experienced by marginalized groups of women. Subsequently, very little data are available about the forms of abuse that exist alongside physical abuse from an intimate partner or sexual assault by a stranger. Furthermore, the research ignores women who experience violence but who do not use traditional services attached to the criminal legal system (where most of the data are collected). There is very little funding for research into women's uses of extralegal approaches to the problem of violence against them or for any woman whose experience falls outside the dominant paradigm, such as women like Tanya, Ms. B, and the New Jersey 4.

Stage Seven: Gender Hegemony and Anti-violence Rhetoric: The Creation of a Popular Discourse

As the historical accounting of the anti-violence movement shows, the work to end male violence against women has unfolded in distinct ways in this country, shaped by many social, cultural, and political forces. Here I turn my attention to how gender hegemony influenced the anti-violence rhetoric in such a way that the mainstream support was solidified at the expense of the social change movement that began with grassroots organizing.

To start, we must return to the rhetoric used to organize at the grassroots level, to shift consciousness to the early 1960s, when discourse erupted regarding intimate partner violence and sexual assault and activists sought to build public support for legal and legislative reforms. This rhetoric established the notion of gender vulnerability as universal. Along with other scholars and activists, I have called this—the creation of a popular public discourse about rape and intimate partner violence that hinged on the generalized risk to all women and children—the "every-woman analysis."[52] In the earliest conceptual formulations, this analysis was an intentional and strategic move to avoid the stereotyping of those who use violence and the women who experience it. Drawing connections between groups ensured that members of privileged, well-resourced communities took the issue of violence against women seriously, and that members of the elite class did not see the problem as limited to groups who were stigmatized by racial identity, class position, or neighborhood.

Originally, this construction of "*any woman could be a battered woman*" and "*rape is a threat to every woman*" was a strategic way to avoid individualizing the problem of domestic and sexual violence and to focus on social dimensions of the problem of gender violence. Later, research established it as a statistical reality as well as the lived experience of most women who—at many points in our lives—change our behavior in anticipation of threatening situations in order to minimize the risk of assault or humiliation. As the anti-violence movement evolved, this generalized construction helped to foster an analysis of women's vulnerability as profound and persistent rather than particular to any racial-ethnic community, socioeconomic position, religious group, or station in life. From college campuses to private corporations, public housing complexes, suburban community centers, and religious institutions, public awareness was growing that violence toward women was an important social problem that required a broad-based response.

Both the earliest activists and those who came later to engage in system advocacy work were relentless in promoting the "everywoman analysis," and in so doing created a very strong and consistent message. Later, during the era of legal and legislative reform when promoting public awareness campaigns and public policy proposals, anti-violence activists used the everywoman analysis to influence those who had the power to create institutional and legal change. Research began to assess the extent of the violence toward "every woman" as opposed to *all* women as a way to convince people in power of the importance of the issue. In most cases, these powerful figures were people who held elected office (typically white, heterosexual men from elite backgrounds) who had influence in judicial chambers or in foundation boardrooms, and who set policy for police precincts and governmental agencies. These elite groups became one of the key audiences for the consciousness-raising messages. The everywoman analysis became a way to persuade those with decision-making authority to respond to the problem or, if they did not, to develop strategies for holding both individuals and institutions accountable.

To be fair, the everywoman analysis was a critical dimension of the early radical campaign to bring attention to the issue of violence against women—to make public what for so long had been understood to be a private problem. The grassroots organizing efforts to make the issue public hung on the notion that any woman or child can be the victim of gender violence. In fact, many advocates today who have done training, public speaking, teaching, and writing on violence against women begin their presentations, drawing the audience in, by saying, "*it can happen to anyone.*" This notion has become a powerful emblem of the anti-violence rhetoric and, some would argue, the basis of the work during every era of the anti-violence movement. By 2010, many people in this country finally understood that their children, mothers, sisters, co-workers, neighbors, and, indeed, they themselves could be victimized by gender violence.[53]

A closer look, in fact, shows that this construction—a hallmark of the mainstream anti-violence movement's rhetorical paradigm—has in fact become almost dangerous insofar as it detracts from the development of a broad social justice analysis of violence against women that might emerge from a contextualized understanding.[54] As the political foundation of the anti-violence movement became more conservative, reflecting the broader social trends, the everywoman rhetoric fell right into the vacuum created by a white feminist analysis that could not successfully incorporate an analysis of race and class.[55] In fact, the assumed race and class neutrality of gender violence—to some extent ignoring the issue of sexuality—led to the erasure from the dominant view of the victimization of lesbians, women of color in low-income communities, and other marginalized groups. State violence and harmful public policies could not fit into the everywoman analytical paradigm of the male violence that focused on individual men. The loss of focus on these groups seriously compromised the transgressive and transformative potential of the anti-violence movement's radical social critique of power, various patriarchies, economic exploitation, and heterosexism.

Put another way, when the national discussion became organized around *"it could happen to anyone,"* "it" was reduced to direct physical assault from household members and stranger rape, and "anyone" came to mean the women with the most visibility, the most power, and the most public sympathy, the citizens whose experience of violence is taken most seriously. This outcome prompts additional concern when the needs are integrated into the public commerce of social service delivery, legal protection, visibility in research studies, and so forth. So, the image of the *everywoman* becomes a white, middle-class woman who can turn to a counselor, a doctor, a police officer, or a lawyer to protect her from abuse. Researchers ask her about her experiences and then describe them in the literature; intervention strategies are based on her needs, she is featured in public awareness campaigns, and she is reflected in the recognized national leadership on the issue of violence against women. In the end, the everywoman analysis, with its unintended consequence of limiting the public understanding of who is included under the rubric of "victims," is a key element in the context that surrounds women like Tanya, Ms. B, and the New Jersey 4.

Stage Eight: Institutionalization: The Benefits and the Costs of Success

Institutionalization is the state of evolution in a social movement's history when questions are asked about the extent to which sufficient progress toward the long-term goals has been made such that sustained change can be claimed. In the case of the anti-violence movement, the question is, of course, "to what extent have we successfully ended violence against women and if so, how have we done that?" It is possible to imagine that we might consider this question from a variety of viewpoints. From the perspective of grassroots activism, we might ask if women are safer and is the problem of violence understood to be one that is linked to other issues of power and domination. A systems advocacy perspective would focus on questions of access to bureaucratic services and improved institutional responses to the problem of male violence. Coalition-builders would want to know about the extent to which violence against women is understood to be part of a broader analysis of the need for social change and legal and legislative reform efforts are evaluated by the extent to which governmental and state authorized changes have had an impact on the problem.

Given how the anti-violence movement evolved—from grassroots activism to a more conservative law enforcement approach that reflects gender hegemony—the process of institutionalization reflected the question "to what extent has a social service system been put into place that offers assistance to those women who have been a victim of one of the crimes that are included in the legal rubric of domestic violence, sexual assault and related crimes of stalking, etc.?" As resources that focus on law enforcement and services became more generous, there was a tendency to respond to the narrow question by affirmatively evaluating services to the exclusion of other questions. Researchers began to explore best practices associated with intervention strategies, and legislative initiatives became solidly embedded in mainstream political processes. There was a sense of entrepreneurialism and professionalism that began to be valued as part of the goal of the work with scant attention to the initial political motivations.

From the point of view of evaluating traditional services, it is noteworthy that by 2004, there were close to 1,500 rape crisis centers and more than 2,000 domestic violence shelters in the United States. Each year, these facilities provide emergency housing and counseling to an estimated 300,000 women and children. A national toll-free domestic violence hotline has been operational for more than 15 years and by July 2005, it was receiving an average of 16,000 calls per month. Operators refer callers to a well-established network of local domestic violence and sexual assault programs. Many communities have counseling services for those who abuse their intimate partners and support groups for victims of these assaults. This range of services is coordinated by a legislated state and federal infrastructure that establishes programmatic policy and provides resources through grants and contracts. Statewide domestic violence and sexual assault coalitions work in partnership with professional associations and systems advocates to monitor these programs.

Accompanying the growth in support services and intervention programs are changing public attitudes that suggest that there have been significant shifts in consciousness about, and intolerance of, violence against some women in this country over the last 30 years. Significantly, this shift has advanced the "everywoman" rhetoric; an image of women as innocent victims of male violence who deserve protection by the state and its agencies.

In addition to increased services and shifts in public consciousness, some broad claims are made about the success of the anti-violence movement, and of legal and legislative changes that have rendered some forms of male violence illegal. As examples, legal scholars look at the public laws covered by Title II, and in the case of intimate partner violence, examples include the Violent Crime Victims' Assistance Act, the Victims of Crime Act, and the Violence Against Women Act. Prohibition against sexual harassment is detailed in Title VII of the Civil Rights Act of 1964, and stalking is covered by state penal codes.

Other observers measure the success and institutionalization of the anti-violence movement by the extent to which academic institutions have defined violence against women as a legitimate field of study and the subsequent growth of a body of literature based on empirical research. Federal agencies such as the Department of Justice, the Department of Health and Human Services, and the Centers for Disease Control have funded numerous studies that have contributed to an impressive national database of information on intimate-partner violence and sexual aggression. There are at least eight peer-reviewed journals that disseminate findings to an audience of violence researchers and scholars, and there are frequent references in the popular press to the victimization of women at the individual level in the private sphere.

It is possible to interpret these social advances as evidence that by 2010, the anti-violence movement had attained a considerable degree of success. However, political disappointment sets in when one realizes that, had the anti-violence movement evolved along a different trajectory, or had the tensions between a social justice and activism approach versus a more professionalized social service approach that relied heavily on law enforcement been resolved differently, things would have turned out differently for women like Tanya, Ms. B, and the New Jersey 4 and other Black women who tragically find themselves in similar situations. Indeed, from some vantage points, it is possible to imagine that if the feminist organizing that led to these changes in research, in the law, in services, and in public awareness had included a broader, more radical and anti-racist agenda, Black women in disadvantaged communities might have been protected. It might be possible to imagine that anti-violence programs would have built coalitions with groups organizing against police brutality in African American communities or with groups working to respond to hate crimes in major urban areas.

However, the stories that frame this book present contrary evidence—that the success of the anti-violence movement in the United States has been unequal, and the ways that it has become institutionalized disproportionately benefit women with social privilege. The institutionalization of the anti-violence movement has its success embedded in the larger social fabric in such a way that it does not threaten the status quo. It closely coincides with a feminist agenda that is more politically neutral, an analysis of gender inequality that does not include attention to class, race, sexuality, and other social markers of identity.

Given the conservative context that surrounded the evolution and institutionalization of the anti-violence movement, it is possible to understand why some women were left so defenseless considering that the forms of abuse that they experienced in nearly every sphere of their lives were beyond the capacity (or the will) of the mainstream anti-violence movement in this country to respond in 2010. That is, despite the tremendous social advances in research, public attitudes, and securing governmental support for emergency services, each of the women was unidentified, unsupported, and unprotected by anti-violence programs in part because the forms of abuse they experienced are inconsistent with the evolving image of an "innocent female victim" of individual male violence.

An accounting of the ways that institutionalization led to the anti-violence movement's inability to offer safety or protection to poor women, lesbians, or victims of police brutality is linked to the ways that gender inequality does not occupy a central place in the consciousness of some communities of color. In fact, incest, rape, battering, and other forms of violence against Black women and girls continue to be such a low priority in neighborhoods like theirs that the profound silence around gender violence could be interpreted as evidence that even today, racial solidarity continues to subordinate any demands for attention to and accountability for gender oppression or social disenfranchisement based on sexuality.[56] At the same time that residents are organizing against state policies leading to the dismantling of public housing, the lack of affordable health care, the erosion of community infrastructure caused by the mass incarceration of Black male youth, and persistent and intergenerational poverty, they are ignoring the particular conditions that disadvantage women and girls.[57]

It is easy to comprehend why this is the case if we consider the extent to which low-income neighborhoods in this country continue to be systematically disadvantaged by an aggressive public policy agenda. Indeed, by 2003, scholars generally agreed that not only are the cumulative negative impacts of the policies more pronounced than ever, but the long-term entrenchment of social inequalities will be very difficult to overcome.[58] Disparities in income, educational attainment, health status, and other markers are challenging Black community leaders to take urgent action. The ensuing problem, however, for Black women who live in socially and economically marginalized communities, is that certain forms of male violence are ignored. Much the same as during my earliest involvement in anti-violence work, it is *still* the case that community problems are cast in racially specific but gender-neutral macro terms, and mainstream anti-violence work is based on a gender-specific but racially neutral microanalysis of individual harm. As a result, those Black women who are most vulnerable to male violence remain unprotected, disbelieved, and unsupported by institutionalized programs, unexposed to prevention messages, cut off from the crisis intervention services that the movement had fostered, and marginalized in their communities.

In sum, the prevailing analysis of gender inequality that does not incorporate an understanding of related inequalities fails to provide a full explanation of these women's dangerous and complicated circumstances. Their communities are distracted by deteriorating social circumstances, and the racial injustice rhetoric of community leaders leads to complacency about gender violence. State institutions and public services are unsympathetic, at best, to these women's plight. Combined with the evolution of the anti-violence movement into a more conservative specialized field, it was not only possible but also perhaps inevitable that women like Tanya are so quickly labeled heartless Black teenage girls, that Ms. B's abuse was invisible, and that the New Jersey 4 were prosecuted for their victimization. As the anti-violence movement is proclaiming its success and communities argue for racial justice, the population of Black women whose experience is at the center of this book are left in desperate and dangerous situations.

Conclusion

Why, given the many social advances in the area of violence against women, are Black women in low-income communities so vulnerable to multiple forms of abuse in so many spheres of their lives?

While the anti-violence movement has evolved into a highly organized set of formal responses to the problem of violence against women that has led to an increase in safety for *some* women, this progress has not benefited all women equally. As the work has evolved, the more radical and transformative dimensions of the movement's initial goal—to end violence against women and gender-based oppression in the broader spheres of their lives—was diminished. Today, as the broader political discussion about crime, violence, and justice is more conservative, a number of women in positions of power within the anti-violence movement made a series of strategic decisions, moving to work inside the system rather than against it. Subsequently, Black women and other women of color, lesbians, immigrant women, human rights activists, women involved in prostitution, and outspoken survivors of battering and rape continue—30 years later—to find themselves in conflict with other leaders in the anti-violence movement.

We won the mainstream but lost the movement because of key events, decisions, and political influences shaped by the broader social context that resulted in institutionalization. Indeed, the cumulative effect of grassroots activism, system advocacy, legal changes, legislative reforms, research, and the creation of institutions that offer relief and recourse for women has meant that countless women are safer today than they would have been without the progress I document in this chapter. At the same time, the elements of progress that benefit some women (the every-woman who has social privileges) simultaneously disadvantage others. The movement has responded to some of the problems of male violence, but it has ignored those which are conceptually written out of what we understand our work to be. We won the mainstream by making a series of strategic decisions based on the idea that benefits for some were more important than the possible disadvantages for others. We lost the movement by accepting that compromise.

To make matters worse, this process was occurring alongside of the building up of the prison nation in the United States. Some might argue that the coincidence was unforeseeable. Others might say that the social movement *decided* to move away from radical organizing around male violence as a social justice issue, and in so doing we left some women who experience male violence squarely in the path of the buildup of America's prison nation. I take up this assertion in the next chapter.

4

Black Women, Male Violence, and
the Buildup of a Prison Nation

Activists and advocates, who are part of the Chicago Taskforce on Violence against Girls and Young Women, called for the Cook County (Chicago) State's Attorney to drop charges against Tiawanda Moore and release her from jail, where she is detained after being arrested and charged with two counts of eavesdropping and a domestic dispute. According to a report in the *New York Times*,[1] Ms. Moore, aged 20, used her Blackberry (cell phone) to record encounters with the Chicago police officers without the officer's permission, a Class 1 felony in Illinois. Importantly, the conversation that Ms. Moore recorded was taking place in Police Headquarters with Internal Affairs officers while she attempted to file a sexual harassment complaint against another officer.

For a difficult year before her arrest, Ms. Moore and her live-in boyfriend were visited frequently by the police, who were called to their home because of their fighting. On one incident, the couple was being interviewed separately, which at face value is understood to be "good police practice," except that during the private discussion, one of the officers allegedly fondled Ms. Moore and gave her his personal telephone number. She handed over the phone number to the authorities as evidence of misconduct a few days later, when she attempted to file a complaint against the officer. After Ms. Moore was repeatedly and aggressively discouraged from filing a complaint by Internal Affairs officers, she began recording the conversations on her phone. When the police officers discovered that they were being recorded, they arrested Ms. Moore and charged her with eavesdropping.

The interface between violence against women, law enforcement intervention, the use of technology, the boundaries between citizen rights and institutional policies, and the creation of laws that regulate all of the above collided in this case in a way that disfavored Ms. Moore. Local activists responded aggressively to her case with calls for justice, which ultimately resulted in an acquittal. Still, discussions with advocates for women in prison describe cases like this with troubling frequency.

The criminalization of Kelley Williams-Bolar is another case in which a woman who was attempting to protect herself was punished by the state. Ms. Williams-Bolar was arrested, charged, and sentenced in Ohio for what could be understood as "stealing an education for her children."[2] A single mother of two adolescent girls, Ms. Williams-Bolar decided, following several threatening circumstances in which her family's safety was at risk, (including a violent break-in to her public housing apartment), that she needed to move in with her father, where her daughters could live in a safer community and attend a better school in Akron, Ohio. Ms. Williams-Bolar had a good job as a teaching assistant for children with special needs and was in college studying to become a teacher. After an aggressive investigation that included videotaped surveillance, the jury was not convinced even by W-2 forms addressed to Ms. Williams-Bolar at her father's residence, or other evidence, that they were in fact residents of the school district. She was convicted of falsifying resident records of two children, which was a third degree felony. Ms. Williams-Bolar was sentenced to 10 days in jail, two years probation, and community service.

The punishment extends beyond these formal sanctions. According to Ohio law, you are not allowed to become a teacher with a felony conviction, which means that the verdict took away her long-term ability to care for herself and her children. The danger that caused her to seek an alternative living situation and her attempts to secure a safe educational environment for her children cost her not only the time associated with the official punishment, but the secondary negative consequences resulting from employment policy related to licensing teachers. In the end, her attempts to be safe and self-sufficient were thwarted by the state, which permanently disenfranchised her, even though the felony convictions were eventually reduced to misdemeanor charges.

These cases illustrate the broader context of a prison nation that surrounds the evolution of the anti-violence movement as it transformed from a radical grassroots social movement to an institutionalized set of social services that relies heavily on the remedies offered by the legislative process and the criminal legal system. Analysis of the broader context is critical to an understanding of what happens to Black women who experience male violence when highly specialized institutional services are inaccessible because *their* experiences of male violence are inconsistent with the oversimplified classifications that result from hegemonic discourse *and* because of their precarious positions in a prison nation. The precarious situations that I am referring to are those that are created when (1) communities are suspicious of law enforcement because of aggressive tactics and occasional maltreatment; (2) when women whose gender performance, life circumstances, and/or sexuality threatens normative standards; (3) when women attempt to protect themselves; and (4) for women whose victimization and risk of violence is so severe that they are forced to choose among very bad options to protect their own safety.

This contextualization of the anti-violence movement as evolving from within and adapting to a prison nation situates the understanding of the experiences of Black women from disadvantaged communities who experience male violence within the context of conservative political ideology and punitive public policy where institutionalized victims' services cannot reach them. This approach makes it possible to argue (1) that the evolution of the anti-violence movement toward a more conservative set of intervention strategies and public policy reforms is, in part, a reflection of a broader set of conservative social trends in the United States that occurred during the same time period; and (2) that an analysis of the problems associated with male violence against Black women and society's response to it will be advanced significantly if we use a conceptual frame that takes those conservative trends into account. This chapter will show that the *nature* of male violence against Black women in contemporary society and *the extent to which it occurs in the multiple contexts* are a direct result of *both* the evolution of the anti-violence movement, described in the previous chapter, *and* simultaneous changes in political and social ideology associated with the buildup of a prison nation. The combination of these conservative trends and the narrow images of women (without attention to issues of race, sexuality, and class) by the anti-violence movement results in pernicious and persistent male violence toward Black women (who live in disadvantaged communities which are socially marginalized).

In addition, the prison nation framework helps to explain the convergence of repressive shifts in social policy and conventional feminist rhetoric around violence against women, a rhetoric that privileges a gender-specific analysis while virtually ignoring how race, class, and sexuality can create particular vulnerability to violence. This convergence creates a significant disadvantage for Black women in low-income communities where persistent poverty and more general problems of crime exacerbate the experience of male violence. That is to say, the concept of a prison nation is helpful insofar as it illuminates the links between (1) intimate-partner violence, community violence, state violence, and the harm caused by public policy; (2) structural inequality, institutionalized racism, and patriarchal power; and (3) the anti-violence movement's commitment to an increasingly conservative state and subsequent unwillingness to take up these two problems, leaving socially marginalized Black women increasingly vulnerable to male violence.

Following a fuller description of the concept of a prison nation, I will turn my attention to the specific pre-conditions necessary for society to orient itself in that direction. Specifically, this discussion will focus on how America's prison nation reorganizes social structures and relationships in society in ways that disadvantage Black women who have fewer economic resources, less social capital, more social stigma, and who also experience male violence. The reorganization necessary for the buildup of a prison nation occurs in three ways: (1) through a process of community divestment and the subsequent concentration of disadvantage, (2) through the co-optation of the strategies that advocates might have used to resist divestment, and (3) by isolating and criminalizing Black women who experience forms of male violence that are outside of the context of the dominant everywoman paradigm that relies on a monolithic notion of gender oppression. Following this discussion of how the buildup of America's prison nation influences Black women who experience male violence, I will discuss how a prison nation works to influence two social problems that are associated with male violence for disadvantaged women: persistent poverty and control of sexuality. An exploration into these issues will point to the opportunities for a Black feminist response to male violence that includes developing a broad new analysis designed to end direct physical abuse and assault, as well as community and state-sanctioned violence against women.[3] This new strategic paradigm is presented in chapter 5.

Conceptualization of a Prison Nation

In this framing of Black women's experience of male violence, I am using the notion of a prison nation metaphorically. I borrow the notion from scholars who use the term more literally to signal the situation in which a neoliberal, law-and-order-oriented social agenda has supplanted the state's willingness to provide basic material resources and opportunity for self-sufficiency for low-income groups.[4] This trend has been called mass incarceration or imprisonment,[5] lockdown,[6] the prison industrial complex,[7] carceral archipelago,[8] the celling of America,[9] the American gulag[10] and the New Jim Crow.[11] In most of these analyses, the notion of a prison nation alludes to the political process whereby enforcement strategies, criminal justice policy, the creation of new laws, and mass incarceration are used strategically as part of a larger social agenda aimed at maintaining the power of economic elites through the control of marginalized groups.[12] This is accomplished through the deployment of public policies that rely on a socially constructed understanding of the "crime problem," which the public accepts without question.

Extending this to the problem of violence against Black women, we understand that the ultimate shift in the work to end male violence became embedded in a broader set of conservative social dynamics aimed at creating a law-and-order society. Aggressive punishment of norm violations was used to help maintain the existing social order rather than changing society to benefit the most disadvantaged Black women. The buildup of a prison nation that surrounded the anti-violence movement enacted a set of public policies that favor the creation of a more conservative, punishment-oriented state, replacing a liberal notion of the role of government in a welfare state. The ideology that undergirds the creation of a prison nation requires a departure from a philosophy that characterized the early eras of the anti-violence movement in which the state was understood to be responsible for protecting women in crisis, facilitating long-term access to safety, and expanding opportunities for citizens who are most vulnerable to abuse.

More specifically, the work of a prison nation is to reinforce state authority and to reassert hegemonic values under the guise of "preventing crime," which co-opted the more radical goals of ending women's oppression. The co-optation that I am describing depends on two related societal mechanisms: (1) a set of practices that overtly or unintentionally advance the interests and protection of powerful elites at the expense of marginalized groups who are victimized, and (2) the assignment of responsibility for creating anti-violence policy to a group of advocates who operate outside of (and hence are not accountable to) constituents in the social domain within which the most pernicious impact of social policies is felt. In the case of the anti-violence movement, the evolution from grassroots organizing to institutionalization was a move *away from* leadership by women who had experienced male violence directly, leaving the work to professionals who were more oriented toward organizational development, legal reform, bureaucratic management, evidence-based research, and best practices and other activities geared toward legitimizing the issue of violence against women. As a result, for some of the new, more professionally oriented leaders, there is an indisputable tendency to locate their concern about violence against women in more neoliberal conservative contexts of the anti-crime dimensions of the buildup of America's prison nation. This makes it possible for them to ignore the more radical call to action on behalf of disadvantaged Black women, whose lives are complicated by race, class, immigration status, or sexuality; conceding the broader social justice agenda related to women's liberation that characterized the early days of grassroots activism. Professional anti-violence leadership thereby support lawmakers who make decisions to use strategies to end violence against women that end up controlling their behavior through law enforcement, limited resources to activist cause, or constrained opportunities for those women who are hurt but who are deemed "unworthy" of mainstream support. Unlike other eras, the goal of the legislation, public policy, and intervention developed during the buildup of America's prison nation is to procure and distribute benefits to those women who are important to people in power in order to maintain the status quo *rather than* to prevent or remedy the range of social problems associated with male violence for those who are most socially isolated, economically disadvantaged, or politically powerless.

So by 2010, punitive public policy, criminalization of deviations from hegemonic social norms, the erosion of the social support system for disadvantaged groups, and increased surveillance and monitoring of people who are most at risk of the negative effects of poverty, heterosexism, and racism *as well as* gender violence were deeply entrenched in social ideology, and the anti-violence movement was deeply influenced by it. As neoliberal anti-violence leadership is celebrating successes that enhanced some women's safety, the three related pre-conditions necessary to solidify the buildup of America's prison nation were set in motion: (1) divestment from low-income communities and the subsequent concentration of disadvantage among poor Black women, (2) co-optation of resistance strategies that activist anti-violence groups were using, and (3) isolation and criminalization of Black women like Tiawanda Moore, Kelly Williams-Bolar, and others whose stories are told in this book who are attempting to survive violence and other forms of abuse.

The First Pre-condition for the Prison Buildup: Divestment from and Concentration of Disadvantage in Marginalized Communities

The buildup of America's prison nation around Black women who experience male violence begins with political and economic divestment from low-income communities and results in a concentration of disadvantages. Divestment starts with public policies that eliminate social programs that were intended to provide a social "safety net" to remedy social problems,[13] leaving communities that rely on public assistance and governmental support more isolated and destitute. As a result, people who live in these communities struggle to survive despite persistent poverty,[14] chronic health problems,[15] family disruption,[16] vulnerability to aggressive law enforcement,[17] internalized oppression,[18] and gender violence.[19]

The divestment process is a strategic one. Its intent is to eliminate services that were designed to provide a minimum standard of income, housing, health, and education. I am using the notion of divestment here to represent the aggregate decisions to advance a national neoliberal policy agenda that reduces budgets for social and health services and terminates community development programs. The term "divestment" implies some political intentionality—active decisions to implement a comprehensive change in society's orientation toward its most marginalized citizens. This change in orientation is both substantive and ideological and, as such, must be understood to be motivated by a change in politics and assumptions about disadvantaged groups.

Details of this change are noteworthy. Prior to the buildup of the prison nation that surrounded the evolution of the anti-violence movement described in chapter 3, the ideological assumption that guided the social policy of the 1960s and 1970s was that the state could be called on to protect basic human rights and advance a liberal social agenda that promised to equalize access to opportunity and resources.[20] Optimistic public attitudes supported the belief that the government should allocate resources to solve problems, including those related to inequality. Programs associated with this liberal social agenda include Head Start, Medicaid, Food Stamps, Community Action Programs, and other initiatives that were designed to minimize disadvantages associated with poverty and, secondarily, racial inequality.[21] While gender violence was not at the center of public discussion of social welfare debates at the time, even a superficial review of the programs that emerged from policy initiatives of the 1960s and 1970s reveals that most social programs were understood to be strongly associated with the needs of particularly vulnerable members of disadvantaged communities, including women and children.

Without overstating the actual governmental commitment to practices that advanced social justice, some measurable progress toward social equality can be attributed to the liberal policy that characterized the 1960s and 1970s. It should be noted that in great measure that progress was a direct result of mobilization by social movements that included the civil rights movement,[22] the women's movement, the anti-poverty movement, the gay and lesbian rights movement, and later the feminist anti-violence movement. A core political position of these movements and the subsequent implementation of these liberal policies and programs was that all citizens were entitled to protective services from the state.[23] Theoretically, that would include Black women in low-income communities who experienced male violence. The right to services, resources, and protection from the state was a *guaranteed* right, not one that had to be earned by particular behavior or accommodation to a set of social norms. The prevailing doctrine was that it was the responsibility of the government to make sure that people were cared for, that they had the opportunity to improve their condition (e.g., United States Social Security Act, 1935; Aid to Families with Dependent Children (AFDC), 1936; Supplemental Security Income (SSI), 1974), and that public resources should be allocated on the basis of that ethic. The "everywoman rhetoric" that suggests that all victims of male violence deserve protection, as I described in chapter 3, is a reflection of this assumption. As I previously established, there were benefits and consequences of assuming this naive, racially neutral rhetorical position about violence against women, even during a more liberal political era.[24]

A closer, more critical examination of social policy that was advanced in the 1960s and expanded in the 1970s reveals subtle punitive, moralistic assumptions that resulted in attempts to control communities through programs based on narrow definitions of family, work, gender roles, and childhood, particularly for Black women in low-income communities.[25] Indeed, while the state has always been a protector of some rights, it has also been an agent of control of people who are more socially marginalized—including pregnant women, public housing residents, young queer women, and others who threaten hegemonic norms. Even during political eras when more liberal ideology prevailed, social programs that looked like they were designed to increase social equality and expand opportunity subtly authorized the state use of its authority to control marginalized groups. As such, these reform efforts are not designed to significantly change relationships of power between the ruling class and those who serve and support it though low-paid wages, traditional gender relationships, and so forth. In fact, some social theorists and policy analysts argue that it is *because of* the progress of short-sighted social initiatives and ineffective programs that critics were able to mobilize for divestment in the 1980s, in opposition to the more progressive agenda for change that characterized the 1960s and 1970s.

Indeed, in the early 1980s, as anti-violence leaders were focused almost exclusively on legal and legislative strategies, a new set of questions and a more conservative point of view about the nature of social problems emerged. Conservative scholars, religious leaders, and lawmakers began to argue that social problems (including violence) were based more on personal choices and immoral behavior than persistent lack of resources and structural arrangements.[26] Accompanying this perspective were shifts in the values about work and family and a renewed commitment to social arrangements based on assumptions of meritocracy. These developments dramatically affected the social perception of women who were hurt by men in their lives; by their boyfriends, husbands, employers, strangers, or agents of the state, like the police.

By the early 1990s, the progress toward divestment was significant and the subsequent disadvantages were becoming concentrated in low-income communities of color, with a particular impact on women. The principal architects of America's prison nation—conservative policymakers, religious leaders, and corporate decision-makers—were joined by more neoliberal supporters of a more limited governmental role in improving conditions in communities. There was a decided sense that the state had "overstepped its role" in providing resources and that individuals had to take responsibility for their social conditions, regardless of the circumstances that led to them. The erosion of entitlement programs, long-term benefits, exemptions, and other policy revisions are evidence that the sense of a collective responsibility was being replaced by stringent limitations on what the government would provide. Importantly, the shift was *not only* in terms of reallocating material resources and opportunities in such a way that it appeared that the state was abandoning a commitment to social advancement and equality. There was growing evidence that the state was also rejecting its commitment to social equality by using its ideological power to reassert hegemonic values about gender through social welfare reforms. Time limits on eligibility for welfare benefits, promotion of marriage as mandatory programming, stringent work requirements, and the like are evidence of this.[27]

In sum, the first pre-condition to the buildup of America's prison nation around the anti-violence movement exists when the state is infused with power to reproduce and then uphold white patriarchal privilege by divesting from low-income communities and relying on neoliberal political ideology to support that divestment plan. A system of beliefs and conservative values about social life influences the thinking and practices of institutions and ultimately reorganizes society through public policy. The ideology about Black women is influenced by narratives about race (white dominance), about gender (nuclear family), about sexuality (heterosexual reproduction), and about class (the value associated with paid work). Black women who experience male violence in communities that have been divested of social and material resources become undeserving of support because they are marginalized in the same ways that their communities are, while they are ignored by mainstream anti-violence leadership.

The Second Pre-Condition for the Buildup of a Prison Nation: Co-optation of Resistance Strategies and Analytic Sites of Resistance

The divestment and subsequent concentration of disadvantage that established the foundation for the buildup of America's prison nation required the manipulation of the progressive social values that dominated public sentiment in the 1960s and 1970s. First, those leaders who were invested in the buildup of a prison nation had to co-opt the political rhetoric that shaped the social movements of the times. Second, the architects of divestment strategies needed to refocus the prevailing social analyses of conditions that led to inequality from blaming structural conditions to ones that focused on individual failure. Third, the social movements that challenged dominant structures of power and the assumptions that supported them were undermined, discredited, and otherwise compromised. Finally, social movements become co-opted and lose their potency through backlash.[28] Most relevant to this discussion of the buildup of America's prison nation that surrounds male violence against Black women are the ways that feminist organizing and black liberation movements lost their focus—both rhetorically and politically—on the issues of social justice and equity for Black women who experience male violence, arguing instead for a kind of legitimacy. That is, the social movements that demanded rights based on either race or gender failed to argue for the importance of both.[29]

The case implicating the co-optation of white feminist organizations in the buildup of America's prison nation is best made by looking at how the dominant analytical frames that evolved over time did not seriously attend to issues of institutionalized racism, cultural difference, or the mediation of sexism through structures of racial images and identities (with noted exceptions discussed in chapter 2).[30] It is instructive here to return to the discussion in chapter 3 about the rhetorical dependence on the notion of the innocent victim that argues that any woman and any child can be the victim of gender violence. This *"it can happen to anyone"* rhetoric has become a powerful emblem of the anti-violence movement. It was successful insofar as it allowed the creation of a public perception that any woman could be victimized by male violence.

This construction of *"any woman could be a battered woman"* and *"rape is a threat to every woman"* was initially adopted as a political strategy to avoid individualizing the problem of domestic and sexual violence and to focus instead on the social dimensions of the problem of gender violence. This generalized, monolithic construction of women's universal subordinated status was an analytic site of resistance insofar as it helped to foster a belief that women's vulnerability was profound and persistent, rather than particular to any racial-ethnic community, socioeconomic position, religious group, or station in life.

And yet, as the policies associated with divestment began to take hold, the race/class-neutral analysis was wholly inadequate. It failed to explain that for Black women who experience abuse along a continuum that includes physical, sexual, and social mistreatment in their households, community, and from the state. It was epistemologically unable to account for class differences and all that racism brings to the problem of male violence against women. Indeed, when the national discussion became organized around the "it could happen to anyone," the "ones" with the most visibility, the most power, and the most public sympathy are the "ones" whose needs are taken most seriously. Professional leadership in the anti-violence movement was drawn into the aura of being legitimate when powerful elites like then Attorney General Ashcroft and now Vice President Biden began to acknowledge the importance of violence against women that they might know. This created pressure to continue the focus on this elite group and to ignore the more complicated needs of others. Furthermore, the lure of being respected professional feminists was very strong and pulled women away from issues that would challenge the status of powerful elite men.

In a similar vein, the rhetorical strategy that informed the dominant struggle for racial justice led by male political elites continued to focus on the issue of race to the near exclusion of gender.[31] Some scholars refer to this as the master race narrative, the analysis of racial injustice that framed the struggle for racial justice in the United States. This takes two related forms. First, the situation for Black women who experience male violence is complicated by the emergence of a community narrative that considers Black men's subordinated social status to be worse than Black women's vulnerability.[32] Second, the growing call for "decency" in the Black community that ultimately calls for the reinscription of heterosexual, nuclear families with concomitant gender and generational hierarchy has become popularized by high-profile Black leaders and national organizations. From this perspective, part of the solution to violence, imprisonment, joblessness, and poverty is the re-ordering of gender relationships in the Black community in favor of patriarchal structures.[33]

This pre-condition—the concurrent co-optation of critical analysis of race, gender, class, and social inequality, combined with overly simplistic analyses emerging from social movements—redirected the white-dominated feminist and Black power movements from comprehensive social change goals to more conservative agendas for social reform and the establishment of respectability through individual change. It gave way to processes of individual blame of disadvantaged communities and their members, enabling America's prison nation to adopt a strategy of criminalization. Paradoxically, the social commitment to incapacitation, surveillance, and criminal justice sanctions, which were not originally key elements of the anti-violence movements' radical agenda, were accepted as necessary strategies in order to benefit some women at the expense of others who are less advantaged. Once divestment has begun and movements are being co-opted, isolation and criminalization constitute the final and most significant aspect of the buildup of a prison nation and its impact on Black women who experience male violence.

The Third Pre-condition for the Buildup of a Prison Nation: Isolation and Criminalization

Black women who experience male violence in communities of concentrated disadvantage and who face increasingly conservative rhetoric about poverty, sexuality, and their role in their own victimization, face disproportionate negative consequences from the public policy shifts associated with the buildup of a prison nation. Key among those consequences is a social dynamic called criminalization, whereby instead of benefiting from advances in state protection when they are in danger, Black women from low-income communities become isolated from mainstream services, blamed for the abuse they experience, and then sanctioned by state agencies for the harm they endured.[34] This paradoxical political dynamic—in which victims are isolated and subsequently treated as social deviants or criminals—operates at several levels in a prison nation, most notably the criminalization of poverty and non-normative sexuality.

The Criminalization of Poverty and Violence against Black Women

In the last decade, social scientists and political theorists have written a great deal about the criminalization of poverty.[35] Generated in great part by activists who work on economic justice issues, this interdisciplinary body of literature explores the ways that the consequences of being poor in contemporary society extend far beyond the obvious one—merely having insufficient resources to take care of oneself and one's family. In the current era, the ideological shifts associated with the buildup of America's prison nation conspire with increased economic inequality to create a situation where poverty is understood to be caused by moral failings, faulty decision-making, negative cultural values, and errant behavior *as opposed to* being associated with structural conditions or lack of equal opportunity. In the buildup of America's prison nation, the poverty that results from divestment from low-income communities as society is reordered is accepted as an inevitable consequence of individual pathology. Indeed, the very use of the term "personal responsibility" in the title of the 1996 legislation that transformed welfare policy is evidence of the strength of this ideological assumption about the individual nature of the problem and its ultimate solution. The Personal Responsibility and Work Opportunity Reconciliation Act of 1996 (PRWORA) shifts responsibility from the state to the person, which justifies the serious limitations placed on the amount of time, money, children, and the circumstances that individuals can have in order to receive financial relief from structural poverty.

A number of prominent feminist scholars have focused their recent work on the impact of welfare reform on Black women from marginalized communities who experience male violence during the buildup of America's prison nation. Anna Marie Smith makes an important contribution in her book *Welfare Reform and Sexual Regulation* through a close look at both the mechanical workings and the ideological underpinnings of welfare reform policy.[36] She argues, "poor women are extraordinarily exposed to the coercive powers of the state today. Obviously they are the ones who bear the brunt of the neo-liberal cuts in social programs and who are most vulnerable to male violence. They are the women who are targeted, first and foremost, where conservative family values projects and disciplinary interventions are concerned."[37] Smith provides evidence of the ways that the state uses welfare policy to force or coerce poor, Black women and other women of color to conform to what she calls a "one-size-fits-all heteropatriarchal model of kinship relations"[38] through family caps, coerced adoption, paternity notification, marriage provisions, abstinence programs, and the like. Each of these policy initiatives leaves women victimized by male violence even more vulnerable. Criminalization of poor women through welfare reform works in America's prison nation to the extent that women lose their rights to privacy and are forced to make information public that might put them at risk of abuse, they are vulnerable to moral judgments and criminal sanctions because their social position is understood as a part of their moral failing, and then are ultimately left to fend for themselves once they experience male violence. It is tantamount to policing of women's obedience to society's gender laws—laws that are a part of the broader project of conformity to hegemonic roles—and the criminalization of those who threaten or deviate from them.

Religious conservatism in both Black and white communities (and its influence on politics) are a significant part of the criminalization of poor Black women insofar as much of the social control apparatus and the ideological rhetoric are linked to traditional heteronormativity of families. This is articulated by leadership of right-wing conservative religious organizations as well as by conservative, high-profile African American religious leaders. The growing social conservatism that blames poverty on poor people has a profoundly gendered dimension to it, as evidenced by the focus on young Black girls, Black single mothers, and Black women who work in the sex industry, all of whom face particular vulnerability to male violence.[39]

Legal scholar Dorothy Roberts has provided one of the clearest social analyses of how poverty and ideology about race and gender work against Black women who are socially marginalized through removing children from the custody of Black families. In both of her books, *Killing the Black Body* and *Shattered Bonds: The Color of Child Welfare*, she forcefully argues that the contemporary child welfare system has roots in a social agenda that sees poor Black women as immoral, dangerous parents. In her extensive documentation of Black women's experience in the Child Welfare agency in Chicago, she exposes how the system works in discriminatory ways that ultimately destroy Black families and marginalize Black women. From the perspective of the buildup of America's prison nation where women are abused, it is important to note that this positioning is not only about parenting, but also about sexuality, class, and male violence. That is, losing one's children through actions of the state pushes women outside of the sphere where they are considered "real women" deserving of "real protection," however paternalistic that protection might be. As such, if they are also experiencing male violence, as is the case with a majority of women who lose custody of their children, they are not considered "real women victims." In several other important essays that examine the relationship between domestic violence, poverty, and the child welfare system, feminist scholars continue to argue that race is as central to the analysis of what is happening to women as class; being criminalized because they are poor is tantamount to institutionalized racism.

Dana Ain Davis has taken the general analysis of the gendered criminalization of poverty and explicitly links it to institutionalized racism and male violence. Her ethnographic work provides a microanalytic look at impacts of welfare policy on Black women who are abused by their partners. Davis's work supports the link between intimate partner violence and women's poverty. Given the dynamics of class in contemporary society, Black women are particularly vulnerable to this linkage.[40] Even with the option provided to states to ignore some of the requirements for women who experience male violence, referred to as the Family Violence Exemption, new rules for public assistance increase the likelihood that women will be harmed. For example, abusers sabotage women's ability to go to work, and then the time limits policy found in the PRWORA forces them out of eligibility for benefits. Similarly, the family cap rule has disproportionate impact in cases where abusive boyfriends force women to become pregnant, which can result in losing benefits. Because more than half of the women receiving welfare benefits have been victims of male violence, these and other provisions have a disproportionately negative effect—discriminating against Black women who experience male violence by leaving them in a particularly dangerous place where their eligibility is threatened by the nature of the abuse they experience.[41]

The threats to public housing provide another illustration of how poverty is criminalized. Intimate-partner violence and homelessness are significantly correlated according to many national studies,[42] and a disproportionate number of the residents of public housing are Black women. One of the key dimensions of neoliberal social policy was to create "zero-tolerance policies" for people living in public housing; this means that if a family member of any resident uses violence, the family will be immediately evicted. This creates serious disadvantages for Black women whose male partners use violence against them.[43] Other examples include the maintenance of central registries of people who use social services, the fingerprinting of people who receive public assistance, use of that data in crime registries, and enhanced penalties for "welfare fraud" which women may use to protect themselves or their families. In the aggregate, these initiatives, which apply sanctions to women for their attempts to avoid violence and manage their economic circumstances, have a disproportionate impact on Black women who are more likely to be poor and disadvantaged during the buildup of America's prison nation.[44]

The Criminalization of Non-normative Sexuality and Gender Roles as an Influence on Male Violence against Black Women

Even with what some scholars and activists understand as an increased tolerance for diversity in gender roles and sexual identities in some spheres, there is strong evidence that for the most marginalized groups, deviance from hegemonic gender and sexuality norms continues to be associated with negative consequences.[45] It is important to emphasize that the negative impact extends beyond individuals who are "queer" to those who simply do not conform to traditional standards because of their appearance, their work, their family structure, or their behavior.[46] The risks that come with nonconformity to hegemonic expectations around gender and sexuality include being stigmatized and discriminated against by social institutions, victimized by aggressive hate crimes, isolated and invisible in communities, and, increasingly, criminalized. Punishing people for their nonconformity to gender roles is a key aspect of the ideology behind the buildup of America's prison nation.

Social and political pressure forces individuals to conform to normative gender expectations of masculinity and femininity; to establish and maintain households of nuclear, self-supporting (middle-class) families, and to organize these families around gender and generational hierarchies. All of this is intended to reinforce heterosexual patriarchy.[47] This idealized type is just that—an image of a family that is driven by hegemonic gender ideology and seldom realized in real life. Still, the expectations inform how social policy is written and how social institutions operate. For example, social policy expects the following from women who have children: (a) they have them in the setting of an intimate relationship with the children's other biological parent; (b) they have them as part of a long-term relationship; (c) both biological parents will be involved in the children's lives as co-parents, but with very different roles based on gender; (d) the co-parents are married heterosexuals; and (e) the families will not be abusive. Interestingly, this final expectation is protective of women in violent relations as long as the other pre-conditions are met. Beth Silken Catlet and Julie E. Artis[48] state, "Research shows that domestic violence is a central reality for the very population that marriage promotion policies necessarily target—namely low-income families." They go on to say that "the stated goals of the PRWORA including ending the dependence of needy parents on government benefits by promoting . . . marriage and encouraging the formulation of and maintenance of two-parent families."[49]

Public policy requirements are linked to each of these expectations and, as such, define what a legitimate family is and is not. Because they are not "real women" living in "real families," single women, lesbians or transsexuals, incarcerated women, adolescent parents, and other groups who deviate from the expectations do not benefit from the public policy protections if they experience male violence. In fact, the greater the deviance, the more women are targeted as illegitimate and illegal.[50] These expectations are deeply embedded in the cultural belief system that is supported by state institutions. Feminist scholars have explored the consequences of deviance from hegemonic gender roles and queer sexuality, but have not focused on how race complicates the consequences, one of which might be gender violence. The literature does establish that the pressure to conform to these standards is stronger for marginalized groups, and deviations are not tolerated for people with higher status, but without sufficient depth to explain what happens to Black women who live on the margins of society.

During the buildup of a prison nation, the state monitors deviations from gender expectations. Andrea Ritchie has conceptualized this dynamic as the policing of gender, whereby women who deviate from norms find themselves under law enforcement surveillance in new ways. For example, according to these new standards, prostitution, which has always been illegal but frequently overlooked, is punished more harshly by elevating it in some instances to the level of a felony sex crime.[51] Hate crimes constitute another example of how ideology and conservative rhetoric buttress the criminalization of sexuality. Hate crimes toward lesbians like the New Jersey 4 tend to be under-reported in part because the state has denied statutory protection to GLBTQ people in the form of sodomy laws and bans of gay marriage.[52]

Speaking more generally, Black women who experience male violence have more difficulty achieving the hegemonic expectations of gender and sexuality. Compared to their white counterparts, they are less likely to subscribe to traditional gender roles, to marry, to depend on men for economic support and live with their children's biological father, or to present as innocent victims and report abuse to law enforcement officers.[53] While a considerable amount of variance can be attributed to class as opposed to race, the fact remains that the process of criminalization of sexuality disproportionately affects Black women. They are subjected to heightened negative media attention, stereotypical reactions from the public, and increased blame and scrutiny from their community for social problems. As the case of the New Jersey 4 showed, hate crimes are more likely to be tolerated when sexual identity, class, and race motivate them. Women who, like Tanya, are breaking with one of the fundamental assumptions regarding womanhood—being a protective mother—are described with disgust because of their response to pregnancy.[54] Ms. B was understood by the social institutions that she interacted with as being in need of "discipline" and therefore more at risk of punishment by the state.

The Impact of the Prison Nation on Violence against Black Women

First, poor Black women tend to live in segregated communities where they are isolated and therefore are less likely, in general, to be protected by governmental agencies. Complicating this, the mainstream white-dominated feminist rhetoric and subsequent policies that organize the institutional response to male violence are not relevant to them, in part because of Black women's lack of adherence to hegemonic standards of womanhood. That is, they are not considered "real victims of male violence" because their victimization "looks different," state authority does not legitimize their relationships, and they are not "real women."[55]

A considerable body of literature has documented the radical differences in relational status among women of different racial/ethnic and class groups. Black women who experience male violence may not be married to or cohabitating with their partners. Their household may be a multi-generational unit of extended family with limited biological connections, and their financial resources may be earned from non-traditional sources and communally shared. The unpredictability of the social environment may create instability and stress that is misinterpreted as self-defeating behavior. It should be noted that other groups, besides Black poor women, are positioned outside of the hegemonic norm. Immigrant women, military families, individuals with substance abuse problems, queer couples and others have trouble "fitting into" the social expectations around which the parameters of male violence are drawn. These variations, however well understood by some social scientists, Black family advocates, and community leaders, have not been very successfully integrated into anti-violence prevention, intervention, and policy strategies. Instead, their "deviant" family arrangements, their "non-normative" sexuality, and their "inadequate" parenting are used as excuses for their victimization.

As a result, Black women who report male violence to state officials are more likely to encounter uninformed service providers, unsympathetic community members, and rigid representatives of the state who blame them for their experiences and ignore the structural pre-conditions that surround them and their families.[56] This leads to a response that addresses only the particular incident of male violence rather than the broader context within which it occurs. Finally, research on factors that lead to escalation of violence indicates that if agencies can't (or won't) help and women are left under-served, the violence will become more serious.[57] The social dynamic of America's prison nation and its impact on Black women, who live in divested communities, where resistance is co-opted and where they are blamed and criminalized, is made clearer by returning to the cases presented in the introduction of this book.

Lack of Protection

Black women who are hurt by male violence, have limited social capital, social support, and opportunities for self-efficacy. Some are young, isolated by the experience of being sexually assaulted, and controlled by their boyfriend. In addition to their marginalized position because of their race and gender, women like Tanya are being raised in a household without adequate economic resources where adults' ability to protect their children is compromised. They are preoccupied with basic survival needs. As I previously noted, the community rhetoric regarding the vulnerability of Black men supersedes the needs that Black women face. This is furthered by the anti-violence movement's over-reliance on the criminal legal system that targets young African American men. The combination of these factors leaves these young women unprotected, and easy prey for the men in their lives.

Ms. B lived in a neighborhood from which the city had intentionally divested its resources. As the city was tearing down the public housing complex that she lived in, the community leadership that was preoccupied with promises of middle-class benefits was deploying a rhetoric that co-opted some advocates for economic justice who had once considered themselves allies of public housing residents. These allies and community organizers began to believe that the "plan for transformation" would not, in fact, have such deleterious consequences for poor people who lived in public housing. As the rhetoric became more convincing, more and more services could be legitimately cut, and Ms. B and her neighbors were further marginalized. The geographic and demographic changes that accompanied the massive displacement further marginalized the neighborhoods. Ms. B's delay in moving was interpreted by the powerful Housing Authority (a state agency influenced by profit-driven private contractors) as obstinant, misguided resistance to the accepted social agenda around housing. This relegated her to the status of "deserving victim" of state abuse.

The New Jersey 4 walking in New York City crossed geographic, political, and ideological boundaries that left them vulnerable and unprotected. First, as working-class, young, Black women in a neighborhood that is increasingly white and middle class, it was almost as if they were trespassing in new, more conservative space. Their sexual identity and their performance of nonhegemonic gender roles made them even more like "outlaws." While the immediate homophobic assault happened as one incident of male violence, the court's decision to consider them undeserving of protection was undoubtedly influenced by legislation that denies them the right to be in open, intimate relationships with one another. Indeed, their social marginalization in a white middle-class community mirrors their isolation as queer young women in Black communities, evidenced by the continued silence about their case by the established Black political leadership that is decidedly not interested in advancing the rights of Black queer youth.[58]

Lack of Responsive Services

Like the hundreds of situations they represent in which Black women from disadvantaged communities experience intimate partner violence, assault in their neighborhood, or state-sanctioned violence, the women whose stories are recounted in this book are denied redress and supportive services despite the fact that their cases are made public. Ms. B made several attempts to get help from a rape crisis center. The cases that made up the composite of Tanya show evidence of young women trying to talk to the adults in their lives about the abuse they experience and their sympathetic understanding toward the men who are harming them. Appeals were made to anti-violence service providers to intervene on the behalf of the New Jersey 4. Indeed, in each case, people with some authority knew what was going on. For various reasons associated with the positioning of the anti-violence movement in the buildup of America's prison nation, no one intervened. For one thing, there are far too few anti-violence programs that understand the relationship between poverty and violence against women. When we add the dynamics of age, sexuality, and multiple perpetrators, the opportunities for support narrowed. The impact of the dynamics of America's prison nation clearly shapes Black women's experience of male violence; however, most programs are not responsive to this broader set of problems. The New Jersey 4 were left vulnerable by the lack of anti-violence agencies willing to aggressively take on either street violence or sexuality, and Ms. B faced agencies' reluctance to intervene in police brutality cases because of their attempts to build relationships with law enforcement. In each of these cases the political hesitation was exacerbated by the lack of culturally competent services, another significant factor in these women's inability to get help.[59]

Further complicating this is important evidence that suggests that Black women may be less likely to rely on formalized reporting systems when they are in crisis for a number of reasons. In those instances when they do make reports to helping agencies, it is less likely that they will receive a serious response.[60] The lack of response has been empirically linked with nonresponsive services that ultimately blame women for their victimization.[61] The research suggests that when experiences of victimization are not legitimized by external forces, which is the case for many Black women, then they are more likely to be blamed and the violence is likely to escalate.[62]

Ultimately Black Women Who Are Victimized Are Blamed

Women in aggregated situations like Tanya's are clearly blamed by both the media and the court for the circumstances they find themselves in and their responses to it. Attempts to explain the decision to break the law in response to victimization are very limited for young, Black pregnant teenagers. Instead, America's prison nation's prevailing social ideology about family, motherhood, sex, and race make it easy to attribute responsibility to these young women for their predicament.

As people learned about Ms. B's case, many asked, "why didn't she leave?" or "why did she allow herself to experience so much victimization?" These questions, and the assumptions behind them, clearly suggest that Ms. B did something to position herself as vulnerable to the police brutality that she experienced and, moreover, she should have done something to remove herself from that position. These assumptions clearly reflect a misunderstanding of how poverty, fear, and violence immobilize people in the face of state violence and how deeply flawed public policy is regarding housing relocation. The lack of understanding makes it easy to blame women like Ms. B for the abuse that they experience.

With respect to the New Jersey 4, the public record documents questions that imply that they had some responsibility for the attack. What were they doing in Greenwich Village? Why did they "flaunt" their sexuality? What did they expect? Why did they have to "get loud"? These and other questions reflect the tendency to supplant the fundamental issue—that they were attacked—with explanations that blame them.

The most overt manifestation of this blame is the arrest of women who are victimized by male violence. As discussed in chapter 3, the legal changes that include zero tolerance and mandatory arrest policies contributed significantly to the number of women being charged with crimes.[63] More subtly, when women fail to cooperate with law enforcement or do not report abuse to authorities, they are held accountable for what happens to them, even though solid evidence has established the reasons why it is quite reasonable that Black women might avoid interactions with protective or service agencies that do not protect them. The ideological and political apparatus of America's prison nation and the pre-conditions that lead to it turn their abuse into blame, and they are left even more vulnerable to violence.

The blame easily morphs into criminalization, the process by which Black women are turned into virtual social outlaws through excessive monitoring, surveillance, limitation of rights and privileges, and ultimately the belief that they are undeserving of help and that the abuse they experience is their fault. As in the cases of women like Tanya, Ms. B, and the New Jersey 4, criminalization leads to disenfranchisement that is serious and long-lasting.[64] Vulnerability for women like Tanya was furthered by the stigma and perceived "undeservedness" for services that young women who are poor and pregnant receive from contemporary society. Because they were "out of place" as working-class, queer, Black women, the New Jersey 4 could not be defended in court. And even though Ms. B won her class action suit, she continues to live a life of seclusion and fear because of her experience of male violence from agents of the state.

Conclusion: The Buildup of a Prison Nation and Male Violence against Black Women

The previous discussion establishes the factors that contribute to the buildup of America's prison nation and how they disadvantage Black women who experience male violence. Much more could be said about how broader state policies deny statutory protection to women who are queer, poor, young, and Black, but here the important conclusion is that the buildup of America's prison nation—in terms of both ideology and public policy—leaves Black women who experience male violence at heightened risk that their victimization will be criminalized as opposed to their rights being protected. It is also possible to extend the argument beyond Black women to include other vulnerable groups. The point here is that for Black women, the evolution of the anti-violence movement during the buildup of America's prison nation has brought paradoxical results. While some women are temporarily or situationally safer because the anti-violence movement had not evolved as it did to rely heavily on criminalization of male violence,[65] those women whose experience falls outside of the mainstream are in as much danger as ever because of the buildup of America's prison nation. Black women who do not fit into the traditional image of an innocent victim because they are an adolescent defendant charged with neonaticide, a lesbian who resists a sexually aggressive stranger, or a resident of public housing who is a victim of police brutality rather than interpersonal violence, will not receive the protection of a prison nation. And, if she is a prostitute, an active substance abuser, a woman who has lost custody of her children because of neglect, an undocumented immigrant, or simply a woman who has learned that the state will not protect her, she is even *less likely* to be served by the criminal legal system's very general response to male violence. Indeed, they are not "real women."

Black women who are most vulnerable in our society are subjected to the political processes whereby social policy is used strategically as part of a larger social agenda aimed at maintaining the power of elites through the control of marginalized groups. As state authority attempts to reassert hegemonic values about class, gender, sexuality, and criminalization under the guise of maintaining social order, Black women like them are at heightened risk because of conservative ideology. Individuals like them are blamed and held accountable for their suffering through moral sanctioning and criminalization. A Black feminist response to male violence must include attention to the factors that lock Black women into America's prison nation as well as the dynamics that create the opportunity for violence at the individual and community levels.

5

The Matrix

A Black Feminist Response to
Male Violence and the State

Tamika Huston was 24 years old when she went missing in Spartanburg, South Carolina in May 2004.[1] Natalee Holloway was 19 when she disappeared almost a year later during a high school graduation trip to Aruba. Originally from a wealthy suburb of Birmingham, Alabama, Natalee Holloway was a member of the National Honor Society and was planning to attend the University of Alabama on a full scholarship after a trip full of abandon and fun. Despite reports of circumstances that suggest that she and her fellow students were not well supervised during the trip, once it was confirmed that she was missing, Special Agents from the FBI, members of the Dutch military, and hundreds of volunteers joined her family and their influential network of friends in the search for the missing young woman. Holloway's case immediately received national attention by the United States' news media, and soon after, her story became an international media sensation. The ongoing investigation, arrests and re-arrests of various suspects, and progress made toward solving the crime, were lively topics of national news broadcasts (CNN), TV documentaries, and Internet websites, and soon the case will be made into a television movie based on the book by her mother Beth Holloway called *Loving Natalee*.

Returning to Tamika Huston, despite the similar profiles of the young women on almost every measure, Tamika's case was not considered "worthy" of the kind of attention that Holloway received. Tamika was also an accomplished student, she came from a loving family, and she had plans for her future that included raising the child that she was carrying. In her case, however, when she was reported missing, the local police investigation was slow to start and was not joined by national agencies, likely subjects (like her former boyfriend) were not interviewed, her parents had to "beg" for media attention, and the national media was particularly slow to respond. In the end, tragically, both women were the victims of young men, and the disregard for their lives could be read into the individual patterns of the crimes. For Huston, however, the source of her disregard extended far beyond the person who murdered her to the social, political, and legal responses to the case of her being missing. So profound was the difference in how the media covered the cases—the saturation of coverage for the young white woman and the blatant disregard for the young Black woman—that some high-profile reporters (Gwen Iffel from CNN, for example) described the phenomenon as the Missing White Woman Syndrome to illustrate how violence against women is taken seriously *only* insofar as it has an impact on those groups of women with social privilege.

Beyond the considerable attention given to this controversial example of how the media and law enforcement respond to and treat Black women who are in dangerous situations with more disregard than their white counterparts, the story of Tamika Huston is also one that illustrates how Black women create structures of resistance by taking matters into their own hands. This was the case for Derrica Wilson, one of the founders of Black and Missing Foundation,[2] a national organization whose mission it is to "provide an Equal opportunity for all missing." The group works to increase attention to the disproportionate number of Black people who are among the "missing" (women and children in particular) and the layers of oppression that Black people experience, especially Black women, that make it easy for the state to ignore this particular form of inequality. They do so based on an analysis of structural inequality, with a fierce commitment to justice, and because they understand that individual danger for Black women needs to be understood as part of a larger pattern of social neglect based on their race, gender, and other socially stigmatized identities that are marginalized in contemporary society.

In this chapter, I present a Black feminist analysis of male violence against Black women as an alternative conceptualization of the problem that takes into account the buildup of America's prison nation. A Black feminist analysis not only provides a much better explanation of the multiple dynamics of race, sexuality, gender, and class; it also accounts for the various forms of violence women experience and the multiple contexts within which it simultaneously occurs. A Black feminist analysis helps to show how the mainstream anti-violence movement achieved success, while at the same time the radical work to end violence against women diminished. Finally, a Black feminist analysis points to the manner in which the work to dismantle America's prison nation will advance the anti-violence agenda in fundamental and critical ways. To provide a background to this discussion, I will draw on the work of a number of Black feminist scholars to delineate the tenets of Black Feminist Theory that are most relevant to the work to end violence against women.[3] I will then apply the theoretical argument directly to what I am calling "the male violence matrix." I conclude with a compendious presentation of Black feminist work to end violence against women: the seminal research, writing, and activism that have paved the way for a much more political understanding of what happened to vulnerable groups of Black women who experience male violence.

Black Feminist Theory

Black Feminist Theory is a political and intellectual intervention developed by women activists and scholars challenging the traditional body of knowledge about Black women and the ways that it is produced and validated.[4] Recognizing that most research about Black women and representations of their lives are far from objective, Black feminists worked both inside and outside of the academy to advance a theoretical framework designed to subvert what was accepted as "real science," "empirical evidence," or "truth" about Black women's lives and the circumstances that we live within.[5] Scholars who utilize Black Feminist Theory understand that even progressive intellectuals and more critical studies have the tendency to skew scholarly and political understandings toward the hegemonic norm.[6] Black Feminist Theory is both an epistemological approach and a call for engaged praxis with the overall goal of political empowerment and social justice. In that way, it is particularly well suited to this discussion of male violence against Black women and the buildup of a prison nation. Prior to applying Black Feminist Theory to those issues specifically, I will review the five tenets of Black Feminist Theory that are most relevant to this discussion.

Interlocking Oppression

A cornerstone of Black Feminist Theory is the understanding that the oppression of Black women is complex and layered. As a marginalized group, Black women are subjected to a tangled web of concentrated structural disadvantages that are profoundly intense and forceful in their ability to stigmatize and create subordinate social status. Sexism, for example, is experienced differently by Black women than white women in part because it is not the only source of oppression that Black women face; it is complicated by institutional racism and the particular way that white patriarchy imparts racial hierarchy on Black bodies. The combined effect of sexism and racism is linked to uniquely disparaging images of Black women's sexuality, and it is emboldened by the ways that state power controls opportunity on the basis of race as well as gender. A similar argument has been made about how an overly simplistic view of racialized oppression of Black people often fails to consider the particular ways that gender roles and relationships are invoked as part of the system of white racism in the United States imaginary.[7]

Highly critical of these overly simplified, additive models of oppression, Kimberlé Crenshaw is one of the most often cited scholars who discuss the interlocking oppressions associated with Black Feminist Theoretical analyses. In an article in the *Stanford Law Review*, Crenshaw lays out a schema that shows why Black women's identities cannot be compartmentalized into discrete categories of gender, class, social status, and the like.[8] On the contrary—intersectional arguments claim that Black women's bodies are simultaneously marked by racial, gender, sexual, color, historical, class, and other stigmas; these stigmatized identities and the subsequent oppressions are not hierarchical or additive; they are intersectional. One of the most important contributions of Black feminist theory is the notion of how intersectionality is relational, structural, political, and ideological, and thus explains male violence as complex and multi-dimensional, as the matrix will show.

Standpoint Epistemology

A second theoretical guidepost of Black Feminist Theory is the notion that in research and representations of Black women, *their* experience should be at the center of the analysis.[9] The authenticity of interpretations is enhanced when scholars and activists can link "what one thinks" about something to "what one does" about it. Standpoint epistemology assumes that knowledge that is generated by people who are closer to the experience they are analyzing will be more accurate than knowledge generated by researchers who claim to be objective or impartial because of their distance from the object of study. In fact, Black Feminist Theory gives little credence to the very concept of objectivity because it is understood to be an impossible intellectual stance, given how knowledge reflects relationships of power and the entrenchment of stigma and stereotypical judgments in society. Instead, Black Feminist Theory argues for the utility of an "interested standpoint," whereby those who understand the phenomenon under exploration are in the best position to evaluate and make claims about the meaning of it.[10]

This assumption presents a deep challenge to research, politics, and activism on the issue of male violence against Black women. By implication, it suggests that those who claim authority (in the traditional sense of scholar, policymaker, lawyer, social worker) must yield expertise to the often-subordinated group of Black women who are victimized in the multiple ways described in chapter 2 within the context of a prison nation. This has important implications both for the understanding of violence against black women like Tanya, Ms. B, and the New Jersey 4 (in these cases, members of subordinated groups) and for the architects of the buildup of America's prison nation (those who occupy positions of ideological or state authority).

Everyday Knowledge

Interpretation of experiences and the attribution of common meaning to those experiences is an important tenet of Black Feminist Theory. Like standpoint theory, privileging everyday knowledge is an attempt to locate authority or expertise with those who experience a circumstance rather than generating it from scholars, policymakers, or other outsiders who lack access to authentic understanding of events, relationships, behaviors, values, or historical antecedents to current phenomena. The idea that the collective wisdom of people with shared experiences is the most accurate source of data is a frequently added element of the notion of how important everyday knowledge is. And standpoints are not static. As Patricia Hill Collins states: "A recognition of the connection between experience and consciousness that shapes the everyday lives of individual African-American women often pervades the works of Black women activists and scholars."[11]

Dialectical Images

There are other theoretical dimensions of Black Feminist Theory that must be understood as nonstatic or reflecting dynamic qualities. One of the most common is that images of Black womanhood are dialectical. This means that while it is generally agreed that "within the U.S. imaginary, Black women have typically represented 'deviant womanhood,'"[12] the *particular* negative image that is most common and/or damaging at any historical moment depends on the context in which such an image is being constructed. Black Feminist Theory understands that there are varying images of Black womanhood that shape Black women's identity and social positioning. So, for example, Black women can be strong (and therefore not at risk of violence), castrating (and therefore incapable of heteronormative intimacy), hypersexual (therefore ill-suited for long-term relationships or parenting), or criminal (and therefore unworthy of protection or support).[13] Importantly, Black Feminist Theory allows for an analysis that suggests that Black women can be all of these things at once. This fluid image, the dialectic, is almost always in conflict with dominant notions of hegemonic femininity that imagines women to be passive, nurturing, and relationship-oriented, and thus "innocent victims" when they experience male violence. It also contradicts the ideologically based assumptions that all the forces associated with the buildup of America's prison nation disadvantage and criminalize Black women like those whose stories are described in this book.

Social Justice Praxis

The final precept of Black Feminist Theory that is critical to the discussion of male violence against Black women and the buildup of America's prison nation is the role that social justice praxis assumes in responding to it. This notion insists that research on Black women be linked to efforts at changing conditions that subordinate them and their communities.[14] This commitment is reflected in language that permeates Black feminist texts; Patricia Hill Collins uses the term empowerment, Bernice Johnson Regan talks about coalition-building, and other Black feminist activists like Barbara Ransby, Julia Sudbury, and Joy James discuss engaged scholarship and social justice.[15]

The assumption behind these concepts is that scholarly work should be in service to activism and that the beneficiaries of research findings, policy recommendations, or theoretical insights should be those most affected, in this case Black women who experience male violence within the context of a prison nation. This might be accomplished through challenging hierarchies of power, transforming academic institutions, advancing a new kind of organizational leadership, and reinvigorating grassroots mobilization efforts for social change.

Understanding Male Violence from a Black Feminist Perspective Using the Violence Matrix

Black Feminist Theory greatly enhances the ability to interrogate the problem of male violence against women in several ways. First, given the multiple forms and contexts in which Black women are harmed, an evaluation of the interlocking oppressions that Black women face allows for a much more comprehensive understanding of the kind of violence that vulnerable groups of Black women in the United States experience. In each case, an intersectional analysis helps to focus on the ways that their non-normative images and disadvantaged social status created particular vulnerabilities to multiple forms of male violence, including structural violence associated with America's prison nation. Black Feminist Theory also provides a method of exploring how structural conditions interacted with ideology to leave Black women at risk of the serious harm that they endure. A Black feminist theoretical standpoint that understands women's experiences to be valid and important (as opposed to understanding them in relation to white women or Black men) offers them a more effective remedy—a remedy that is consistent with the justice-oriented principal goal of Black Feminist Theory.

The alternative Black Feminist conceptual framework I present here assumes that for most Black women like those whose stories I told in the introduction to this book, an analysis of their experiences must take into account the community, institutional, and social contexts within which male violence is nested. Specifically, the male violence matrix I am advancing here does two things. First, using a Black feminist standpoint, the matrix makes it possible to comprehend the tenacious grip that male violence has on Black women and the ways that the various kinds of abuse in multiple contexts line up to leave Black women uniquely vulnerable. Equally important, the male violence matrix highlights the intersectional relationship between male violence and ideology around race, gender, sexuality, and class. In particular, it allows us to consider the consequences when ideology shifts in more conservative directions, when resources are constrained, and communities of color are disadvantaged by the buildup of a prison nation.

The first dimension of the violence matrix locates the forms of abuse that women experience, described in chapter 2, along a continuum, reflecting a dialectical orientation.[16] At one end of the continuum are direct physical assaults against women, including hitting, punching, kicking, attacks with weapons, and other displays of physical force that injure, threaten, or intimidate women and their bodily integrity. Being slapped, thrown down stairs, burned, chased by a car, physically restrained, and forced to consume drugs or alcohol are among the endless examples of this form of abuse that women have reported.[17]

The second point on the continuum contains the range of sexual aggressions from sexual harassment to rape, including forcing women

The Violence Matrix

	Physical Assault	Sexual Assault	Emotional Manipulation
Intimate households	1. Direct physical assaults by intimate partners	2. Sexual assaults and aggression toward Black women by their intimate partners.	3. Emotional manipulation of Black women and the creation of a hostile social environment by their intimate partners
Community	4. Direct physical assaults by community members	5. Rape, sexual harassment, and sexual aggression toward Black women from their community	6. Emotional manipulation of Black women and the creation of a hostile social environment in their communities
State	7. Direct physical assault of Black women by state agencies and public policy	8. Sexual exploitation and aggression toward Black women who are in state custody and by public policy	9. State authority and public policy that enables emotional manipulation and the creation of a social environment that is hostile to Black women

to have sex with multiple people or animals, preventing women from using birth control or sterilizing them without their consent, videotaping and capitalizing on degrading sexual acts, forced prostitution, or coerced involvement in the sex industry, and other forms of sexual terror. Although these two forms are not mutually exclusive—clearly sexual abuse has a physical aspect to it—the violence matrix provides a way to think about direct physical assaults and sexual aggressions as forms of abuse that are dialectically linked and separate, with differing impact.

The third point along the continuum is the emotional manipulation that results from the creation of a hostile social environment. In other paradigms, described in the literature review in chapter 2, this form of abuse is called psychological or emotional abuse.[18] In the violence matrix, I have broadened the concept to reflect the more general idea that part of the abusive dynamic that some Black women face in disadvantaged communities is the creation of a tense and threatening *social* environment, beyond the psychological realm. In addition to emotional cruelty, some women must adjust to adverse, demeaning, and humiliating living conditions. They are subjected to misdirected anger, their mobility is threatened, and they are kept under constant surveillance, and must engage with unsympathetic community members or institutional authorities who make them feel ashamed or punish them for their social circumstances. The effect of living in hostile environments over time limits women's ability to function not only emotionally, but socially, financially, and politically as well. The continuum between direct physical attacks, sexual abuse and aggression, and the creation of a hostile social environment is dynamic; the points of the continuum are not static, and, as the following discussion will show, these forms of abuse create and reinforce a powerful negative impact on women's lives. All along the continuum, from direct physical assaults to the creation of a hostile social environment, the Black feminist analysis upon which the matrix is predicated shows that Black women experience abuse in ways that are specific to their position as racialized subjects and bodies. When we add to the conceptualization *the context* within which male violence exists, this specificity becomes clear.

Contexts of Abuse: Households, Community, and the State

In addition to the three forms of abuse, a Black feminist analysis of the violence matrix introduces the notion of context, identifying the three contexts within which the forms of abuse occur. The first context is where abuse happens in intimate households, which includes abuse from partners, family members, and others who have constant access to a person because of shared domestic space. This category includes boyfriends, parents, live-in partners, and co-parents who come and go with some regularity. The primary distinguishing feature of this context, which reflects a Black feminist orientation, is that it is *not* solely based on hegemonic notions of intimacy in the relationship, but physical proximity, which emerges from the everyday lived experiences of Black women. This is analytically meaningful because of the mutual dependency associated with shared living space and shared position with respect to external forces and conditions (like attempting to raise children in impoverished circumstances together).

The second context that the male violence matrix considers is the community—the geographic area that surrounds the household, in terms of both the actual neighborhood and also public areas like parks, schools, storefronts, bus stops, and other informal public spaces that people share. The matrix directs attention to the community context as a way to account for the danger that Black women face as they navigate public life in the areas that surround their intimate household. In this context, the notion of community also has an extra-geographic meaning. It takes into account the reference group or collective wisdom of Black women that establishes ways of understanding, provides moral maps that inform one's decisions and judgments, and directs expressive behavior. In this sense, "the community" includes the symbolically important people beyond those who share neighborhood space or live in proximity to one another.

The third context that the male violence matrix takes into account is the state and the ways that public governmental agencies create structural conditions that harm Black women. The conceptualization of state violence includes abuse that women experience while they are in the custody of institutions like prisons, hospitals, drug treatment centers, or schools *as well as* abuse by people who are in positions of authority in social agencies that women are required to engage with or depend on, including police brutality and sexual manipulation by public assistance workers and other employees of public institutions who, because of their formal role, wield tremendous power over women's vulnerable lives and their futures. Analysis of state violence enables an exploration of the ways that Black women are assaulted, manipulated, and not protected by institutions and the individuals who act on their behalf, and of the development of corresponding social justice praxis.

The conceptualization of the context of the state also includes the structural harm resulting from neoliberal public policy, such as decisions made at the local, state, or federal level that disadvantage women in such a way that they cannot get help when they are harmed. It also includes the rules and regulations that take away Black women's authority and self-determination and leave them dependent on hostile or ineffective state agencies.

In the visual representation of the male violence matrix shown in the table, readers will note that the three forms of abuse (direct physical assaults, sexual aggression, and creation of a hostile social world), and the three contexts within which violence against women occurs (intimate household, community, and state), are portrayed in discrete boxes or cells. This visual representation allows a fuller display of the impact of male violence on the lives of Black women within a prison nation. Insofar as it shows how the context and forms line up, cell by cell, one can begin to see how an intersectional Black Feminist analysis is possible. Importantly, as ordered as they may appear in the diagram, the lived experience of Black women reveals that the boundaries of the cells are actually permeable; the forms and contexts flow into each other as women experience violence in various ways and places. The nine cells of the violence matrix are surrounded by the various elements of America's prison nation; the ideological and political conditions that operate to reinforce power and privilege of elite groups in profound ways. It is here, at the intersection of the nine cells, where the layers of degradation pile up within America's prison nation, that readers can appreciate the distinctly Black feminist analysis of male violence against Black women who populate marginalized groups in society.

The Problem of Intimate Household Violence in the Lives of Black Women Living in a Prison Nation: Cells 1, 2, and 3

The first three forms of the male violence that are included in the matrix encompass the physical, sexual, and emotional assaults most commonly referred to as intimate partner violence described in chapter 2. A Black feminist analysis broadens the conventional understanding to include abuse by adults where there is a current or historical romantic, sexual, familial, or otherwise intimate or household relationship. In this formulation, cells 1, 2, and 3 capture the dynamics that reflect the myriad of circumstances in which Black women find themselves where shared space or living in the same household facilitates access to a potential victim. This would include circumstances where there are mutual responsibilities for dependents (as in the case of co-parents of minor children), where resources are assumed to be common property (food, money, furniture, telephones), and where there is a social expectation that the household unit operates according to some standard of mutual interests or care (sexual intimacy, shared decision-making, protection, etc.). Concretely, these relationships can include a woman's husband or boyfriend (regardless of whether they live together), people who have children together but are not legally married, adult siblings, and same-sex partners. From a Black feminist theoretical perspective, the distinctions that are important here are (a) historical or episodic feelings of intimacy, connectedness, or dependency, even if they are not current or reciprocal; (b) the social perception by outsiders that the individuals form some type of intimate unit, even if it is not a fully positive one; and (c) the routine access of the partners to each other's physical and, to some extent, emotional space.

The combination of these characteristics engenders a particular vulnerability to physical assaults, sexual aggression, and emotional manipulation. Indeed, the ideological conditions associated with America's prison nation, including the regulation of women's sexuality, reproduction, and hegemonic expectations regarding gender roles and relationships are essential factors in creating Black women's vulnerability to the layers of violence described in cells 1, 2, and 3 of the violence matrix. For, while the most blatant forces that are activated in the buildup of a prison nation are directed toward dynamics in the *public sphere*, relationships in the *private* sphere are necessarily invoked in the process of controlling marginalized households and the women who live in them. A Black feminist analysis enables this understanding of how intimate partner violence against women is dialectically linked to conditions that force particular household arrangements that endanger Black women, including subordinated Black patriarchy.[19]

Community Violence toward Black Women Who Live in a Prison Nation: Cells 4, 5, and 6

The data described in chapter 2 establish that, in addition to violence within intimate household arrangements, Black women are also at considerable risk of direct physical assault, sexual abuse and aggression, and a form of emotional manipulation that leads to social degradation by members of their communities. Cells 4, 5, and 6 consist of the kinds of individual harm that results when households and neighborhood dynamics in disadvantaged communities converge to create dangerous and degrading circumstances for Black women. It is important to establish a context of America's prison nation for the discussion of these three cells. The populations of Black women who are most vulnerable to male violence in all of its forms reside in the most dangerous communities in our country where disadvantages are concentrated.[20] The strategic divestment that characterizes the buildup of America's prison nation has meant that their neighborhoods are characterized by high rates of unemployment, low rates of home ownership, and inadequate health and human services to meet the needs of disadvantaged families. Some residents of neighborhoods where disadvantage is concentrated have developed strategies—some more effective than others—for coping with conditions of serious social and political disenfranchisement, including turning rage toward those members of the community who are most vulnerable—in this case Black women and girls. In addition, most analyses of cumulative neighborhood effect confirm that alienation is one of the results of structural racism which, when combined with limited social capital, has a serious negative effect, including intra-racial violence.[21] Indeed, while neighborhood associations, religious institutions, activist groups, and informal networks can serve as important sites of strength and resistance to these overwhelming disadvantages, it is fair to say that America's prison nation is built, many low-income African American neighborhoods face a level of despair that surrounds even those families and individuals who are faring well.[22] This renders dormant the activism, resistance, or coordinated response that might have otherwise characterized a Black community responding to aggression. A Black feminist analysis can easily account for how community violence layers onto intimate partner violence when the forces associated with the buildup of America's prison nation are operating.

Violence Inflicted by State Institutions and Policy Initiatives in a Prison Nation that Disadvantage Black Women Who Experience Male Violence: Cells 7, 8, and 9

In some instances, conditions in state-run institutions and public policies further the negative impact of household and community violence. For those Black women whose social status in America's prison nation is precarious, there are unique vulnerabilities to multiple threats from state institutions, including risk of direct physical assault, injury caused by sexual assault, and hardship created by a hostile social environment and neoliberal public policy initiatives.[23] Yet, because the same state agencies that create vulnerability either through direct harm or neglect are also primarily responsible for data collection about violence, it is difficult to find quantitative evidence of the violations found in cells 7, 8, and 9. Indeed, almost no data exist regarding physical or sexual abuse of women by state or governmental agencies, and there is very limited research on the direct effects of public policy on Black women's health and safety. At best, the literature addresses the ways that the state's lack of response leaves women vulnerable, as in the case of what happens when police do not respond to calls from battered women or when women who have been raped are re-traumatized via insensitive examinations by health-care providers.[24] To be sure, these are important contributing factors to the disproportionate rate of violence against Black women and the serious consequences victimized women face. The Black feminist analysis put forward by the male violence matrix, however, demands a more rigorous and in-depth analysis of how state institutions and neoliberal public policies interact with and deepen the harm caused by household and community violence.[25]

Beyond the overt harm caused by state agencies and people who represent them, attention to the violence that would fit into cells 7, 8, and 9 frames a way to capture the harm caused by those governmental and other public agencies that are officially authorized to offer services, monitor behavior, and maintain social order, but fail to protect Black women in vulnerable communities. These official agencies use their authority in different ways based, in part, on the positioning of the groups and individuals under their auspices. While it is generally assumed that these entities work on behalf of the citizens of any given locale, there is a body of research that documents the ways that the neoliberal state and its institutions have varying commitments and agendas about which social groups are protected and which are threatened and controlled. In a prison nation, more-privileged groups enjoy legal protection, guaranteed access to public services, safeguarded rights, and a set of economic benefits that maintain their secure status. In most instances, these privileges of citizenship are distributed through government policy and institutional practices. In other ways, the apparatus of the state operates indirectly by advancing a set of social expectations that clearly benefits and protects certain groups and individuals, distinguishing them from "others."

In America's prison nation, the "others"—the less privileged groups—experience the state and its practices in a very different way. For some groups, governmental agencies threaten individual liberty, constrain opportunity, limit resources, and serve to disenfranchise.[26] An analysis of the impact of the state in the lives of people with less social standing—groups like the working poor, people who rely on governmental assistance, immigrants, and battered women—reveals this discrepant role of state institutions.[27] Arguably, those who most need the support and protection of the state are the most vulnerable to its controlling and limiting dimensions.

This aspect of the violence matrix—including structural violence against Black women—is a unique contribution that emerges from a Black feminist analysis. It is important because although all women face a vulnerability to abuse from state institutions, the overrepresentation of Black women under the supervision of, surveillance by, or in dependent relationships with state institutions leaves them *disproportionately* vulnerable to the forms of abuse I describe in cells 7, 8, and 9. A Black feminist understanding shows how male violence toward Black women in America's prison nation that occurs in this context is distinct and different from abuse suffered in intimate personal and household relationships or inflicted by community members. For, while it may be the case that an individual employee or worker actually inflicts the assault, the state agency that he or she works for is complicit with the abuse by either condoning it or ignoring it. There is usually a set of institutional conditions that exacerbates Black women's vulnerability to victimization when it occurs within social institutions.

A Black Feminist Analysis of the Forms and Contexts of Male Violence against Black Women in the Context of a Prison Nation
The New Jersey 4

The attack on the New Jersey 4 was not random. They were targeted because of their non-normative display of gender, their overt queer sexuality, and their presence in a community that was increasingly closing its boundaries to those with less class privilege. Indeed, they were victims of a hate crime that was based on several forms of oppression that were operating in America's prison nation to regulate their social behavior, and when they resisted in self-defense, they were arrested. The interplay between sexism, racism, heterosexism, and subordinate class status allowed the court to criminalize them. A Black feminist analysis would point to the ways that the women were punished by the attack and later penalized by the criminal legal system's response because they did not reach the threshold of heteronormativity established by dominant cultural forces. Their experience as marginalized members of the Black community, compounded by the disrespect they experienced from society in general, dramatically worsened their experience of sexual harassment and physical assault.

Ms. B

A critical backdrop to Ms. B's experience of male violence was the country's divestment from low-income black communities represented by aggressive public policies and the plan to dismantle public housing complexes in cities like Chicago. The structural conditions in her neighborhood positioned her at odds with dominant institutions understood to be responsible for responding to victimization that the prison nation has transformed into institutions of social control—most obviously law enforcement. The more traditional social service system—including mainstream anti-violence programs—was reluctant to help her because of their relationship with state agencies, including the police department who perpetrated the abuse against her. A Black feminist analysis of male violence against women would place her experience in several cells in the male violence matrix as a way to conceptualize the impact of multiple abuses in several contexts. For example, it would include issues of police brutality in order to understand Ms. B's experience not only as physical abuse, but as harm caused to her already stigmatized image and the insult of having her requests for assistance denied. A Black feminist response would also take into account the history of prior victimization from members of her community and the dialectical feelings of protectiveness of Black men, on the one hand, and her betrayal by them on the other.

Tanya

The multiple forms of abuse that women like Tanya experience—from various perpetrators across the lifespan—is evidence of interlocking oppressions that are associated with violence against Black women within America's prison nation. They are targeted for abuse by men in their intimate households *not only* because they are girls/children, but because of their moral upbringing as Black women and their unconditional loyalty to Black men. A Black feminist analysis would engender a discussion about how the community's rhetoric of the men's vulnerability to dominant social institutional forces compromised Black women's ability to get help. In addition, it would show how they ended up in harm's way because of their position in a prison nation.

Black Feminist Activism and Resistance

The women's stories that frame the introduction to this book are desperate but not uncommon ones, representing circumstances and events faced by many Black women who experience male violence during the buildup of America's prison nation. A Black feminist analysis of their stories is incomplete, however, without consideration of Black women's proactive responses. Therefore, in the concluding section of this chapter, I highlight the ways in which Black women have not only survived but also—in many instances—prevailed in the face of male violence and the buildup of America's prison nation.

What follows is a description of the forms of resistance that characterized Black women's response to male violence during the era that the prison nation was being built and the anti-violence movement was most active. The review is not intended to be comprehensive. Instead, I follow the same time frame described in chapter 3 and provide a brief illustrative account of what Black women have done to resist physical, sexual, and emotional violence in their households, within their communities, from state institutions, and from public policy decisions that negatively impact their lives. The examples I present here are evidence that, unlike what transpired in the evolution of the more mainstream anti-violence movement, Black anti-violence activists responded to the tightening web of male violence and buildup of America's prison nation by sharpening their analysis, building coalitions, and fighting back. While white feminist leadership was winning the mainstream, Black feminist activism was gaining momentum and, in part because of Black women's more marginalized position, it was not as easily co-opted by the promise of legitimization.

Readers will note that in this chapter I use the concept of activism to refer to a range of activities designed to change the social arrangements that privilege those in power at the expense of more marginalized groups. For example, when institutions failed us, Black women supported one another in autonomous self-help groups. We sought to change repressive anti-violence laws through electoral politics, and when material needs arose, we pooled resources. In addition, Black feminist anti-violence praxis responded to being silenced by mainstream organizations, by organizing our own national groups, taking great risks by speaking out against racial and gender injustice in our communities and in larger social venues. As the following discussion will show, Black women writers have given voice to our struggle through essays, poetry, and fiction. Black women scholars have chronicled other Black women's experiences of violence in books and journal articles. Significant partnerships sprung up between "everyday experts working at the grassroots level" and radical Black women intellectuals. These partnerships and groups have actively resisted intimate household, community, and state violence both in concrete terms and by honing an analysis of Black women's unique position at the intersections of racism, sexism, classism, and heterosexism. Many Black women have employed multiple tools and talents in defiance of male violence in their homes and communities, in defiance of neoliberal public policies, and importantly, in defiance of the mainstream feminist movement that has so blatantly denied our leadership, our analysis, and our unique needs for safety and autonomy.[28]

The individuals and the Black feminist groups I discuss in the remainder of this chapter represent only a fraction of the voices that have contributed to the ever-growing presence of Black feminist anti-violence activists. This sampling is based on a review of Black feminist writing since 1970 and of the various organizations that shaped the activist movement against male violence and prison buildup. It is important to remember that this is only a sampling of the women, some living in small towns and isolated urban neighborhoods across the country, who have been engaged in daily acts of resistance to male violence in their lives, and the long reach of America's prison nation into their communities. These highlights reflect a broad set of resistance strategies that have long been characteristic of Black women's struggles in a hostile social, political, economic, and ideological world.

Setting the Contemporary Stage: The Civil Rights and Women's Movements

During the 1960s, the United States was embroiled in a struggle for African American civil rights, a movement led by men and women whose opportunities had been constrained by the history of slavery and Jim Crow segregation.[29] Even though few achieved the recognition or notoriety of their male counterparts, many Black women were central figures in the political activity of that era.[30] A central theme in Black women's activism at the time was the glaring contradiction found in the oppressive treatment that women received from their male comrades in civil rights activist communities.[31]

A considerable body of historical literature by Black feminist historians and political scientists describes how the commitment to the goals of racial justice and the fevered rhetoric of the civil rights movement gave way to the contemporary women's rights movement.[32] The initial political appeal of the women's rights movement for Black women was the focus on gender subordination and challenges to patriarchy. However, despite their activism and participation in the second-wave feminist movement, Black women were quickly discouraged because the dominant feminist agenda *at the time* was overwhelmingly based on the needs and desires of middle-class white women. Black women's voices and contributions were often marginalized.[33]

As a result, a distinct Black feminist consciousness was articulated from the margins of the women's rights and civil rights movements. Informed by the historical struggles for both gender and racial justice, these articulations focused on the simultaneous and overlapping sexism within the Black community and racism within the white feminist movement. Unable and unwilling to organize solely around their identity of "Black" or "woman," Black feminist anti-violence activists chose a third path, one that has led to a more radical anti-violence and anti-prison agenda.[34]

1970s–Early 1980s: Organizing as Black Feminists

The explosion of Black feminist anti-violence activity in the 1970s and early 1980s was in no small part a result of outrage at the long legacy of private degradation and public despair caused by racial and gender subordination that was being articulated publicly by the individuals who were forming political and social collectives. These years witnessed the rise of several Black feminist organizations that focused on male violence. For example, in 1968, the Third World Women's Alliance (TWWA; later the Black Women's Alliance) began as a part of the Student Nonviolence Coordinating Committee (SNCC) to bring a Black feminist analysis to the organization's gender-neutral goal of racial justice. Specifically, the early feminist organizers of TWWA set out to dispel the myth of the Black matriarch within the community, to prioritize work that responded to the ongoing oppression of Black women, and to legitimize Black women's role in the revolutionary struggle for civil rights.[35]

The agenda to reframe the Black freedom movement to include challenges to male dominance and unequal power related to gender roles also motivated the formation of the National Black Feminist Organization (NBFO) in 1973, which began with a call to Black women who wanted to discuss the positioning of feminist politics within the struggle for Black liberation. As one of the first national organizations that specifically validated Black experiences and needs, the NBFO led to the founding of other groups like the National Alliance of Black Feminists.[36] Their agenda included a focus on street harassment in order to support the educational aspirations of Black girls; they also coordinated health fairs to address disparities in care that included treatment for violence, and planned employment seminars that included attention to workplace violence. The NABF also created a rape crisis hotline to serve Black women dealing with sexual violence.[37]

The Combahee River Collective is an example of a local effort that emerged during this era to advance the agenda initially set by national organizations like the NBFO. Their work focused on the community domain, importantly incorporating a class analysis into an understanding of Black women's experiences. The Collective produced the now infamous "Black Feminist Statement," which boldly outlines the struggle of Black women to overcome the disabling impact of racism, sexism, and classism, and calls for a political, material, and spiritual response to oppression.[38] This statement has been reprinted in numerous anthologies and has served as a guidepost for many Black feminist organizations because of its clear articulation of a Black feminist agenda. Black Women Organized for Action, which began in San Francisco in 1973, is another example of an organization that evolved to support Black women's leadership and to express the concerns of Black women in the public arena, including, but not limited to, responding to male violence.[39]

By the early 1980s, these and other Black feminist organizations formed a strong foundation of resistance that continues to inform our understanding of Black women's experiences of male violence and the buildup of America's prison nation. *Their response* to male violence distinguishes their viewpoint from the more contemporary white feminist analysis in great part because the Black feminists addressed issues of community violence and harm caused by state policy, as described in the matrix in chapter 4.

Writing as Black Feminists

Kitchen Table: Woman of Color Press stands out as one of the most significant institutions that helped shape Black feminist analyses, serving not only as a publishing outlet, but as an organizing vehicle for critical analysis of issues like violence against women. They were a catalyst for scholarly and popular articles discussing various aspects of Black feminist struggle for justice and equality, including sexuality, male violence, and the impact of public policy on Black women's health and well-being.[40] In the early 1980s, a number of texts were published that specifically identified violence as an issue for Black women. For example, in 1981, bell hooks' *Ain't I a Woman: Black Women and Feminism*, was published alongside

Angela Davis's *Women, Race and Class* and poet-activist June Jordan's book of essays entitled *Civil Wars*. This was also the year that the first of three notable anthologies of writing by women of color was released, all of which included discussions of male violence. Most noted among these was *This Bridge Called My Back*,[41] edited by Cherie Moraga and Gloria Anzaldúa, which included contributions by Black feminists Audre Lorde, Barbara Smith, and Toni Cade Bambara. The next year, writer-activist Barbara Smith co-edited an anthology with Gloria Hull and Patricia Bell Scott entitled *All the Women Are White, All the Blacks Are Men, But Some of Us Are Brave: Black Women's Studies*,[42] which was followed a year later by *Home Girls: A Black Feminist Anthology*. Each of these collections and the single-author texts before them showcased the writing of Black women who use a broad feminist lens across disciplines and in various genres. Together they form an important and still-influential body of literary, theoretical, and empirical work on race and politics in general and on gender and male violence in particular.

During the same time period (the 1970s and early 1980s), several Black women authors published fictionalized accounts of the physical, sexual, and emotional abuse Black women experienced in their households, relationships, in their communities, and from institutions. Importantly, in addition to the vivid portrayals of male violence as described in chapter 2, these stories also depicted Black women's strategic resilience and capacity for love in the face of violence and degradation. The stories are not only accounts of brutal violence, but also rich descriptions of families, communities, and Black women's relationships to broader social institutions. This literature provides keen insights into the multiple forces of oppression Black women face, while reminding readers of Black women's capacity for personal growth and for social transformation.

Among the most widely read novels is Toni Morrison's *The Bluest Eye*, published in 1970, which tells the story of a young girl who equates beauty with whiteness, survives a violent sexual assault by her father, and finds little support to help her resist her own descent into madness. The themes of vulnerability to violence and survival despite degrading circumstances are echoed in Ntozake Shange's 1977 *For Colored Girls Who Have Considered Suicide/When the Rainbow is e'nuf*, a choreopoem that enacts a series of poetic monologues discussing the trials and joys of being a Black woman. In some ways, these early texts set the stage for Alice Walker's acclaimed 1982 novel *The Color Purple*, set in rural Georgia and narrated by a woman named Celie. Celie's story reflects a range of violent experiences in multiple contexts: sexual violence at the hands of her father, physical violence by her husband, and a vivid picture of the racist environment within which her Black community manages to survive. In a similar way, Gloria Naylor's *The Women of Brewster Place*, published in 1983, focuses on the hardships of seven Black women from various class backgrounds, and with different sexual identities. Also in 1983, *I Know Why the Caged Bird Sings* recounted Maya Angelou's own story of her painful childhood, including sexual violence, community violence, and racism.

There are many other novels, short stories, poems, and films that include accounts of male violence within Black women's fictional life stories. It is important here to note that alongside the development of Black women's grassroots anti-violence organizing and the proliferation of Black feminist essays and anthologies, a range of voices articulated Black women's resistance to male violence in fiction and creative writing. While the mainstream anti-violence movement has not recognized or attended to this form of public education or the audience that consumes it, there are untold numbers of Black women whose feminist consciousness was nurtured by these influential texts. Again, they are noteworthy because they are suggestive of a more contextualized, nuanced understanding of the experience of male violence in the lives of women, an understanding that is consistent with a Black feminist theoretical orientation. They describe an experience of abuse that is embedded in a cultural rhetoric, a set of racialized experiences and particularities of community and social conditions that links intimate partner violence much more closely to public policy and community violence than does the dominant white feminist analysis found in the contemporary social science literature.

1980s: Black Women in the Anti-Violence Movement

The Black feminist literature I described above was produced during the grassroots anti-violence organizing that characterized the beginning of the contemporary U.S. anti-violence movement in the 1970s.[43] By the mid-1980s, as more formal structures were being created, Black women volunteered for, staffed, and provided leadership to the many women's collectives, hotlines, shelters, and other support services for women experiencing male violence. Indeed, despite the structural racism embedded in organizational practices, and the general lack of acceptance of gender-specific anti-violence work in Black communities such as discriminatory hiring practices and culturally naïve intervention models, Black women labored at both the neighborhood and the institutional levels.[44] A significant part of this work was Black women forcefully articulating the divergent needs of women of color who were dealing with violence in their homes and communities.[45] For example, Black feminists argued for attention to the forms of abuse that result from the racist and classist social context in which they lived, as in cells 7, 8, 9 in the violence matrix.[46] More generally, Black women challenged the strategies and decision-making structures of white-dominated institutions and protested imbalances in power in feminist anti-violence organizations, drawing attention to the ways that anti-violence work was reflective of general trends associated with the buildup of America's prison nation.

By most accounts, these early challenges were met with openness by key leaders in the anti-violence movement. The early anti-violence collaborations between Black women, other women of color activists, and white feminists were characterized by a sense of optimism and possibility. That is, although being disenfranchised by organizations was not an unfamiliar or unexpected experience for Black women, many of these women recall feeling a sense of possibility for more egalitarian relationships precisely because of the early anti-violence rhetoric that focused on social and racial justice. In this time of openness, Black women and other women of color worked *within* established organizations to strategize solutions to the problem of violence against women in their communities and to offer anti-racist leadership to white feminist organizations. An example of this leadership took place at the annual conference for the National Coalition Against Domestic Violence (NCADV) in 1982 that I mentioned in the introduction to this book, which featured a one-day Women of Color Institute called "Building a Colorful Coalition."[47] This event marked the beginning of the Women of Color Caucus, a forum through which women of color could explore their own understanding of violence within their communities, discuss the ever-present racism within the mainstream movement, and demand equal power. The First National Conference on Third World Women and Violence, held in 1980, also provided a space for Black women and other women of color to develop an analysis of violence that went beyond interpersonal violence to discuss state-sanctioned violence.[48] It is important to note that initially, this work was undertaken with the belief that the anti-violence movement would, in fact, be an anti-racist movement. Women of color assumed, perhaps naively, that their autonomous organizing would always be considered a legitimate, necessary, and implicitly valued part of the anti-violence movement's work. However when, as chapter 3 chronicled, the anti-violence movement became more invested in appeasing policymakers than in challenging the state, real alternatives to existing gender and racial relationships that were based on broader structural arrangements became less viable. White women in positions of power felt threatened, and Black women were reminded of the pernicious racism within feminist organizations.[49]

Still, since the early 1980s, Black women have played leadership roles in NCADV and the National Coalition Against Sexual Assault (NCASA), as well as in other organizations, relentlessly asserting a radical agenda within a rapidly mainstreaming movement. Various critiques of both Black politics and anti-violence organizing chronicle the challenge of doing so, as noted by Richie,[50] Burns,[51] and others. These were among the first articulations of the untenable dilemma for politically active Black women in the 1980s—the seemingly conflicting goals of promoting the strength of Black communities while demanding a response to male violence against women—in all forms—in those communities.

Black Feminist Analysis Confronts the State

As Black feminists developed an intersectional analysis of male violence that incorporated race, class, and gender subordination, and argued for attention to both institutional and interpersonal racism from the mainstream anti-violence movement, other Black activists were responding to the tightening grip of America's prison nation. Most notably, Black feminists like Angela Davis, a celebrated scholar and activist, Safiya Bukhari-

Alston, a leader of the Republic of New Afrika, Assata Shakur, a leader in the Black Liberation Army, and Ramona Africa of MOVE worked against the state's racist, capitalist policies and actions. Asha Bandele, Paula Fishman, and others wrote about trauma and abuse of Black women as the impact of incarceration on families and communities began to take hold. The leadership of these Black women scholars, writers, and activists set the stage for contemporary Black feminist analysis of male violence that is linked to the buildup of America's prison nation. It is important for readers to recall here the dynamics that were surrounding the evolution of the mainstream anti-violence movement as described in chapter 3. The once-radical leadership was being co-opted by the lure of legitimacy that was promised by legislative and legal advances. Activities that were initially designed to challenge and change how the state responded to male violence were now more geared toward reform efforts. Organizations became institutionalized to the extent that they relied on professionally trained, credentialed, hierarchically organized staff and, perhaps more important, conservative rhetoric and images regarding gender, violence, and appropriate responses to it.

1990s: Breaking the Silence of Black Women's Suffering

Indeed, the late 1980s saw the advancement of a formidable conservative backlash agenda that affected Black feminist organizing as much as the more mainstream white feminist anti-violence movement. The national consciousness about many social issues was shifting far to the right of the positions feminists and other activists had assumed in the 1960s and 1970s. Consistent with these conservative politics, concerns about and responses to male violence became more about individual "crime" victims rather than about systemic gender oppression, as described in chapter 3. Even as more Black women were hired into professional positions in increasingly white-dominated anti-violence programs, these mainstream programs did not reflect a radical Black feminist analysis of male violence that encompassed all of the forms of violence covered by the matrix, including the process of criminalization described in chapter 4. In great part this is because in America's prison nation, crime is associated with race (Black) and class (poor). Still, despite the backlash and mainstreaming of intervention programs, Black women continued to name and resist the violence they experienced from within their own communities while attempting to redirect the conservative momentum of the anti-violence movement. Several organizations played a key role in this struggle.

In 1990, Evelyn C. White edited *The Black Women's Health Book*, which recounts the development in the mid- to late-1980s of the National Black Women's Health Project (NBWHP) under the leadership of Byl-lye Avery.[52] Credited as one of the first national groups to recognize that Black women's health was greatly impacted by interpersonal violence from within homes and communities, as well as by the ever-grinding pressure of living in a racist, sexist, and classist society, the goal of the NBWHP was to break the multiple silences that so forcefully damaged Black women's health. The NBWHP advocated a holistic response to health as a resistance strategy.

Another key organization that emerged in the 1990s was African American Women in Defense of Ourselves (AAWIDO), a national network that organized in response to Anita Hill's testimony at the congressional hearings to confirm Supreme Court Justice Clarence Thomas, who had been accused of sexual harassment. The range of responses to the hearings are documented in the book *Race-ing Justice, En-gendering Power: Essays on Anita Hill, Clarence Thomas and the Construction of Social Reality*, which focuses a wide political lens on Anita Hill's accusations of sexual harassment against Justice Thomas.[53] In this collection, Black feminist scholars including Kimberlé Crenshaw and Paula Giddings exposed the ways in which Black women are treated by state institutions like the Supreme Court as well as the mechanisms by which women are silenced within the Black community in an effort to create the illusion of racial solidarity.

In addition to the scholarly writing, Black feminists Elsa Barkley Brown, Deborah King, and Barbara Ransby drafted the influential "African American Women In Defense of Ourselves" statement, which denounced the seating of Clarence Thomas, bemoaned the treatment of Anita Hill, and clearly articulated the bind in which Black women found themselves. Over 1,600 women of African descent signed the statement, which appeared in the *New York Times* as a full-page advertisement. Like the Combahee River statement, its publication was significant because it addressed multiple levels of impact: interpersonal violence against women, the community-level changes that were required to improve Black women's lives, and the policy impact on Black women of confirming a conservative Supreme Court justice. That Clarence Thomas was Black illuminated the point that the state colludes with patriarchal power in Black communities to the disadvantage of Black women.[54] The organizing that surrounded the AAWIDO was emblematic of the broadness and comprehensiveness of 1990s Black feminist activism against male violence. Another important collective statement regarding Black women and male violence is Beverly Guy-Sheftall's *Words of Fire: An Anthology of African-American Feminist Thought*.[55] The publication of this anthology in 1995 reasserted the voice of Black feminists at the close of the conservative Reagan/Bush years and broke new ground by including historical writings by Black women beginning in 1831. It provides ample evidence that the legacy of Black feminist consciousness that began in the nineteenth century continues today. Many of the entries in *Words of Fire* include references to male violence from a Black feminist perspective.

Late 1990s: Healing by Sharing Black Women's Stories

During the 1990s, many Black women activist researchers set about documenting the experiences of Black women in order to provide both qualitative and quantitative evidence for the Black feminist analysis of male violence that had been developing in the previous decades.[56] Both the resulting social science research and the popular literature that gives voice to Black women's stories paint a vivid picture of the conditions under which Black women experience male violence. These texts also discuss how male violence makes Black women vulnerable to harsh treatment by state agencies, including those implicated in the buildup of America's prison nation.[57] This literature forms a distinctive subfield of research on violence against women, as chapter 3 describes. It presents the consequences associated with victimization, as well as the impact of the lack of response from a defensive Black community and a racist and classist society. In addition to giving voice to pain, the studies also document accounts of Black women's resistance, strength, and hope.

In *Crossing the Boundary: Black Women Survive Incest*, Melba Wilson breaks the silence around her experience of sexual abuse, revealing the myths and misconceptions that leave Black children vulnerable to incest.[58] All of the stories contribute to Wilson's development of a Black feminist understanding of incest, an essential contribution to the literature.

In *Compelled to Crime*,[59] I share the voices of battered Black women who are incarcerated. These stories reveal the links between gender identity development within Black communities, women's experiences of domestic abuse, and the reasons behind their involvement in criminal activities.[60] I use the term "gender entrapment" to describe the conditions that compel women to crime and implicate an overly punitive criminal justice system that ignores conditions in which women are often revictimized as a result of persistent poverty and violence. Charlotte Pierce-Baker[61] shares her story of survival in *Surviving the Silence*, recounting her rape experience and relating it to 11 Black women's stories of sexual violence. In an effort to include men in the process, she also interviews several Black men who are friends or family of rape survivors. Lori Robinson takes a similar approach in *I Will Survive*.[62]

Taking the notion of healing one step further, Traci West[63] focuses on Black women's stories of intimate violence and the broader context of systemic violence in which intimate partner violence occurs.[64] West discusses Black community responses to violence and the denial of its importance, and suggests strategies for enhanced communal resistance. In addition, she looks at the cultural messages that create a hostile social environment in which Black women are considered deserving of abuse and degradation associated with their social position. Similar accounts appear in *Violence in the Lives of Black Women: Battered, Black, and Blue (Women and Therapy)*; *No Secrets No Lies: How Black Families Can Heal from Sexual Abuse* by Robin Stone; *Chain, Chain, Change: For Black Women in Abusive Relationships* by Evelyn C. White; *Stolen Women: Reclaiming Our Sexuality, Taking Back Our Lives* by Gail Wyatt; and *Strong at the Heart: How It Feels to Heal from Sexual Abuse* by Carolyn Lehman.

In addition to describing Black women's resistance and healing in books and articles, Black women have used videography to document a range of experiences. Among the most notable are the video "NO" by Aisha Simmons, which documents Black women's experience of rape, and "A Long Walk Home," a photography exhibit and performance by Shalimisha Tillbet about recovering from sexual abuse.

2000–2010

In the first decade of the twenty-first century, Black women's activism was characterized by coalition-building and multi-issue organizing. Around the United States, Black women were working with other women of color to end intimate-partner and community violence and to join forces in their resistance to state-sponsored violence against communities of color.[65] In 2000, the Color of Violence Conference in Santa Cruz, California, brought together 1,000 women of color activists from around the country and the world. Black women's visionary leadership helped to shape this event, and Black women's work featured prominently in the workshops. At the conference, Black women discussed not only intimate partner violence, but also their analyses of abuses against Black women from police, from the prison industrial complex, and from the healthcare system.[66] Together with other women of color, Black women validated their beliefs about abuse from within their communities and from the larger society.

The energy built at this conference launched Incite!, a national organization of women of color working to end violence against women. Since 2000, Incite! chapters have formed in 11 states around the country. Incite! also partners with sister organizations like Sista II Sista in New York, Sisters in Action for Power in Portland, Domestic Workers United in the Bronx, and Sisters Organizing Against Sexual Assault. Sista II Sista is a group of young women of color in Brooklyn, New York, working to end violence against women and girls. Sisters in Action for Power organizes to improve the lives of young people of color in Portland. Domestic Workers United fights for domestic workers' rights in the New York area, and the national organization called Sisters of Color Ending Sexual Assault has created a powerful voice of resistance that challenges interpersonal as well as structural violence.

In addition to their collaborations with sister organizations, Black women and other women of color have collaborated with Critical Resistance (CR), a movement to dismantle America's prison industrial complex. In 2001, Incite! and CR produced a joint statement that criticized the anti-violence movement for feeding the prison industrial complex and criticized the anti-prison movement for ignoring or minimizing the violence women experience in prisons. Like the Combahee River Collective statement and AAWIDO, the CR/INCITE Statement is a bold articulation of radical feminist politics about gender violence and racism.[67]

In addition to organizing with other groups, like the Black Church and Domestic Violence Project and the Women of Color Network, Black women are disseminating radical statements and producing groundbreaking scholarship. They are engaging in critical feminist activism work that focuses on the intersections between race, class, and gender, and uncovers complex relationships between violence in the home, in the community, in state institutions, and in social policy. *Policing the National Body*, edited by Jael Silliman and Ananya Bhattacharjee, Andrea Richie, Joey Mogul, and Kay Whitlock in *Queer (In)justice*, and *Global Lockdown*,[68] edited by Julia Sudbury, bring together voices of women working against unjust legal systems around the world. In *Domestic Violence at the Margins*, researchers and activists contribute studies and scholarship on intimate violence in communities of color. The Institute on Domestic Violence in the African American Community includes Black women and men, scholars and practitioners, activists, survivors, and community leaders who understand the broad ways in which male violence and aspects of the buildup of America's prison nation impact Black communities.[69] The leadership of young Black women activists, particularly on the issues affecting the queer community, is noteworthy here.

A Look to the Future

There are many other organizations, texts, videos, and individuals that I could have included in this review of Black women's anti-violence activism and resistance to the buildup of America's prison nation. The ones I mentioned here are illustrative of a broad network of resistance-oriented activists and organizations that have endeavored to save the lives of Black women. Each year, new organizations and forms of resistance are emerging. Technology has made it possible for Black feminist activists to share experiences, build cyber-coalitions, create analyses through blogs, and respond to incidents of violence against Black women perpetrated by individuals, the media, and state institutions. These and other activists' responses have paved the way for a different, more radical social justice-oriented response to Black women who experience male violence during the buildup of America's prison nation.

6

Conclusion

December 22, 2010 marked the tenth anniversary of Kemba Smith's release from Danbury Correctional Facility, a Federal Prison for women in Connecticut, where she served six-and-a-half years on a felony conspiracy charge. Kemba's story, which has received international attention, brought into sharp focus the way that violence against Black women was impacted by the public policy shifts associated with the buildup of America's prison nation. Ms. Smith walked out of prison ten years ago, flew home to her waiting family in Richmond, Virginia, and almost immediately began a crusade to challenge both the violence that young Black women experience and the criminal justice policies that entrapped her and so many of her peers in this country. In her case, it was the mandatory minimum sentencing guidelines that she challenged. She is now an outspoken critic of harsh legal penalties, draconian sentencing policies, and the gender dynamics in Black communities that propel some young women into violent relationships and crime. As an insightful survivor of horrific abuse from her boyfriend and a formerly incarcerated woman who has dedicated her life to bringing to light the conditions that led to her spend six years behind bars, Kemba has turned her experiences of violence, degradation, and injustice into a compelling set of lessons for change. She emerged strong and passionate, and is now happily living with her new husband and children.

During her sophomore year as a student at Hampton University in Virginia, Kemba became involved with a very persuasive, very manipulative, very dangerous man eight years her senior who coerced her involvement in his illegal drug activity through violence and threats to harm her family. Not only was he abusive and controlling, he was connected with a very dangerous network of associates, which earned him a position on the FBI's 15 most wanted list. Kemba was literally trapped in a nightmare of fear, pain, and degradation, but because of the ways that criminal legal policies work in America's prison nation, Kemba was arrested on a conspiracy to distribute cocaine charge, tried, and sentenced to 24 1/2 years with no possibility of parole. Despite the fact (1) that she tried to leave the man several times, (2) that she feared for her life, (3) that she was 7 1/2 months pregnant, and (4) that she had no prior criminal record, there was no consideration given to the conditions of her life when she was sentenced. Instead, like an increasing segment of women who are trapped by policy and abuse, she faced excessive prison time because of the violence and the criminal legal policies. As a result of a national legal advocacy campaign, Kemba was released and her story became an iconic symbol of the deleterious impact of harsh sentencing as well as the danger faced by young women who are preyed upon by men who are deeply involved in the trafficking of illegal substances. Indeed, there is a great deal to learn from Kemba Smith's story (told in her recent book *Poster Child: The Kemba Smith Story*), including the power of organizing and resistance efforts that Black feminist and other social justice activists have been involved in to enact change.[1]

The preceding chapters have illuminated the complex relationship between the various forms of male violence that Black women experience in several contexts, the qualified success of the anti-violence movement in response to that violence, and the ways that ideology about race, sexuality, age, and class have resulted in disadvantaged political, legal, social, and interpersonal status for Black women in marginalized positions. A Black feminist analysis of the convergence of two important trends—(1) the anti-violence movement's relinquishing of its radical rhetoric and praxis, and (2) the buildup of America's prison nation that concentrated disadvantages in low-income communities—shows how Black women whose experience is not consistent with the hegemonic norms and expectations about gender, sexuality, and family have been left in dangerous positions. Indeed, that analysis serves as the foundation for the development of the violence matrix, which shows that the more socially disadvantaged Black women are, the more they will be stigmatized by or, worse, punished, for their victimization.

This chapter will recommend strategies that promise much more effective, justice-oriented solutions to the problem of ending male violence against Black women during the buildup of America's prison nation. Elaborating on the case histories presented in the introduction, chapter 2 reviewed the theoretical literature and presented the empirical data that establish the extent and consequences of violence against Black women. In chapter 3, I described how, despite important successes that benefited some women, the anti-violence movement was distracted from its radical origins by the pressure to become legitimate in the eyes of a growing conservatism associated with the buildup of America's prison nation. Co-opted by state funding, skeptical attention from conservative policymakers, and the false sense of confidence created by conditional gains, the mainstream anti-violence movement became more conservative, turning to over-reliance on the state for remedies to the problem of violence against women. Bear in mind that this was a state that was divesting from communities where disadvantage was concentrated.[2]

As discussed in chapter 3, a critical aspect of the process of winning support from a mainstream public audience was an abandonment of attention toward those women whose social position left them outside of the hegemonic normative standards of gender roles and sexuality, standards that are deeply embedded with race and class imagery in the United States. The leadership of the anti-violence movement left unchallenged the structural racism, the imposition of rigid gender roles, the assumptions of heteronormative sexuality, and America's persistent invisibility of class inequality in the analysis (all features of the prison nation), presumably as a strategy to win continued support from an increasingly conservative state. At different times, leadership made a series of strategic decisions at the national, state, and local levels, including (1) to advocate for mandatory arrest laws despite warnings from women of color activists about the consequences of mass incarceration in communities of color; (2) to accept funding that would forbid crisis intervention services for women who have a felony background despite co-occurrence of male violence and women's involvement in illegal activities; (3) to avoid discussion of lesbian battering; and (4) to remain silent about state violence, like police brutality. These strategic moves represented an acceptance of externally imposed limits on the anti-violence movement's radical political work. Indeed, it could be argued that the very success of the anti-violence movement is predicated on its adoption of conservative positions within a growing conservative state—America's prison nation.

In chapter 5, I presented the argument for a Black feminist analysis of male violence as a way to reverse this conservative tendency. Such an analysis is based on the assumption that gender subordination, structural racism, class inequality, and pressures to conform to heteronormative sexuality undergird violence against Black women. Furthermore, only through knowledge-generating mechanisms that privilege an understanding of how this works every day can lead to the kind of radical social change required to end violence against Black women. In my view, this analysis offers a much better explanation of the interpersonal, social, political, and ideological dynamics at hand. When applied to the analysis of the various forms of male violence against Black women within the context of a prison nation, a Black feminist theoretical analysis does three essential things. First, it makes it impossible to ignore the way that male violence against Black women occurs in multiple contexts simultaneously—the dialectic of violence against Black women and the buildup of America's prison nation. Second, a Black feminist analysis helps to show how mainstream success was won at the expense of radical work to end violence against women. Third, and perhaps most important, it points out that to end violence against women, we must work to dismantle the prison nation that has been built up in the United States during the same time that the anti-violence movement was evolving into a more conservative social service delivery system. To do otherwise would be to continue to put Black women who experience male violence in dangerous, isolated, dehumanized situations, positions not much changed from 30 years ago when I began to understand Black feminist activism in Harlem.

To argue that position with full conviction requires some elaboration in the form of concrete recommendations. I offer the following five broad propositions to stimulate creative thinking, to foster more dynamic discussions, and to encourage more serious strategic debates in the anti-violence movement around race, class, sexuality, gender, violence, and political organizing. I do so humbly, as an insider/outsider whose commitment to the anti-violence movement is as strong as my critique of it.

The starting point for a Black feminist anti-violence praxis is obvious; future anti-violence activism should incorporate the tenets of the Black feminist theoretical approach I described earlier. This approach, which could be accomplished through the use of the male violence matrix to respond to violence against Black women, would employ an intersectional analytical paradigm that centers on Black women's everyday experiences. Such an approach would be able to respond to concrete expressions of violence toward Black women as well as the subtle ways that racialized images of gender and sexuality harm those Black women who are most socially and personally disadvantaged. It would also address the broader contextual issues that come along with the buildup of America's prison nation. By using a Black feminist theoretical approach, activists would no longer be able to ignore those women's experiences that fall outside of the mainstream "everywoman analysis" to define anti-violence work during the buildup of America's prison nation and an increasingly conservative state.

I would even go so far as to argue that a Black feminist analysis of male violence using the male violence matrix would extend benefit to women whose circumstances seem to be quite different from the women whose stories frame the central argument of this book. Take, for example, the issue of male violence toward non-Black, Latina immigrant women. First, a Black feminist analysis would facilitate an understanding of how some immigrant women's partners control them as much by isolating them from family, community resources, and agencies concerned with immigrant rights as through direct physical assault by using an intersectional Black Feminist analysis enabled by the male violence matrix. This important insight would, for example, expose reasons that an immigrant woman without legal status might not report the physical assault or sexual aggression because of fear that the Immigration and Customs Enforcement will deport her, her children, and/or the abusive partner or community member. In this way, a Black feminist analysis using the violence matrix would be able to link the individual abuse, the fear generated by family members and neighbors, the loyalty to one's community, and the violence that women experience at the hands of ICE in border towns and in detention facilities operated by the U.S. government.[3] Each of these forms of abuse, in the entire context of America's prison nation, is harmful to immigrant women and requires a social justice intervention.

A second example might be a new way to understand women who are trafficked into the sex industry by abusive men. Many activists have argued that sex workers—regardless of their race, sexual orientation, class, or age—would benefit if the anti-violence movement were to broaden its analysis to include the violence that women experience in international prostitution rings, as part of street hustling, on Internet pornography, and in degrading music videos and other entertainment venues that foster sexist attitudes toward women.[4] A Black feminist analysis provides such a theoretical link between these contemporary settings by pointing to the ways that in America's prison nation, capitalism and patriarchy conspire to seriously disadvantage women. This would bring into focus as an example of male violence the fact that the state has offered very limited protection to women forced into prostitution, instead creating laws that protect those with the most economic power to exercise their "free market right" to buy sex from women in vulnerable circumstances. In these, and in other examples, the multiple forms of violence that women experience in the context of a prison nation would be recognized as individual crises and at the same time be responded to as social justice issues.

The second recommendation that I offer emerges from the emphasis on praxis in the Black feminist theoretical approach. A central conclusion of the Black feminist analysis put forward in this book is that a much more comprehensive set of radical strategies must be used to respond to the problem of male violence toward Black women than state solutions offer. As documented earlier, the particular evolution of the anti-violence movement ensured that most of the attention to remedying the problem of male violence against women has focused on legal reform driven by legislative changes. This tendency to involve the state came quite naturally in some ways, from the advocacy work that demanded that public institutions respond to and protect women who experience violence in a similar manner to other violations. These demands led to a series of changes that included requisite training of first responders, mandatory arrest policies, and pro-prosecution protocols. Law enforcement officers, prosecutors, court officers, judges, and correctional officers became de facto co-interventionists, partnering with anti-violence advocates who were responding to the problem of violence against women. All of this occurred during the era when America's prison nation was simultaneously being built.

There are two primary problems with over-reliance on the criminal legal systems to respond to male violence against women, especially during this time of increased social conservatism. First, state-sponsored solutions are not balanced with other solutions. They are seldom understood to be part of a menu of options for women who are harmed by male violence; rather, they are offered in isolation from other possible responses. Emergency situations do sometimes require intervention from a person who has state-sanctioned power to physically restrain or remove a dangerous individual. Seldom, however, is much thought given to alternative sources of authority over a person who needs to be sanctioned—people like community officials, faith leaders, local advocacy groups, community activists, or family members.

By far, the most serious problem with over-reliance on legal and legislative changes in response to the problem of male violence against Black women during the buildup of America's prison nation is that it precludes the development of a sustained critique of the state's role in causing, complicating, or being complicit with male violence against Black women. As a result, state-sanctioned violence that women experience, a critical compounding layer of harm, is beyond reproach. It must be remembered that a Black feminist analysis illuminates the fact that state-sanctioned violence is particularly harmful to Black women because of structures of institutionalized racism within public agencies. Indeed, while one could argue that a conservative state agenda creates limitations for *all* women, ideological and sustentative control of gender and sexuality are worse for Black women in communities that have been disadvantaged by divestment. This assertion argues that all women would benefit from less reliance on the state to respond to the problem of violence against women if other systems of sanctioning and support were in place and we reinvested resources into communities.

The third recommendation is that when services are provided to Black women who experience male violence, they should be offered in a way that corresponds to abuse they may experience in all parts of the violence matrix rather than those that receive the most attention (physical and sexual abuse by heterosexual partners or acquaintances). Some scholars and practitioners have called this the instinct to "create culturally competent services," suggesting that if services must be offered, they must be provided in a way that reflects the norms, beliefs, and practices of the community that is being served. This understanding of cultural competence would incorporate ensuring that the interventionists are trained to read and respond to nonverbal cues, that different patterns of social interaction and interpretations of social reality are understood and legitimized in the helping process, and that external macro forces that contribute to micro experiences are factored into the analysis and response. There are a number of organizations dedicated to advancing culturally competent service delivery to Black women and their families in the face of male violence, such as the Institute on Domestic Violence in the African American Community.

While a culturally competent approach to service delivery is critical to ensure that Black women who experience male violence are treated fairly when they turn to helping institutions, it alone is insufficient to the task of considering the context of America's prison nation and creating the social changes necessary to end male violence against Black women in all of its forms. A Black feminist approach says direct crisis intervention services must be accompanied by a dialectally informed grassroots mobilization around issues of race, class, gender, and sexuality.

The forth recommendation of a Black feminist theoretical approach is that the grassroots mobilizing work to end violence focus squarely on dismantling America's prison nation. This is a call to re-engage in community organizing strategies that would advance several social change goals. To repeat, it would first require that a Black feminist theoretical understanding be applied through the use of the violence matrix to assess the problem of male violence—all forms of male violence—in the context of a prison nation. Then it would require a deep analysis of the impact of community divestment and subsequent concentration of disadvantages, with particular attention to the impact that conservative state policies have had on Black women's experience of male violence. This analysis should include the notions of social control, co-optation, and criminalization. It must be dynamic and concrete so as to account for both the structural and ideological conditions that harm Black women in America's prison nation. The result would be mobilizing strategies that attend to issues of sexuality, of youth disempowerment, and of pressure toward heteronormativity and sanctions when such pressures are unheeded. The analysis would also include advancing strategies that reinvest in communities in ways that rebuild families and reframe culturally-constructed gender relations. The mechanisms that lead to overly simplistic ideas about culture and community and that re-inscribe patriarchy within the context of racial solidarity must be amended to incorporate issues that Black feminist activism has highlighted.

Instead, Black feminist activists who have been working over the years to respond to violence against women and the buildup of America's prison nation and our allies must think much more creatively to develop new strategic formulations.[5] For example, racial justice initiatives must include attention to gender and sexuality. Coalitions must be built between organizations of young men and groups working on behalf of Black girls and young women. The particularities of how Black women experience poverty, incarceration, and violence must be attended to in campaigns to mobilize against them.

Finally, when America's prison nation is understood to be the contextual backdrop to male violence against Black women, the struggle must become a global struggle. While the focus of this book has been on the United States, it is clear that the forms and contexts within which violence against Black women occurs are connected to the ways that processes of globalization have disadvantaged women who have limited economic, sexual, religious, social, and political freedom around the world. One need only look at the changing demographics of Black sex workers, of incarcerated Black women from the global south, or the impact of war on Black women globally to see how male violence has become internationalized. Or, if one takes seriously the ways that chronic unemployment is a dominant theme in male violence toward Black women from both intimate partners and community members, then it becomes clear why it is necessary to include an analysis of global capitalism as part of the work to dismantle America's prison nation *and* as part of ending violence against women.[6]

From this vantage point, when we accept the global challenges of our work, when we go beyond providing culturally competent services, when

Black feminist analysis using the male violence matrix informs grassroots mobilizations for change, and when we focus on dismantling America's prison nation, then we can see a new opening for engaged scholarship and a new formulation of anti-violence politics will emerge. Indeed, if we are to do our work more critically within the context of a prison nation, then we will be better able to understand women like Tanya and support their children, to find Ms. B a safe, secure place to live in the city that she loves, and to celebrate the New Jersey 4 as they walk and love freely in Greenwich Village. The possibility of a critical Black feminist approach to ending violence against women takes me back almost 30 years to the dream that I had when I started the work that I have described in the book I end here, with the hope that we are finally in a moment of re-imagining justice, freedom, and radical peace for all of us.

Notes

Chapter 1

1. Burns, 1986; Crenshaw, 1991; Richie, 1985.
2. Potter, 2006; Russo, 2002.
3. Boothe, 2007; Brewer and Heitzeg, 2008.
4. Farmer and Tiefenthalter, 2008.
5. The details of the story presented here are an aggregate of 4 cases that share similar characteristics in order to protect the subjects.
6. Neubeck and Cazenave, 2001.
7. Throughout the text, I will use the term *male violence* to signify violence against women that has its roots in patriarchal arrangements. This conceptualization allows for an understanding of violence perpetrated by an individual who has male privilege, as well as by communities, institutions, and agencies that are organized around the consolidation of patriarchal power and male supremacy.
8. Ms. B is a pseudonym. Although the case is in the public record, some of the details have been modified, at her request, to protect her privacy to the furthest extent possible.
9. http://www.thecha.org/pages/the_plan_for_transformation/22.php; Venkatesh et al., 2004.
10. Fischer, 1999.
11. Rodriguez, 2008.
12. Kalven, 2006.
13. Fischer, 1999; Seccombe, James, and Battle Walters, 1998.
14. Referred to as the New Jersey 4, the women whose case is presented here have benefited from a national organizing campaign. More information about the case and the organizing can be found at http://fiercenyc.org/index.php?s=126.
15. Carter, 2004; Duberman, 1993.

16. Associated Press, 2007; Hartocollis, 2007; Martinez, 2007; Melloy, 2008.
17. Hackworth, 2002.
18. Gross, Aurand, and Addessa, 2000; National Coalition of Anti-Violence Programs, 2010.
19. Girshick, 2002; Leventhal and Lundy, 1999; McClennen and Gunther, 1999; Renzetti, 1992.

Chapter 2

1. Acevedo, 2000; Dines, Jensen, and Russo, 1998; Grossman and DeGaetano, 1999; Jhally, Katz, and Earp, 1999; Kilbourne, 1999; Sommerville, 2005.
2. Catalano, 2006; Centers for Disease Control and Prevention, 2006.
3. Tjaden and Thoennes, 2000b.
4. Ibid.
5. Coker et al., 2002; Tjaden and Thoennes, 2000b.
6. The Allstate Foundation Domestic Violence Program and National Network to End Domestic Violence Fund, 2006.
7. Rennison and Welchans, 2000; Tjaden and Thoennes, 2000a.
8. Rand, 1997.
9. Catalano, Smith, Snyder, and Rand, 2009.
10. Rennison and Welchans, 2000.
11. Homicide data are voluntarily reported to the FBI by law enforcement agencies that utilize the Uniform Crime Reporting Program. Offender information is missing in about 1 in ever 3 murders reported (Catalano et al., 2009).
12. Catalano et al., 2009.
13. Mahoney, Williams, and West, 2001:145.
14. Anderson, Miniño, Fingerhut, Warner, and Heinen, 2004.
15. Catalano et al., 2009.
16. National Center for Injury Prevention and Control, 1997.
17. Coker, McKeown, Sanderson, Davis, Valois, and Huebner, 2000.
18. Honeycutt, Marshall, and Weston, 2001.
19. West and Rose, 2000 in West, 2002a: 9.
20. Brown and Gourdine, 1998; Hunt and Joe-Laidler, 2001.
21. Jenkins, 2002; Wyatt, Axelrod, Chin, Carmona, and Loeb, 2000.
22. Larocco, 2010; see also: http://www.pe.com/localnews/publicsafety/stories/PE_News_Local_S_twitter29.41b2f95.html.
23. Miller, 2011.
24. Hampton and Gelles, 1994; Jordan, 2009; Rand, 2009; Rennison and Welchans, 2000.

25. Hutchinson and Hirschel, 1994; Richie, 1996; Sullivan and Rumptz, 1994.

26. National Coalition of Anti-violence Programs, 2004; Tjaden and Thoennes, 2000b.

27. Renzetti and Miley, 1996.

28. National Coalition of Anti-violence Programs, 2004.

29. National Coalition of Anti-violence Programs, 2010.

30. Staples, 1999; Taylor, 2000.

31. Kotz, 2009.

32. Portillo, 2010.

33. National Victims Center and Crime Victims Research and Treatment Center, 1992.

34. Banyard and Graham-Bermann, 1993; West, 2006.

35. Catalano et al., 2009; Raphael and Ashley, 2008.

36. Catalano et al., 2009; Rand, 2009.

37. Bachman, 1995.

38. Catalano et al., 2009.

39. Ferraro, 2003; Kasturirangan, Krishnan, and Riger, 2004; Riger, Raja, and Camacho, 2002.

40. Byrne and Riggs, 2002; Campbell, Sharps, Gary, Campbell and Lopez, 2002; Ferraro, 2003; Graham-Bermann and Eastin, 2001; Sutherland, Sullivan and Bybee, 2001.

41. Graham-Berman, 2002.

42. Muhammad, 2009.

43. Ibid.

44. Richie, 1985.

45. This idea is developed further in chapter 5.

46. Atassi, 2010; Donaldson, 2010.

47. Craven, 1996.

48. Rand, 2009; West, 2006.

49. Truman, 2011.

50. Anderson, 2000; Anderson and Massey, 2004; Pattillo-McCoy, 2000.

51. Anderson, 2008; Pattillo, 2008.

52. Jenkins, 2002.

53. Ibid.

54. Washington, 2001; Wyatt, 1992.

55. Associated Press, 2007.

56. Dalmus and Wodarski, 2000; Pierce-Baker, 1998; Robinson, 2002; Russell, 1990.

57. Wolfer, 2000; Wyatt, 1992.

58. Abraham, 1999: 592.

59. National Victims Center, 1992.
60. Tjaden and Thoennes, 2006.
61. Koss and Harvey, 1991.
62. Tjaden and Thoennes, 2006.
63. Neville and Hamer, 2001; Washington, 2001.
64. Byrne and Riggs, 2002; Campbell et al., 2002; Chicago Coalition for the Homeless, 2002; Sutherland, Sullivan, and Bybee, 2001; Tjaden and Thoennes, 2000b.
65. Campbell et al., 2002; Catalano, 2006; West, 2006; Wyatt, 1992.
66. Tjaden and Thoennes, 2000b.
67. Pierce-Baker, 1998; Robinson, 2003.
68. Bart and O'Brien, 1985; West, 2006.
69. Jhally et al., 1999; Sommerville, 2005; West, 2006.
70. Avakame and Fyfe, 2001; Bhattacharjee, 2001; Nash, 2005; Stone, 2005; West, 2002a.
71. Taylor, 2000; White, 1995; Wyatt, 1992.
72. Steffans, 2010.
73. Swartz, 2009; WSB-TV, 2009.
74. KBMT, 2010; Stephens, 2010.
75. Wyatt, 1992.
76. Brown-Givens, and Monahan, 2005; Coltrane and Messineo, 2000; Mastro and Tropp, 2004; Monahan, Shtrulis, and Givens, 2005; Sekaquaptewa and Thompson, 2003.
77. Stone, 2005.
78. Hunt, 2010; Hunt and Schmitt, 2010; Oliver, 2010; Schmitt, 2010; Swickard and Damron, 2011; Warikoo, Meyer, and Hunt, 2010.
79. Martin, 2009.
80. Ritchie, 2006.
81. Human Rights Watch, 1996.
82. Iovanni and Miller, 2001; Robinson and Chandek, 2000b.
83. Fraser, McNutt, Clark, Williams-Muhammed, and Lee, 2002; Richie, 2003; Robinson and Chandek, 2000a.
84. Beck and Harrison, 2007; Shaylor, 2003.
85. Shaylor, 2003.
86. ACLU National Prison Project, 2005; Beck and Harrison, 2007; Shaylor, 2003.
87. Greenfeld and Snell, 1999.
88. Catalano, 2006.
89. ACLU National Prison Project, 2005; Gaseau and Martin, 2003; English and Heil, 2005.

90. Raphael and Ashley, 2008; Ratner, 1993; Tjaden and Thoennes, 1998.

91. Merrill et al., 1999.

92. U.S. Government Accountability Office, 2008.

93. Collins, 1997.

94. Silliman, Fried, Ross, and Gutierrez, 2004.

95. American Civil Liberties Union, 1994; Banzhaf, 1999; Boonstra, 2000; Chamberlain and Hardisty, 2000; Choice USA, 2002; Hutson and Levin-Epstein, 2000.

96. Shaylor, 2003.

97. Hines, 1989; Sommerville, 2005.

98. Hooper and James, 2010; James, 2010.

99. Dowell, 2008.

100. Renzetti in Miller, 1998, page 184

101. Ward Doran and Roberts, 2002.

102. Raphael, 2001.

103. Barusch et al., 1999.

104. Roberts, 2002.

105. Roberts, 1998.

106. Roberts, 1998, 2002.

107. See chapter 5.

108. Davis and Hagen, 1996; Hunt, 1996; Jarett, 1996; Seccombe, James, and Battle Walters, 1998.

109. Ferraro, 2008.

110. Richie, 2006.

111. Ferraro, 2008: 195.

112. Sokoloff and Dupont, 2005.

113. Sokoloff, 2005.

114. INCITE! Women of Color Against Violence, 2006.

115. Taylor, 2000.

116. White, 1995.

117. Nash, 2005.

118. Carbone-Lopez and Kruttschnitt, 2010; Swan and Snow, 2006.

119. Chesney-Lind, 1989; Miller, 2008.

120. Makarios, 2007.

121. Cossins, 2003; Miller-Young, 2010; Thomas, Witherspoon, and Speight, 2004.

122. Hampton, Oliver, and Magarian, 2003.

123. Waltermaurer, Watson, and McNutt, 2006.

124. Jiwani, 2005.

125. Long et al., 2007; Wesley, 2006.

126. Taylor, 2005.

127. Bryant-Davis, Chung, and Tillman, 2009.

128. Bent-Goodley, 2007; Rodriquez, Valentine, Son, and Muhammad, 2009.
129. Monnat, 2010.
130. Davis, 2006.
131. Holzman, Hyatt, and Dempster, 2001; Tester, 2008.
132. Struckman-Johnson, 2006; Thompson, 2008.
133. Sudbury, 2002.
134. Potter, 2007; Stabile, 2006.
135. Brewer and Heitzeg, 2008.
136. Dehart, 2008; McDaniels-Wilson and Belknap, 2008; Richie, 1996.

Chapter 3

1. September 2003.
2. It is important to clarify that neither the anti-violence movement that I am describing nor the context within which it has developed is static or monolithic (Matthews, 1994; Dobash, 1992). Rather, I am presenting the distinct eras of collective action that occurred, during which the critical questions of leadership arose and the development of resources and organizing tactics and the cultivation of allies shifted. To understand how we won the mainstream but lost the movement, it is important to note these shifts in strategy, and to be aware of decisions that interested stakeholders made about whether and how to expand the analysis of gender violence to include race, class, and sexuality, whether to engage community institutions in the work, and what role state intervention might play.
3. Ryan and Gamson, 2006.
4. Matthews, 1994.
5. Brownmiller, 1975; Martin, 1981.
6. Schechter, 1982.
7. Martin, 1981.
8. Dobash and Dobash, 1988.
9. Martin, 1981.
10. Walker, 1979; Yllö, 1988.
11. www.ncvc.org.
12. Gornick, Burt, and Pittman, 1985.
13. Kurz and Stark, 1988.
14. Matthews, 1994; Riger, 1984.
15. Schornstein, 1997.
16. Koss, 2000.
17. Klein, Campbell, Soler, and Ghez, 1997.
18. Weldon, 2002.

19. Schechter, 1988.
20. Hines and Malley-Morrison, 2001.
21. Piven and Cloward, 1979.
22. Touraine, 2004.
23. Porta and Diani, 2006.
24. Johnson, 1985; Koss and Harvey, 1991; Matthews, 1994.
25. Finn and Colson, 1990; Langen and Innes, 1986.
26. Blackman, 1989; Crenshaw, 1991; Schneider, 2002.
27. Anderson, 2002.
28. Walker, 1979.
29. Rosen, 1986; Walker, 1979.
30. Browne, 1987.
31. Wesley, 2006.
32. Feltey, 2001.
33. Crocker, 2004; Ferraro, 2003.
34. Note: There is solid evidence that violence escalates post-separation.
35. Fagan, 1988; Finesmith, 1983; Sherman and Berk, 1984b.
36. Berk and Loseke, 1980–81.
37. Carrington, 1989.
38. Domestic Abuse Intervention Project, 1981, 1987.
39. Zweig and Burt, 2006.
40. Hirschel, 2008.
41. Marchetti, 2008; McMahon and Pence, 2003; Römkens, 2006.
42. Welch, 2007.
43. MS Foundation, 2003.
44. Roberts, 2006.
45. Jaffe, Wolfe, Wilson, and Zak, 1986; Stark and Flitcraft, 1988.
46. http://www.ovw.usdoj.gov/regulations.htm.
47. Ibid.
48. Hart, 1995.
49. Crowell and Burgess, 1996; Kruttschnitt and McLoughlin, 2004.
50. Ferraro, 2008.
51. West, 2004.
52. Kanuha, 1996.
53. Family Violence Prevention Fund.
54. See chapter 2.
55. Kanuha, 1996; Richie, 2000.
56. Cole and Guy-Sheftall, 2003; Collins, 2006.
57. Hunnicutt, 2009; West, 2003; Sydney, 2005.

58. Hurst, 2007.

Chapter 4

1. Terry, 2011.
2. Canning and Tanglao, 2011; Meyer, 2011.
3. Chapter 2 describes, more fully, community- and state-sanctioned violence.
4. See more in Wright, 2003.
5. Garland, 2001.
6. Parenti, 2000; Sudbury, 2005.
7. Davis, 2003; *Social Justice* Editors, 2000.
8. Foucault, 1995.
9. Burton-Rose, Pens, and Wright, 2002.
10. Dow, 2004; Gilmore, 2007; Rodríquez, 2006.
11. Alexander, 2010.
12. Brewer and Heitzeg, 2008.
13. Allard, Albelda, Colten, and Cosenza, 1997; Brandwein, 1997.
14. Duncan, Harris, and Boisjoly, 1997; Harris, 1993, 1996.
15. Bent-Goodley, 2007; Fiscella and Williams, 2004.
16. Olson and Pavetti, 1996; Pavetti, 1997.
17. Ritchie, 2006.
18. Thomas, Witherspoon, and Speight, 2004.
19. Richie, 1996.
20. Abramovitz, 1996.
21. Schram, Soss, and Fording, 2003.
22. Birnbaum and Taylor, 2000; Kasher, 1996.
23. Danziger and Haveman, 2001.
24. Worcester, 2002.
25. Baca Zinn, 2007.
26. Abramovitz, 1996; Mead and Beem, 2005; Smith, 2007.
27. Many scholars have examined the range of responses to divestment, from communities organizing resistance strategies to individuals' self-destructive, anti-social behavior. Here, it is important to note that the anti-violence movement was decidedly unresponsive to the impact that divestment was having, particularly on Black women in low-income communities who experience male violence. There was very little acknowledgment that this is a population that disproportionately relies on social welfare programs as essential elements to their safety. There was also very little reaction to the negative effects of the public discourse that was being used to legitimate divestment and its impact on Black women who experience male violence. This may result in them being

neglected by—or even harmed by—social policy that benefits the general population, including relatively privileged women who come from more elite backgrounds; white, middle-class women whose victimization mirrors the everywoman analysis (Schram, 1995).

28. Abramowitz, 1996.

29. Boris, 2004.

30. Sokoloff and Dupont, 2005.

31. Cole and Guy-Sheftall, 2003.

32. Collins, 2005.

33. Nash, 2005.

34. Bell and Mattis, 2000; Richie, 1996; West and Rose, 2000.

35. Chunn and Gavigan, 2004.

36. Smith, 2007.

37. Ibid., 9.

38. Ibid., 3.

39. Raphael and Ashley, 2008.

40. Raphael, 1996; Riger and Krieglstein, 2000.

41. Hirsh, 2001.

42. Tolman and Rosen, 2001.

43. Caputo, 2011; Renzetti, 2001.

44. King, 2010.

45. Mogul, Ritchie, and Whitlock, 2011.

46. Ritchie, 2006.

47. Cohen, 2004.

48. Catlet and Artis, 2004.

49. Ibid., 1227.

50. Sharpe, 2010; Toscano, 2010.

51. Halley, Kotiswaran, Shamir, and Thomas, 2006; INCITE! Women of Color Against Violence, 2006.

52. Alden and Parker, 2005.

53. Lipsky, Caetano, Roy-Byrne, 2009; West and Rose, 2000.

54. Fritz, 2008.

55. Bell and Mattis, 2000.

56. Hampton, Oliver, and Magarian, 2003; Nicolaidis et al., 2010.

57. Slote et al., 2005.

58. Recent national debates about gay marriage have revealed a tremendous schism in the Black community on the issue of queer rights.

59. Williams and Tubbs, 2002.

60. Nash, 2005.

61. Bufkin and Bray, 1998, Erez and Belknap, 1998 in Baker, 2003.

62. Nash, 2005.

63. Fedders, 1997; Iyengar, 2007.

64. Allen, Flaherty, and Ely 2010.

65. See chapter 3.

Chapter 5

1. Memmott, 2005; see: http://www.tamikahuston.org/index.html.

2. See: http://www.blackandmissinginc.com/cdad/about-derrica.htm.

3. Potter, 2006; Sudbury and Okazawa-Rey, 2009.

4. Collins, 2000a.

5. White, 2001.

6. Few, 2007; Jordan, 2009; Meyers, 1997; Thompson, 2002.

7. Daly, 1997; Potter, 2006.

8. Crenshaw, 1991.

9. Nash, 2005.

10. Harding, 2003.

11. Collins, 2000a: 24.

12. Townsend Gilkes, 2001.

13. Few, 2007.

14. Zerai and Zakia, 2006.

15. James, 2000; Johnson Regan, 2000; Ransby, 2003; Sudbury and Okazawa-Rey, 2009.

16. Schechter, 1982.

17. American Psychiatric Association, 2000; Byrne and Riggs, 2002; Crosson-Tower 2005; DePrince and Freyd, 2002; Dutton, 1992; Sutherland, Sullivan, and Bybee, 2001; Taylor, 2000; Tjaden and Thoennes, 2000b.

18. Banyard and Graham-Bermann, 1993; Barnett, Martinez, and Keyson, 1996; DePrince, and Freyd, 2002; Dobash, Dobash, Cavanagh, and Lewis, 1998; Domestic Abuse Intervention Project, 1987; Eisenberg, 2011; Taft et al., 2006.

19. Hampton, Oliver, and Magarian, 2003.

20. Brown, 2000; Chicago Coalition for the Homeless, 2002; West, 2004.

21. Anderson, 1990.

22. Alexander, 2010; Clear, 2007.

23. King, 2010; Ritchie, 2006; Taylor, 2005; Waltermaurer, Watson, and McNutt, 2006; Wesley, 2006.

24. Stone, 2004; Warshaw, 1993; West, 2006.

25. Bumiller, 2008.

26. Boonstra, 2000; Choice USA, 2002; American Civil Liberties Union, 1994; Chamberlain and Hardisty, 2000.

27. Hirschel and Buzawa, 2002; Hirschel and Hutchison, 1991; Hirschel, Hutchison, Dean, and Mills, 1992; Holmes and Bibel, 1988; Iovanni and Miller, 2001.

28. West, 2006.

29. Dierenfield, 2008; Romano and Raiford, 2006.

30. Crawford, Rouse, and Woods, 1993; Robnett, 2000.

31. Ling and Monteith, 2004.

32. Alonso, 1993; McMillan, 2008; Sklar, 2000.

33. Collins, 2008.

34. Crenshaw, 1991.

35. Springer, 2005.

36. Ibid.

37. Ibid.

38. Combahee River Collective, 1977 in Guy-Sheftall, 1995: 231.

39. Springer, 2005.

40. Smith, 1989.

41. Moraga and Anzaldúa, 1981.

42. Hull, Bell Scott, and Smith, 1982.

43. Schechter, 1982, 1998.

44. Fraser et al., 2002.

45. Richie, 1985 in Guy-Sheftall, 1995: 398.

46. Ransby and Matthews, 1993 in Guy-Sheftall, 1995: 526.

47. Richie, 1985.

48. Schechter, 1982.

49. Crenshaw, 2005.

50. Richie, 1985.

51. Burns, 1986.

52. White, 1990.

53. Morrison, 1992.

54. Barkley Brown, King, and Ransby, 2000.

55. Guy-Sheftall, 1995.

56. Ibid.; White, 1995.

57. Ammons, 1995.

58. Wilson, 1993.

59. Richie, 1996.

60. Ibid.

61. Pierce-Baker, 1998.

62. Robinson and Boyd, 2003.

63. West, 1999.

64. Ibid.

65. INCITE! Women of Color Against Violence, 2006.

66. Ibid.
67. Critical Resistance—INCITE!, 2001.
68. Sudbury, 2005.
69. Richie, 2005.

Chapter 6

1. Pradia, 2010; The Sentencing Project, 2006; see: http://www.kembasmith-foundation.org/.
2. INCITE! Women of Color Against Violence, 2006.
3. Fregoso, 2006; Rivera, 1997.
4. Raphael and Shapiro, 2004; Sallmann, 2010; Spector, 2006.
5. West, 2004.
6. Sudbury, 2005.

Bibliography

The law enforcement response to family violence: A state-by-state guide to family violence legislation. (1988). New York: Victim Services Agency.

Abraham, M. (1999). Sexual abuse in South Asian immigrant marriages. *Violence Against Women, 5*(6), 591–618.

Abramovitz, M. (1996). *Regulating the lives of women: Social welfare policy from colonial times to the present* (rev. ed.). Boston: South End Press.

Acevedo, M. J. (2000). Battered immigrant Mexican women's perspectives regarding abuse and help-seeking. *Journal of multicultural social work, 8*(3, 4), 243–82.

Alden, H. L., and Parker, K. F. (2005). Gender role ideology, homophobia, and hate crime: Linking attitudes to macro-level anti-gay and lesbian hate crimes. *Deviant Behavior, 26*(4), 321–43.

Alexander, M. (2010). *The New Jim Crow: Mass incarceration in the age of colorblindness.* New York: New Press.

Allard, M. A., Albelda, R., Colten, M. E., and Cosenza, C. (1997). In harm's way? Domestic violence, AFDC receipt, and welfare reform in Massachusetts. Boston: McCormack Institute and Center for Survey Research, University of Massachusetts, Boston.

Allen, S., Flaherty, C., and Ely, G. (2010). Throwaway moms: Maternal incarceration and the criminalization of female poverty. *Affilia, 25*(2), 160–72.

Alonso, H. H. (1993). *Peace as a Women's Issue: A history of the US movement for world peace and women's rights.* Syracuse, NY: Syracuse University Press.

American Civil Liberties Union. (1994). Norplant: A New Contraceptive with the Potential for Abuse. New York: ACLU Foundation.

American Civil Liberties Union. (2005). National Prison Project: 2004–05 Litigation Docket.

American Psychiatric Association. (1980). *Diagnostic and statistical manual of mental disorders* (3rd ed.). Washington, DC: American Psychiatric Association.

———. (2000). *Diagnostic and statistical manual of mental disorders* (4th ed.). Washington, DC: American Psychiatric Association.

Ammons, L. L. (1995). Mules, madonnas, babies, bathwater, racial imagery and stereotypes. *Wisconsin Law Review, 3,* 1003–80.

Amnesty International. (1999). Amnesty International's findings and recommendations relating to Valley State Prison in California: Amnesty International.

Anderson, E. (1990). *Street wise: Race, class, and change in an urban community.* Chicago: University of Chicago Press.

———. (2000). *Code of the street: Decency, violence, and the moral life of the inner city* (repr. ed.). New York: W.W. Norton.

———. (2003). *A place on the corner* (2nd ed.). Chicago: University of Chicago Press.

———. (2008). *Against the wall: Poor, young, black, and male.* Philadelphia: University of Pennsylvania Press.

Anderson, E., and Massey, D. S. (2004). *Problem of the century: Racial stratification in the United States.* New York: Russell Sage.

Anderson, M., and Collins, P. H. (1998). *Race, class, and gender: An anthology* (3rd ed.). Belmont, CA: Wadsworth Publishing.

Anderson, M. J. (2002). From chastity requirement to sexuality license: sexual consent and a new rape shield law. *George Washington Law Review, 70,* 51.

Anderson, R. N., Miniño, A. M., Fingerhut, L. A., Warner, M., and Heinen, M. A. (2004). Deaths: injuries, 2001 (National Center for Health Statistics). National vital statistics reports (Vol. 52). Hyattsville, MD: Center for Disease Control and Prevention. Retrieved from http://www.cdc.gov/nchs/data/nvsr/nvsr52/nvsr52_21acc.pdf.

Anzaldúa, G., and Keating, A. (eds.). (2002). *This bridge we call home: radical visions for transformation.* New York: Routledge.

Associated Press. (2007). At Fla. housing project, rape just another crime. *Crime and Courts on msnbc.com.* Retrieved from http://www.msnbc.msn.com/id/19698132/ns/us_news-crime_and_courts.

Atassi, L. (2010). Cleveland's nightmare on Imperial Ave: One year later. *The Plain Dealer.* Retrieved from Cleveland.com website: http://blog.cleveland.com/metro/2010/10/clevelands_nightmare_on_imperi.html.

Avakame, E. F., and Fyfe, J. J. (2001). Differential police treatment of male-on-female spousal violence: additional evidence on the leniency thesis. *Violence Against Women, 7*(1), 22–45.

Baca Zinn, M. (2007). Feminist rethinking from racial-ethnic families. In S. J. Ferguson (ed.), *Shifting the center: Understanding contemporary families* (3rd ed., pp. 18–27). New York: McGraw-Hill.

Bachman, R., and Saltzman, L.E. (1995). *Violence against Women: Estimates from the Redesigned National Crime Victimization Survey.* Washington, DC: Office of Justice Programs.

Bagdikian, B. H. (1997). *The media monopoly.* Boston: Beacon Press.

Baker, C. K., Cook, S. L., and Norris, F. H. (2003). Domestic violence and housing problems: a contextual analysis of women's help-seeking, received informal support, and formal system response. *Violence Against Women, 9*(7), 754–83.

Banyard, V. L., and Graham-Bermann, S. A. (1993). Can women cope? A gender analysis of theories of coping with stress. *Psychology of Women Quarterly, 17*(3), 303–18.

Banzhaf, M. (1999). *Welfare reform and reproductive rights: talking about connections.* Paper presented at the National Network of Abortion Funds.

Barkley-Brown, E., King, D., and Ransby, B. (2000). African American women in defense of ourselves. In J. James and T. D. Sharpley-Whiting (eds.), *The black feminist reader.* Malden, MA: Blackwell Publishers.

Barnett, O. W., Lee, C. Y., and Thelen, R. E. (1997). Gender differences in attributions of self-defense and control in interpartner aggression. *Violence Against Women, 3*(5), 462–81.

Barnett, O. W., Martinez, T. E., and Keyson, M. (1996). The relationship between violence, social support, and self-blame in battered women. *Journal of Interpersonal Violence, 11*(2), 221–33.

Bart, P. B., and O'Brien, P. H. (1985). *Stopping rape: successful survival strategies.* New York: Pergamon Press.

Barusch, A. S., Taylor, M. J., Abu-Bader, S. H., and Derr, M. (1999). Understanding families with multiple barriers to self sufficiency. Salt Lake City, UT: Social Research Institute.

Baunach, P. J. (1988). *Mothers in prison.* New Brunswick, NJ: Transaction Books.

Bayley, D. H. (1986). The tactical choices of police patrol officers. *Journal of Criminal Justice, 14*(4), 329–48.

Beauboeuf-Lafontant, T. (2003). Strong and large black women? Exploring relationships between deviant womanhood and weight. *Gender and Society, 17*(1), 111–21.

Beck, A. J., and Harrison, P. M. (2007). Sexual victimization in state and federal prisons reported by inmates, 2007: Bureau of Justice Statistics Special Report (Bureau of Justice Statistics, Trans.). Washington, DC: Office of Justice Programs.

Belenky, M., Clinchy, B., Goldberger, N., and Tarule, J. (1997). *Women's ways of knowing: The development of self, voice, and mind* (10th anniversary ed.). New York: Basic Books.

Belknap, J. (1996). *The invisible woman: gender, crime, and justice.* Belmont, CA: Wadsworth Publishing.

Bell, C. C., and Mattis, J. S. (2000). The importance of cultural competence in ministering to African-American victims of domestic violence. *Violence Against Women, 6*(5), 515–32.

Belle, D. (1982). *Lives in stress: women and depression.* Beverly Hills, CA: Sage Publications.

Benowitz, M. (1990). How homophobia affects lesbian response to violence in lesbian relationships. In P. Elliott (ed.), *Confronting lesbian battering: A manual for the battered women's movement.* St. Paul: Minnesota Coalition for Battered Women.

Benson, M. L., Wooldredge, J., Thistlethwaite, A. B., and Fox, G. L. (2004). The correlation between race and domestic violence is confounded with community context. *Social Problems, 51*(3), 326–42.

Bent-Goodley, T. B. (2007). Health disparities and violence against women: Why and how cultural and societal influences matter. *Trauma, Violence, and Abuse, 8*(2), 90–104.

Berk, S. F., and Loseke, D. R. (1980–1981). "Handling" family violence: Situational determinants of police arrest in domestic disturbances. *Law and Society Review, 15*(2), 317–46.

Bhattacharjee, A. (2001). Whose safety? Women of color and the violence of law. Philadelphia: American Friends Service Committee on Women, Population, and the Environment.

———. (2002). *Policing the national body: Race, gender, and criminalization.* Cambridge, MA: South End Press.

Bhavnani, K. (2001). *Feminism and 'Race.'* New York: Oxford University Press.

Birnbaum, J., and Taylor, C. (2000). *Civil rights since 1787.* New York: NYU Press.

Blackman, J. (1989). *Intimate violence.* New York: Columbia University Press.

Blank, R. (1989). Analyzing the length of welfare spells. *Journal of Public Economics, 39*(3), 245–73.

Boonstra, H. (2000). Welfare law and the drive to reduce 'illegitimacy.' *The Guttmacher Report on Public Policy Special Analysis.* New York: The Alan Guttmacher Institute.

Boothe, D. (2007). *Why are so many black men in prison? A comprehensive account of how and why the prison industry has become a predatory entity in the lives of African-American men, and how mass targeting, criminalization, and incarceration of Black male youth has gone toward creating the largest prison system in the world.* Memphis: Full Surface Publishing.

Boris, E. (2004). The gender of discrimination: Race, sex, and fair employment in S. A. Schwarzenbach and P. Smith (eds.), *Women and the U.S. constitution: History, interpretation and practice* (273–91). New York: Columbia University Press.

Bourg, S., and Stock, H. V. (1994). A review of domestic violence statistics in a police department using a pro-arrest policy: Are pro-arrest policies enough? *Journal of Family Violence, 9*(2), 177–89.

Brandwein, R. (1997). *Family violence and welfare reform: the Utah experience and national implications.* Paper presented at the Stafford Lecture, Graduate School of Social Work, University of Utah, Salt Lake City.

Brandwein, R. A. (ed.). (1999). *Battered women, children, and welfare reform: The ties that bind*. Thousand Oaks, CA: Sage Publications.

Breines, W. (2002). What's love got to do with it? White women, black women, and feminism in the movement years. *Signs, 27*(4), 1095–1133.

———. (2006). *The trouble between us: an uneasy history of white and black women in the feminist movement*. New York: Oxford University Press.

Breslau, N., Kessler, R. C., Chilcoat, H. D., Schultz, L. R., Davis, G. C., and Andreski, P. (1998). Traumatic and posttraumatic stress disorder in the community: The 1996 Detroit area survey of trauma. *Archives of General Psychiatry, 55*(7), 626–32.

Brewer, R. M., and Heitzeg, N. A. (2008). The racialization of crime and punishment: criminal justice, color-blind racism, and the political economy of the prison industrial complex. *American Behavioral Scientist, 51*(5), 625–44.

Brown, A. W., and Gourdine, R. M. (1998). Teenage Black girls and violence: Coming of age in an urban environment. In L. A. See (ed.), *Human behavior in the social environment from an African American perspective* (105–24). Binghamton, NY: Hawthorne Press.

Brown, E. R. (2000). Income inequalities and health disparities. *Western Journal of Medicine, 172*(1), 25.

Brown-Givens, S. M., and Monahan, J. L. (2005). Priming mammies, jezebels, and other controlling images: An examination of the influence of mediated stereotypes on perceptions of an African American woman. *Media Psychology, 7*(1), 87–106.

Browne, A. (1987). *When battered women kill*. New York: Free Press.

———. (1999). *How to die and survive: Addiction, crisis, change, and transitions*. Escondido, CA: Truth Seeker.

Browning, C. R. (2002). The span of collective efficacy: Extending social disorganization theory to partner violence. *Journal of Marriage and Family, 64*(4), 833–50.

Brownmiller, S. (1975). *Against our will: Men, women, and rape violence against women, Classic papers*. New York: Simon & Schuster.

Bryant-Davis, T., Chung, H., and Tillman, S. (2009). From the margins to the center: Ethnic minority women and the mental health effects of sexual assault. *Trauma, Violence, and Abuse, 10*(4), 330–57.

Bui, H. N. (2003). Help-seeking behavior among abused immigrant women. *Violence Against Women, 9*(2), 207–39.

Bumiller, K. (2008). *In an abusive state: How neoliberalism appropriated the feminist movement against sexual violence*. Durham, NC: Duke University Press.

Burns, M. C. (1986). Speaking profits us: violence in the lives of women of color. Seattle, WA: Center for the Prevention of Sexual and Domestic Violence.

Burton-Rose, D., Pens, D., and Wright, P. (eds.). (2002). *The celling of America: An inside look at the US prison industry*. Monroe, ME: Common Courage Press.

Butler, P. (1998). (Color) blind faith: The tragedy of "race, crime, and the law." *Harvard Law Review, 111*(5), 1270–88.

Buzawa, E., Austin, T., and Buzawa, C. (1995). Responding to crimes of violence against women: gender differences vs. organizational imperatives. *Crime and Delinquency, 41*(4), 443–66.

Buzawa, E., and Buzawa, C. (2003). *Domestic violence: The criminal justice response.* Thousand Oaks, CA: Sage Publications.

Buzawa, E. S., and Hotaling, G. (2000). The police response to domestic violence: Calls for assistance in three Massachusetts towns: Final report. Washington, DC: National Institute of Justice.

———. (2001). An examination of assaults within the jurisdiction of Orange district court: Final report. Washington, DC: National Institute of Justice.

Byrne, C. A., and Riggs, D. S. (2002). Gender issues in couple and family therapy following traumatic stress. In R. Kimerling, P. Ouimette, and J. Wolfe (eds.), *Gender and PTSD* (382–99). New York: Guilford.

Campbell, D., Sharps, P., Gary, F., Campbell, J., and Lopez, L. (2002). Intimate partner violence in African American women. *Online Journal of Issues in Nursing, 7*(1, Manuscript 4). Retrieved from http://www.nursingworld.org/ojin/topic17/tpc17_4.htm.

Campbell, D. W., Campbell, J., King, C., Parker, B., and Ryan, J. (1994). The reliability and factor structure of the Index of Spouse Abuse with African-American women. *Violence and Victims, 9*(3), 259–74.

Campbell, D. W., Masaki, B., and Torres, S. (1997). Water on rock: Changing domestic violence perceptions in the African American, Asian American, and Latino communities. In M. Ghez (ed.), *Ending domestic violence: changing public perceptions/halting the epidemic* (64–87). Thousand Oaks, CA: Sage Publications.

Campbell, J., Rose, L., Kub, J., and Nedd, D. (1998). Voices of strength and resistance: A contextual and longitudinal analysis of women's responses to battering. *Journal of Interpersonal Violence, 13*(6), 743–62.

Canada, D. (2004). *Fist stick knife gun.* Boston: Beacon Press.

Canning, A., and Tanglao, L. (2011). Ohio mom Kelley Williams-Bolar jailed for sending kids to better school district. *ABC News.* Retrieved from abcnews.com website: http://abcnews.go.com/US/ohio-mom-jailed-sending-kids-school-district/story?id=12763654.

Caputo, A. (2011, September/October 2011). One and Done. *The Chicago Reporter, 40*, 10–16.

Carbone-Lopez, K., and Kruttschnitt, C. (2010). Risky relationships? Assortative mating and women's experiences of intimate partner violence. *Crime and Delinquency, 56*(3), 358–84.

Carrington, F. (1989). Avoiding liability for police failure to protect. *Police Chief,* 56(9), 22–24.

Carter, D. (2004). *Stonewall: The riots that sparked the gay revolution.* New York: St. Martin's Press.

Catalano, S. M. (2004). *Crime victimization, 2003.* Washington, DC: Office of Justice Programs.

———. (2006). *Crime victimization, 2005.* Washington, DC: Office of Justice Programs.

Catalano, S. M., Smith, E., Snyder, H., and Rand, M. (2009). *Female Victims of Violence.* Washington, DC: Office of Justice Programs.

Catlett, B. S., and Artis, J. E. (2004). Critiquing the case for marriage promotion: How the promarriage movement misrepresents domestic violence research. *Violence Against Women, 10*(11), 1226–44.

Centers for Disease Control and Prevention. (2006). Understanding intimate partner violence fact sheet.

Chamberlain, P., and Hardisty, J. (Summer 2000). Reproducing patriarchy: Reproductive rights under siege. *Public Eye Magazine 14*(1). Retrieved from http://www.publiceye.org/magazine/v14n1/ReproPatriarch-12.html.

Chesney-Lind, M. (1989). Girls' Crime and women's place: Toward a feminist model of female delinquency. *Crime and Delinquency, 35*(1), 5–29.

Chesney-Lind, M., and Shelden, R. (1998). *Girls, delinquency, and juvenile justice* (2nd ed.). Belmont, CA: Wadsworth Publishing.

Chicago Coalition for the Homeless. (2002). Unlocking options for women: A survey of women in Cook County Jail. Chicago: Chicago Coalition for the Homeless.

Chicago Housing Authority. (2010). *The plan for transformation.* Chicago: Chicago Housing Authority.

Choice USA. (2002). Welfare reform and reproductive rights. Washington, DC.

Chow, E., Wilkinson, E., and Zinn, M. (eds.). (1996). *Race, class, and gender: Common bonds, different voices.* Thousand Oaks, CA: Sage Publications.

Chunn, D., and Gavigan, S. (2004). Welfare law, welfare fraud, and the moral regulation of the 'never deserving' poor. *Social and Legal Studies, 13*(2), 219–43.

Clear, T. (2007). *Imprisoning communities: How mass incarceration makes disadvantaged neighborhoods worse.* New York: Oxford University Press.

Cohen, C. (2004). Deviance as resistance: A new research agenda for the study of black politics. *Du Bois Review: Social Science Research on Race 1*(1), 27–45.

Coker, A. L., Davis, K. E., Arias, L., Desai, S., Sanderson, M., Brandt, H. M., and Smith, P. H. (2002). Physical and mental health effects of intimate partner violence for men and women. *American Journal of Preventive Medicine, 23*(4), 260–68.

Coker, A. L., McKeown, R. E., Sanderson, M., Davis, K. E., Valois, R. F., and Huebner, E. S. (2000). Severe dating violence and quality of life among South Carolina high school students. *American Journal of Preventive Medicine, 19*(4), 220–27.

Coker, D. (2004). Race, poverty, and the crime-centered response to domestic violence: A comment on Linda Mills's insult to injury: Rethinking our responses to intimate abuse. *Violence Against Women, 10*(11), 1331–53.

Cole, D. (1999). *No equal justice: Race and class in the American criminal justice system.* New York: New Press.

Cole, J. B., and Guy-Sheftall, B. (2003). *Gender talk: The struggle for women's equality in African American communities.* New York: Ballantine Publishing Group.

Collins, P. H. (1990). *Black feminist thought: Knowledge, consciousness and the politics of empowerment.* New York: Routledge.

———. (1998). *Fighting words: Black women and the search for justice.* Minneapolis: University of Minnesota Press.

———. (2000a). *Black feminist thought: Knowledge, consciousness, and the politics of empowerment* (2nd ed.). New York: Routledge.

———. (2000b). Gender, black feminism, and black political economy. *Annals of the American Academy of Political and Social Science, 568*(1), 41–53.

———. (2005). *Black sexual politics: African Americans, gender, and the new racism.* New York: Routledge.

———. (2006). *From black power to hip hop: Racism, nationalism, and feminism.* Philadelphia: Temple University Press.

Collins, P. H. (2008). *Black feminist thought: Knowledge, consciousness, and the politics of empowerment.* New York: Routledge.

Collins, S. (1997). *Black corporate executives: The making and breaking of a black middle class.* Philadelphia: Temple University Press.

Coltrane, S., and Messineo, M. (2000). The perpetuation of subtle prejudice: Race and gender imagery in 1990s television advertising. *Sex Roles, 42*(5–6), 363–89.

Colville, L., Moore, G., Smith, L., and Smucker, S. (1997). A study of AFDC case closures due to JOBS sanctions. Lansing: Michigan Family Independence Agency, Administration for Legislation, Budget, and Analysis.

Combahee River Collective. (1997). A black feminist statement. In L. Nicholson (ed.), *The second wave: A reader in feminist theory* (63–70). New York: Routledge.

Cossins, A. (2003). Saints, sluts and sexual assault: Rethinking the relationship between sex, race and gender. *Social Legal Studies, 12*(1), 77–103.

Craven, D. (1996). Female victims of violent crime. Washington, DC: Office of Justice Programs.

Crawford, V. L., Rouse, J. A., and Woods, B. (eds.). (1993). *Women in the civil rights movement: Trailblazers and torchbearers, 1941–1965 (Blacks in the diaspora).* Bloomington and Indianapolis: Indiana University Press.

Crenshaw, K. (1991). Mapping the margins: intersectionality, identity politics, and violence against women of color. *Stanford Law Review, 43*(6), 1241–99.

———. (2005). Reflection (on Mapping the margins: intersectionality, identity politics, and violence against women of color). In C. M. Renzetti, J. L. Edleson, and R. K. Bergen. (eds.). *Violence against women: Classic papers.* Boston: Allyn and Bacon.

Crocker, Diane. (2004). *Criminal Harassment: Understanding Criminal Justice Outcomes for Victims.* Department of Justice Canada.

Crosson-Tower, C. (2005). *Understanding child abuse and neglect* (6th ed.). Boston: Allyn and Bacon.

Crowell, N. A., and Burgess, A. W. (1996). *Understanding violence against women.* Washington, DC: National Academy Press.

Dalmus, C. N., and Wodarski, J. S. (2000). Trauma-related symptomatology among children of parents victimized by urban community violence. *American Journal of Orthopsychiatry, 70*(2), 272–77.

Daly, K. (1997). Different ways of conceptualizing sex/gender in feminist theory and their implications for criminology. *Theoretical Criminology, 1*(1), 25–51.

Daniels, L. (ed.). (2003). *The state of black America.* New York: National Urban League.

Danziger, S. H., and Haveman, R. H. (eds.). (2001). *Understanding poverty.* New York: Russell Sage Foundation.

Dasgupta, S. D. (1999). Just like men? A critical review of violence by women. In M. F. Shepard and E. L. Pence (eds.), *Coordinating community response to domestic violence: Lessons from Duluth and beyond* (195–222). Thousand Oaks, CA: Sage Publications.

———. (2002). A framework for understanding women's use of nonlethal violence in intimate heterosexual relationships. *Violence Against Women, 8*(11), 1364–89.

Davis, A. (2003). *Are prisons obsolete?* New York: Seven Stories Press.

Davis, D. (2006). *Battered black women and welfare reform: Between a rock and a hard place.* Albany: State University of New York Press.

Davis, L. V., and Hagen, J. L. (1994). Social services for battered women: Are they adequate, accessible, and appropriate? *Social Work, 39*(6), 695–704.

———. (1996). Stereotypes and stigma: What's changed for welfare mothers. *Affilia, 11*(3), 319–37.

DeHart, D. D. (2008). Pathways to prison: Impact of victimization in the lives of incarcerated women. *Violence Against Women, 14*(12), 1362–81.

DeKeseredy, W., and Schwartz, M. (1998). Measuring the extent of woman abuse in intimate heterosexual relationships: A critique of the Conflict Tactics Scales. *Violence Against Women Online Resources.* Retrieved from VAWnet website: http://new.vawnet.org/assoc_files_vawnet/ar_ctscrit.pdf.

DeMaris, A., and Swinford, S. (1996). Female victims of spousal violence: Factors influencing their level of fearfulness. *Family Relations, 45*(1), 98–106.

DePrince, A. P., and Freyd, J. J. (2002). The intersection gender and betrayal in trauma. In R. Kimerling, P. Ouimette, and J. Wolfe (eds.), *Gender and PTSD* (98–113). New York: Guilford.

Derr, M. K. (1997). A study of client non-participation and case closure at Utah's Office of Family Support. Salt Lake City: Social Research Institute, University of Utah.

Díaz-Cotto, J. (1996). *Gender, ethnicity, and the state: Latina and Latino prison politics.* Albany: State University of New York Press.

———. (2006). *Chicana lives: Voices from el barrio.* Austin: University of Texas Press.

Diefenbach, P. (1996). Michigan's project zero: A study of barriers to client employment (Office of Quality Assurance, Trans.). Lansing: Michigan Family Independence Agency.

Dierenfield, B. J. (2008). *The civil rights movement* (rev. ed.). New York: Longman.

Dill, B. (1988). The dialectics of black womanhood. In S. Harding (ed.), *Feminism and methodology* (97–108). Bloomington: Indiana University Press.

Dines, G., Jensen, R., and Russo, A. (1998). *Pornography: the production and consumption of inequality.* New York: Routledge.

Dixon, T. L., and Linz, D. (2000a). Overrepresentation and underrepresentation of African Americans and Latinos as lawbreakers on television news. *Journal of Communication, 50*(2), 131–54.

Dixon, T. L., and Linz, D. (2000b). Race and the misrepresentation of victimization on local television news. *Communication Research, 27*(5), 547–73.

Dobash, R. E., and Dobash, R. P. (1979). *Violence against wives.* New York: Free Press.

———. (1988). Research as social action. In K. Yllö and M. Bograd (eds.), *Feminist perspectives on wife abuse.* Thousand Oaks, CA: Sage.

———. (1992). *Women, violence, and social change.* New York: Routledge.

Dobash, R. E., Dobash, R. P., Cavanagh, K., and Lewis, R. (1998). Separate and intersecting realities: A comparison of men's and women's accounts of violence against women. *Violence Against Women, 4*(4), 382–414.

Dobash, R. E., Dobash, R. P., Wilson, M., and Daly, M. (1992). The myth of sexual symmetry in marital violence. *Social Problems, 39*(1), 71–91.

Dodge, L. (2002). *"Whores and thieves of the worst kind": A study of women, crime, and prisons, 1835–2000.* DeKalb: Northern Illinois University Press.

Domestic Abuse Intervention Project. (1981). Duluth: Minnesota Program Development.

———. (1987). Power and control wheel. Duluth: Minnesota Program Development.

Domestic Abuse Project. (1998). Women who abuse in intimate relationships. Minneapolis: Domestic Abuse Project.

Donaldson, S. (2010). Candlelight vigil in Cleveland neighborhood mourns and honors 11 victims of suspected serial killer. *The Plain Dealer*. Retrieved from Cleveland.com website: http://blog.cleveland.com/metro/2010/10/candlelight_vigil_in_cleveland.html.

Donzinger, S. R. (1996). *The real war on crime: The reports of the national criminal justice commission*. New York: Perennial.

Dow, M. (2004). *American gulag: Inside U.S. immigration prisons*. Berkeley and Los Angeles: University of California Press.

Dowell, L. (2008). Memphis cops brutally beat trans woman. *Workers World*. Retrieved from Workers World website: http://www.workers.org/2008/us/memphis_0717/.

Downs, D. (1996). *More than victims: Battered women, the syndrome society, and the law*. Chicago: University of Chicago Press.

Duberman, M. (1993). *Stonewall*. New York: Dutton.

Duncan, G. J. (1984). *Years of poverty, years of plenty: The changing economic fortunes of American workers and families*. Ann Arbor: University of Michigan Press.

Duncan, G. J., Harris, K. M., and Boisjoly, J. (1997). Time limits and welfare reform: New estimates of the number and characteristics of affected families. *Social Science Review, 74*(1), 55–75.

Dutton, D. (1987). The criminal justice response to wife assault. *Law and Human Behavior, 11*(3), 189–206.

Dutton, M. A. (1992). *Empowering and healing the battered woman: A model of assessment and intervention*. New York: Springer.

Eigenberg, H. M., Scarborough, K. E., and Kappeler, V. E. (1996). Contributory factors affecting arrest in domestic and non-domestic assaults. *American Journal of Police, 15*(4), 27–54.

Eisenberg, F. (2011). *"I could see colors again": How women end emotional abuse by accessing agency*. PhD dissertation, City University of New York. Ann Arbor: ProQuest/UMI. (Publication No. AAT 3466300).

Emerson, R. A. (2002). "Where My Girls At?" Negotiating black womanhood in music videos. *Gender and Society, 16*(1), 115–35.

English, K., and Heil, P. (2005). Prison rape: what we know today. *Corrections Compendium, 30*(5), 1–5, 42–45.

Entman, R. M. (1992). Blacks in the news: Television, modern racism and cultural change. *Journalism Quarterly, 69*(2), 341–61.

———. (1994a). African Americans according to TV news. *Media Studies Journal, 8*(3), 29–38.

———. (1994b). Representation and reality in the portrayal of Blacks on network television news. *Journalism Quarterly, 71*(3), 509–20.

Epstein, S. D. (1987). *The problem of dual arrest in family violence cases.* Meriden: Connecticut Coalition Against Domestic Violence.

Fagan, J. (1988). Contributions of family violence research to criminal justice policies on wife assault: Paradigms of science and social control. *Violence and Victims, 3*(3), 159–86.

Faith, K. (1993). *Unruly women: The politics of confinement and resistance.* Vancouver: Press Gang.

Faludi, S. (1991). *Backlash: The undeclared war against American women.* New York: Crown.

Family Violence Prevention Fund. Congress considers violence against women. Retrieved July 1, 2010, from http://www.endabuse.org/content/features/detail/1504/.

Farley, M. (ed.). (2003). *Prostitution, trafficking, and traumatic stress.* Binghamton, NY: Haworth Maltreatment and Trauma Press.

Farmer, A., and Tiefenthaler, J. (2008). Explaining the recent decline in domestic violence. *Contemporary Economic Policy, 21*(2), 158–72.

Farrell, A. D., and Bruce, S. E. (1997). Impact of exposure to community violence on violent behavior and emotional distress among urban adolescents. *Journal of Clinical Child Psychology, 26*(1), 2–14.

Feagin, J. (1972). "When it comes to poverty, it's still, 'God helps those who help themselves." *Psychology Today, 6,* 101–29.

Fedders, B. (1997). Lobbying for mandatory-arrest policies: Race, class, and the politics of the battered women's movement. *New York University Review of Law and Social Change, 23*(2), 291–96.

Feder, L. (1998). Police handling of domestic violence calls: Is there a case for discrimination? *Crime and Delinquency, 44*(2), 139–53.

Feinman, C. (ed.). (1992). *The criminalization of a woman's body.* Binghamton, NY: Harrington Park Press.

Feld, S. L., and Straus, M. A. (1989). Escalation and desistance of wife assault in marriage. *Criminology, 17*(1), 141–61.

Felson, R. B., and Ackerman, J. (2001). Arrests for domestic and other assaults. *Criminology, 39*(3), 655–76.

Feltey, K. (2001). Gender violence: rape and sexual assault. In D. Vannoy (ed.), *Gender Mosaic.* Los Angeles: Roxbury.

Ferraro, K. J. (2003). The words change, but the melody lingers: The persistence of the battered women's syndrome in criminal cases involving battered women. *Violence Against Women, 9*(1), 110–29.

————. (2008). Invisible or pathologized? Racial statistics and violence against women of color. *Critical Sociology, 34*(2), 193–211.

Few, A. L. (2007). Integrating black consciousness and critical race feminism into family studies research. *Journal of Family Issues, 28*(4), 452–73.

Few, A. L., and Bell-Scott, P. (2002). Grounding our feet and hearts: Black women's coping strategies in psychologically abusive dating relationships. In C. West (Ed.), *Violence in the lives of black women: Battered, black, and blue* (59–77). New York: Haworth.

Finesmith, B. K. (1983). Police responses to battered women: a critique and proposal for reform. *Seton Hall Law Review, 14*, 74–109.

Finn, P., and Colson, S. (1990). Civil protection orders: Legislation, current court practice, and enforcement (National Institute of Justice, Trans.) *Issues and Practices in Criminal Justice*. Washington, DC: U.S. Department of Justice.

Fiscella, K., and Williams, D. R. (2004). Health disparities based on socioeconomic inequities: Implications for urban health care. *Academic Medicine, 79*(12), 1139–47.

Fischer, P. (1999). Section 8 and the public housing revolution: where will the families go? Chicago: The Woods Fund of Chicago.

————. (2003). Where are the public housing families going?: An update. Chicago: National Center on Poverty Law.

Flavin, J. (2001). Of punishment and parenthood: family-based social control and the sentencing of black drug offenders. *Gender and Society, 15*(4), 611–33.

Foucault, M. (1995). *Discipline and punish: The birth of the prison*. New York: Vintage Books.

Fox, J. A., and Zawitz, M. W. (2000). Homicide trends in the United States: intimate homicide (Bureau of Justice Statistics, Trans.). Washington, DC: U.S. Department of Justice.

Fraker, T., Nixon, L., Losby, J., Prindle, C., and Else, J. (1997). Iowa's limited benefit plan. Washington, DC: Mathematica Policy Research.

Fraser, I. M., McNutt, L., Clark, C., Williams-Muhammed, D., and Lee, R. (2002). Social support choices for help with abusive relationships: perceptions of African American women. *Journal of Family Violence, 17*(4), 363–75.

Fregoso, R. L. (2006). The complexities of "feminicide" on the Border. In INCITE! Women of Color Against Violence (ed.), *Color of violence: The INCITE! anthology*. Cambridge, MA: South End Press.

Fritz, M. J. (2008, April). *Race and gender in the* Department of Housing and Urban Development v. Rucker: *Constructing the racialized family in federal public housing*. Paper presented at the Annual Meeting of Midwestern Political Science Association, Chicago, IL.

Fyfe, J. J., Klinger, D. A., and Flavin, J. (1997). Differential police treatment of male-on-female spousal violence. *Criminology, 35*(3), 455–73.

Gallo, L. C., and Matthews, K. A. (2003). Understanding the association between socioeconomic status and physical health: Do negative emotions play a role? *Psychological Bulletin, 129*(1), 10–51.

Garfield, G. (2005). *Knowing what we know: African American women's experiences of violence and violation.* New Brunswick, NJ: Rutgers University Press.

Garland, D. (2001). *The culture of control: Crime and social order in contemporary society.* New York: Oxford University Press.

Gary, F. A., and Campbell, D. W. (1998). The struggles of runaway youth: Violence and abuse. In J. C. Campbell (Ed.), *Empowering survivors of abuse: Health care for battered women and their children* (156–73). Thousand Oaks, CA: Sage.

Gaseau, M., and Martin, K. (2003). Secrets behind bars: Sexual misconduct in jails—jails take pro-active role to prevent illegal behavior. Retrieved September 20, 2008, from http://database.corrections.com/news/results2_new.asp?ID=4707.

Gilbert, P. R. (2002). Discourses of female violence and societal gender stereotypes. *Violence Against Women, 8*(11), 1271–1300.

Gilens, M. (1996). 'Race coding' and white opposition to welfare. *American Political Science Review, 90*(3), 593–604.

Gilmore, R. W. (2007). *Golden gulag: Prisons, surplus, crisis, and opposition in globalizing California.* Berkeley and Los Angeles: University of California Press.

Girshick, L. (1999). *No safe haven: Stories of women in prison.* Boston: Northeastern University Press.

———. (2002). *Woman-to-woman sexual violence: Does she call it rape?* Boston: Northeastern University Press.

Golden, R. (2005). *War on the family: Mothers in prison and the families they leave behind.* New York: Routledge.

Gondolf, E. W., and Fisher, E. R. (1988). *Battered women as survivors: An alternative to treating learned helplessness.* Lexington, MA: Lexington Books.

Goodman, L. A., Koss, M. P., and Russo, N. F. (1993). Violence against women: Physical and mental health effects. Part I: Research findings. *Applied and Preventive Psychology, 2*(2), 79–89.

Goodwin, J., and Jasper, J. (eds.). (2003). *The social movements reader: Cases and concepts.* Malden, MA: Blackwell Publishing.

Gornick, J., Burt, M. R., and Pittman, K. J. (1985). Structure and activities of rape crisis centers in the early 1980s. *Crime and Delinquency, 31*(2), 247–68.

Graham-Berman, S. A. (2002). Child abuse in the context of domestic violence. In J.E.B. Myers, L. Berliner, J. Brier, C. T. Hendix, C. Jenny, and T. A. Reid (eds.), *The APSAC Handbook on Child Maltreatment.* Thousand Oaks, CA: Sage.

Graham-Bermann, S. A., and Eastin, J. (2001). Stress and coping. In J. Worell (Ed.), *Encyclopedia of women and gender* (1101–11). San Diego, CA: Academic Press.

Greenfeld, L. A., and Snell, T. L. (1999). Women offenders (Bureau of Justice Statistics, Trans.). Washington, DC: U.S. Department of Justice.

Griffin, F. J. (2000). Black feminists and Du Bois: respectability, protection and beyond. *Annals of the American Academy of Political and Social Science, 568*(1), 28–40.

Gross, L., Aurand, S. K., and Addessa, R. (2000). The 1999–2000 study of discrimination and violence against lesbian women and gay men in Philadelphia and the Commonwealth of Pennsylvania: The Philadelphia Lesbian and Gay Task Force. Philadelphia: Philadelphia Lesbian and Gay Task Force.

Grossman, D., and DeGaetano, G. (1999). *Stop teaching our kids to kill: A call to action against TV, movie and videogame violence.* New York: Crown Publishers.

Guy-Sheftall, B. (ed.). (1995). *Words of fire: An anthology of African-American feminist thought.* New York: New Press.

Hackworth, J. (2002). Postrecession gentrification in New York City. *Urban Affairs Review, 37*(6), 815–43.

Halley, J., Kotiswaran, P., Shamir, H., and Thomas, C. (2006). From the international to the local in feminist legal responses to rape, prostitution/sex work, and sex trafficking: Four studies in contemporary governance feminism. *29 Harvard Journal of Law and Gender 335,* 340.

Hamberger, L. K., and Guse, C. E. (2002). Men's and women's use of intimate partner violence in clinical samples. *Violence Against Women, 8*(11), 1301–31.

Hamberger, L. K., Lohr, J., and Bonge, D. (1994). The intended function of domestic violence is different for arrested male and female perpetrators. *Family Violence and Sexual Assault Bulletin, 10*(34), 40–44.

Hamberger, L. K., Lohr, J., Bonge, D., and Tolin, D. F. (1997). An empirical classification of motivations for domestic violence. *Violence Against Women, 3*(4), 401–43.

Hamby, S. L. (2000). The importance of community in a feminist analysis of domestic violence among American Indians. *American Journal of Community Psychology, 28*(5), 649–69.

Hampton, R. (1991). *Black family violence: Current research and theory.* Lexington, MA: Lexington Books.

Hampton, R., and Gelles, R. J. (1994). Violence toward Black women in a nationally representative sample of Black families. *Journal of Comparative Family Studies, 28*(6), 105–19.

Hampton, R., and Gullotta, T. (eds.). (2006). *Interpersonal violence in the African American community: Evidence-based prevention and treatment practices.* New York: Springer.

Hampton, R., Oliver, W., and Magarian, L. (2003). Domestic violence in the African American community: An analysis of social and structural factors. *Violence Against Women, 9*(5), 533–57.

Harding, S. (ed.). (2003). The feminist standpoint theory reader: Intellectual and political controversies. New York: Routledge.

Harris, A. P. (2000). Gender, violence, race, and criminal justice. *Stanford Law Review, 52*(4), 777–807.

Harris, K. M. (1991). Teenage mothers and welfare dependency: Working off welfare. *Journal of Family Issues, 12*(4), 492–518.

———. (1993). Work and welfare among single mothers in poverty. *American Journal of Sociology, 99*(2), 317–52.

———. (1996). Life after welfare: Women, work, and repeat dependency. *American Sociological Review, 61*(3), 407–23.

Harris, P. (1997). *Black rage confronts the law.* New York: NYU Press.

Hart, B. J. (1995). The Violence Against Women Act: identifying projects for law enforcement and prosecution grants: FY '95. Harrisburg, PA: Battered Women's Justice Project and the National Resource Center on Domestic Violence.

Hartocollis, A. (2007). Woman in gang assault trial says man started the fight, *New York Times.* Retrieved from http://www.nytimes.com/2007/04/14/nyregion/14assault.html?ex=1177128000&en=a1ea123367fd1a57&ei=5099&partner=TOPIXNEWS.

Hatty, S. (2000). *Masculinities, violence, and culture.* Thousand Oaks, CA: Sage.

Haviland, M., Frye, B., Rajah, V., Thukral, J., and Trinity, M. (2001). *The Family Protection and Domestic Violence Act of 1995: Examining the effects of mandatory arrest in New York City.* New York: Urban Justice Center.

Heise, L. L. (1998). Violence against women: an integrated, ecological framework. *Violence Against Women, 4*(3), 262–90.

Herman, J. (1992). *Trauma and recovery: the aftermath of violence--from domestic abuse to political terror.* New York: Basic Books.

Hill, H., Hawkins, S., Raposo, M., and Carr, P. (1995). Relationship between multiple exposure to violence and coping strategies among African American mothers. *Violence and Victims, 10*(1), 55–71.

Hines, D. (1989). Rape and the inner lives of Black women in the Middle West. *Signs, 14*(4), 912–20.

Hines, D., and Malley-Morrison, K. (2001). Psychological effects of partner abuse against men: a neglected research area. *Psychology of Men and Masculinity, 2*(2), 75–85.

Hirsch, A. (2001). "The world was never a safe place for them": abuse, welfare reform, and women with drug convictions. *Violence Against Women, 7*(2), 159–75.

Hirschel, D. (2008). Domestic violence cases: what research shows about arrest and dual arrest rates (National Institute of Justice, Trans.). Washington, DC: U.S. Department of Justice.

Hirschel, J., and Buzawa, E. (2002). Understanding the context of dual arrests with directions for future research. *Violence Against Women, 8*(12), 1449–73.

Hirschel, J., and Hutchinson, I. (1991). Police-preferred arrest policies. In M. Steinman (ed.), *Wife battering: Police responses.* Cincinnati, OH: Anderson.

Hirschel, J., Hutchinson, I., Dean, C., and Mills, A. (1992). Review essay on the law enforcement response to spouse abuse: Past, present, and future. *Justice Quarterly, 9*(2), 247–83.

Holmes, W., and Bibel, D. (1988). Police response to domestic violence: Final report (Bureau of Justice Statistics, Trans.). Washington, DC: U.S. Department of Justice.

Holzman, H. R., Hyatt, R., and Dempster, J. M. (2001). Patterns of aggravated assault in public housing: Mapping the nexus of offense, place, gender, and race. *Violence Against Women, 7*(6), 662–84.

Honeycutt, T. C., Marshall, L. L., and Weston, R. (2001). Toward ethnically specific models of employment, public assistance and victimization. *Violence Against Women, 7*(2), 126–41.

hooks, b. (2000). *Feminist theory: From margin to center.* Cambridge, MA: South End Press.

Hooper, J., and James, S. D. (2010). Scott Sisters: Road 'Long and Hard' to prison release. *ABC World News with Diane Sawyer.* Retrieved from abcnews.com website: http://abcnews.go.com/US/scott-sisters-released-mississippi-prison-condition-donates-kidney/story?id=12563876.

Hubbard, J. (2010). Outrage follows arrests in rape of 7-year-old New Jersey girl. *ABC World News with Diane Sawyer.* Retrieved from abcnews website: http://abcnews.go.com/WN/charged-trenton-gang-rape-year/story?id=10283128.

Hull, G., Bell Scott, P., and Smith, B. (eds.). (1982). *All of the women are white, all of the Blacks are men, but some of us are brave: Black women's studies.* Old Westbury, NY: Feminist Press.

Human Right Watch Women's Rights Project. (1996). All too familiar: sexual abuse of women in US state prisons. New York: Human Rights Watch.

Hunnicutt, G. (2009). Varieties of patriarchy and violence against women: Resurrecting "patriarchy" as a theoretical tool. *Violence Against Women, 15*(5), 553–73.

Hunt, A. (2010). In the fatal shooting case, what each side says. *Detroit Free Press.* Retrieved from Detroit Free Press website: http://www.freep.com/article/20100602/NEWS01/6020303/In-fatal-shooting-case-what-each-side-says.

Hunt, A., and Schmitt, B. (2010). Detroit police investigate grenade use in fatal raid. *Detroit Free Press.* Retrieved from Detroit Free Press website: http://www.freep.com/article/20100517/NEWS01/100517054/Detroit-police-investigate-grenade-use-fatal-raid.

Hunt, G., and Joe-Laidler, K. (2001). Situations of violence in the lives of girl gang members. *Health Care for Women International, 22*(4), 363–84.

Hunt, M. O. (1996). The individual, society, or both? A comparison of Black, Latino, and White beliefs about the causes of poverty. *Social Forces, 75*(1), 293–322.

Hurst, C. (2007). *Social inequality: forms, causes, and consequences.* Boston: Allyn and Bacon.

Hutchinson, I. W., and Hirschel, J. D. (1994). Family violence and police utilization. *Violence and Victims, 9*(4), 299–313.

Hutson, R. Q., and Levin-Epstein, J. (2000). Linking family planning with other social services: The perspectives of state family planning administrators. Washington, DC: Center for Law and Social Policy.

INCITE! Women of Color Against Violence. (2001). Statement on gender violence and the prison industrial complex, from http://incite-national.org/index.php?s=92.

———. (2006). *Color of Violence: The INCITE! Anthology.* Cambridge, MA: South End Press.

Iovanni, L., and Miller, S. L. (2001). Criminal justice responses to domestic violence: Law enforcement and the courts. In C. M. Renzetti, J. L. Edleson, and R. K. Bergen (eds.), *Sourcebook on violence against women.* Thousand Oaks, CA: Sage.

Iyengar, R. (2007). Does the certainty of arrest reduce domestic violence? Evidence from mandatory and recommended arrest laws. NBER Working Paper #13186.

Jacobson, M. (2005). *Downsizing prisons: How to reduce crime and end mass incarceration.* New York: NYU Press.

Jaffe, P., Wolfe, D., Wilson, S. K., and Zak, L. (1986). Similarities in behavioral and social maladjustment among child victims and witnesses to family violence. *American Journal of Orthopsychiatry, 56*(1), 142–46.

James, J. (2000). Radicalizing feminism. In J. James and T. D. Sharpley-Whiting (eds.), *The Black feminist reader.* Malden, MA: Blackwell Publishers.

———. (ed.). (2002). *States of confinement: Policing, detention, and prisons.* New York: Palgrave Macmillan.

James, S. D. (2010). Scott sisters kidney donation threatens organ transplant laws. *ABC World News with Diane Sawyer.* Retrieved from abcnews.com website: http://abcnews.go.com/Health/scott-sisters-kidney-donation-threatens-organ-transplant-laws/story?id=12515616.

Janzen, F. V. (1997). *Risk factors of CT and DP clients by education level* (Unpublished table). Social Research Institute. Salt Lake City: University of Utah.

Jarrett, R. L. (1996). Welfare stigma among low-income African American single mothers. *Family Relations, 45*(4), 368–74.

Jenkins, E. J. (2002). Black women and community violence: Trauma, grief, and coping. *Women and Therapy, 25*(3 and 4), 29–44.

Jhally, S., Katz, J., and Earp, J. (Writers). (1999). Tough guise: Violence, media, and the crisis in masculinity. United States: Media Education Foundation.

Jipguep, M., and Sanders-Phillips, K. (2003). The context of violence for children of color: Violence in the community and the media. *Journal of Negro Education,* 72(4), 379–95.

Jiwani, Y. (2005). Walking a tightrope: The many faces of violence in the lives of racialized immigrant girls and young women. *Violence Against Women,* 11(7), 846–75.

Johnson, A. G. (2005). *Privilege, power, and difference* (2nd ed.). Columbus, OH: McGraw-Hill.

Johnson, E. P., and Henderson, M. G. (eds.). (2005). *Black queer studies: A critical anthology.* Durham, NC: Duke University Press.

Johnson, K. (1985). *If you are raped: What every woman needs to know.* Holmes Beach, FL: Learning Publications.

Johnson, M. P. (1995). Patriarchal terrorism and common couple violence: Two forms of violence against women. *Journal of Marriage and the Family,* 57(2), 283–94.

Johnson, P. (2003). *Inner lives: voices of African American women in prison.* New York: NYU Press.

Johnson Reagon, B. (2000). Coalition politics: turning the century. In B. Christian (ed.), *Home girls: A black feminist anthology.* New Brunswick, NJ: Rutgers University Press.

Jones, C., and Shorter-Gooden, K. (2003). *Shifting: the double lives of black women in America.* New York: HarperCollins.

Jones, D. A., and Belknap, J. (1999). Police responses to battering in a progressive pro-arrest jurisdiction. *Justice Quarterly,* 16(2), 249–73.

Jones, N. (2004). "It's not where you live, it's how you live": How young women negotiate conflict and violence in the inner city. *Annals of the American Academy of Political and Social Science,* 595, 49–62.

Jordan, C. E. (2009). Advancing the study of violence against women: Evolving research agendas into science. *Violence Against Women,* 15(4), 393–419.

Joseph, J. (1997). Woman battering: a comparative analysis of black and white women. In G. Kantor and J. L. Jasinski (eds.), *Out of darkness: Contemporary perspectives on family violence.* Thousand Oaks, CA: Sage.

Judiciary of Rhode Island. (2001). DV cases arrests, dual arrest and multiple involvement.

———. (2001). DV case arrests by gender.

Kalven, J. (2006). Kicking the pigeon. Retrieved from http://www.viewfromthe-ground.com/archive/2006/05/ktp-index.html.

Kanuha, V. (1996). Domestic violence, racism, and the battered women's movement in the United States. In J. L. Edleson and Z. C. Eisikovits (eds.), *Future interventions with battered women and their families.* Thousand Oaks, CA: Sage.

Kasher, S. (1996). *The Civil Rights Movement: A photographic history 1954–68*. New York: Abbeville Press.

Kassel, P. (1985, August). Ironic consequences of domestic violence law. *National Lawyers Guild Anti-Sexism Newsletter*, 1(2), 4.

Kasturirangan, A., Krishnan, S., and Riger, S. (2004). The impact of culture and minority status on women's experience of domestic violence. *Trauma, Violence, and Abuse*, 5(4), 318–32.

Kasturirangan, A., and Williams, E. N. (2003). Counseling latina battered women: A qualitative study of the latina perspective. *Journal of Multicultural Counseling– Development*, 31(3), 162–78.

Kaufman Kantor, G., and Jasinski, J. L. (1998). Dynamics and risk factors in partner violence. In J. L. Jasinski and L. M. Williams (eds.), *Partner violence: A comprehensive review of 20 years of research*. Thousand Oak, CA: Sage.

Kaufman Kantor, G., and Straus, M. A. (1987). The "drunken bum" theory of wife beating. *Social Problems*, 34(3), 213–30.

Kay, P., Estepa, A., and Desetta, A. (eds.). (1998). *Things get hectic: teens write about the violence that surrounds them*. New York: Touchstone.

KBMT. (2010). UPDATE: Sheriff says man killed woman with hammer, dragged her about a quarter mile. Retrieved from 12newsnow.com website: http://www.12newsnow.com/story/12606231/update-sheriff-says-man-killed-woman-with-hammer-dragged-her-about-a-quarter-mile?redirected=true.

Kelley, L. (1996). Beyond victim to survivor: sexual violence, identity, feminist theory and practice. In V. Merchant (ed.), *Sexualizing the social: The social organisation of power*. London: Macmillan.

Kelley, R. (1997). *Yo' mama's disfunktional!: Fighting the culture wars in urban America*. Boston: Beacon Press.

Kilbourne, J. (1999). *Deadly persuasion: why women and girls must fight the addictive power of advertising*. New York: Free Press.

Kilmartin, C., and Allison, J. (2007). *Men's violence against women*. Mahwah, NJ: Lawrence Erlbaum Associates.

Kilpatrick, D. (2004). What is violence against women? Defining and measuring the problem. *Journal of Interpersonal Violence*, 19(11), 1244–51.

Kimmel, M. S. (ed.). (1990). *Men confront pornography*. New York: Crown Publishers.

King, T. L. (2010). One strike evictions, state space and the production of abject female bodies. *Critical Sociology*, 36(1), 45–64.

Klein, E., Campbell, J., Soler, E., and Ghez, M. (1997). *Ending domestic violence: Changing public perceptions/halting the epidemic*. Thousand Oaks, CA: Sage.

Klinger, D. (1995). Policing spousal assault. *Journal of Research in Crime and Delinquency*, 32(3), 308–24.

Koss, M. P. (2000). Blame, shame, and community: Justice responses to violence against women. *American Psychologist, 55*(11), 1332–43.

Koss, M. P., and Harvey, M. (1991). *The rape victim: clinical and community interventions.* Newbury Park, CA: Sage.

Kotz, P. (2009). Tiffany Wright, 15 and pregnant, shot at Charlotte bus stop. *True Crime Report.* Retrieved from True Crime Report website: http://www.truecrimereport.com/2009/09/tiffany_wright_15_and_pregnant.php.

Kruttschnitt, C., and McLoughlin, B. (eds.). (2004). *Advancing the federal research agenda on violence against women.* Washington, DC: National Academies Press.

Kurz, D., and Stark, E. (1988). Not-so benign neglect: The medical response to battering. In K. Yllö and M. Bograd (eds.), *Feminist perspectives on wife abuse.* Thousand Oaks, CA: Sage.

Lamb, S. (1999). Constructing the victim: Popular images and lasting labels. In S. Lamb (ed.), *New versions of victims: Feminists struggle with the concept.* New York: NYU Press.

Langen, P. A., and Innes, C. A. (1986). Preventing domestic violence against women: Discussion Paper (Bureau of Justice Statistics, Trans.). Washington, DC: U.S. Department of Justice.

Larocco, P. (2010). New murder trial denied for Riverside woman supported by Demi Moore. *The Press-Enterprise.* Retrieved from The Press-Enterprise website: http://www.pe.com/localnews/publicsafety/stories/PE_News_Local_W_wkruzan17.46f8c6d.html.

Lavizzo-Mourey, R., and Knickman, J. R. (2003). Racial disparities—the need for research and action. *New England Journal of Medicine, 349,* 1379–80.

Lawrenz, F., Lembo, J. F., and Schade, T. (1988). Time series analysis of the effect of a domestic violence directive on the number of arrests per day. *Journal of Criminal Justice, 16*(6), 493–98.

Lee, R., Thompson, V. L., and Mechanic, M. B. (2002). Intimate partner violence and women of color: A call for innovations. *American Journal of Public Health, 92*(4), 530–34.

Lehman, C. (2005). *Strong at heart: How it feels to heal from sexual abuse.* New York: Farrar, Straus, and Giroux.

Lein, L., Schexnayder, D. T., Douglas, K. N., and Schroeder, D. G. (2007). *Life after welfare: Reform and the persistence of poverty.* Austin: University of Texas Press.

Leonard, E. (1982). *Women, crime and society: A critique of criminology theory.* New York: Longman.

———. (2002). *Convicted survivors: The imprisonment of battered women who kill.* Albany: State University of New York Press.

Leventhal, B., and Lundy, S. E. (eds.). (1999). *Same-sex domestic violence: Struggles for change.* Thousand Oaks, CA: Sage.

Ling, P. J., and Monteith, S. (eds.). (2004). *Gender and the civil rights movement.* New Brunswick, NJ: Rutgers University Press.

Lipsky, S., Caetano, R., and Roy-Byrne, P. (2009). Racial and ethnic disparities in police-reported intimate partner violence and risk of hospitalization among women. *Women's Health Issues,* 19(2), 109–18.

Lischick, C. W. (1999). *Coping and related characteristics delineating battered women's experiences in self-defined, difficult/hurtful dating relationships: A multicultural study.* Unpublished doctoral dissertation. Newark, NJ: Rutgers University, State University of New Jersey.

Lockhart, L., and White, B. (1989). Understanding marital violence in the black community. *Journal of Interpersonal Violence,* 4(4), 421–36.

Long, L. M., Ullman, S. E., Starzunski, L. L., Long, S. M., and Mason, G. E. (2007). Age and educational differences in African American women's sexual assault experiences. *Feminist Criminology,* 2(2), 117–36.

Loprest, P. J., and Acs, G. (1996). Profile of disability among families on AFDC. Washington, DC: Urban Institute.

Mahoney, M. R. (1994). Victimization or oppression? Women's lives, violence, and agency. In M. Myktiuk, F. Albertson, and R. Albertson (eds.), *The public nature of private violence: The discovery of domestic abuse.* New York: Routledge.

Mahoney, P., Williams, L. M., and West, C. M. (2001). Violence against women by intimate relationship partners. In C. Renzetti, J. Edleson, and R. K. Bergen (eds.), *Sourcebook on violence against women* (143–78). Thousand Oaks, CA: Sage.

Majors, R., and Billson, J. (1992). *Cool prose: the dilemmas of black manhood in America.* New York: Touchstone.

Makarios, M. D. (2007). Race, abuse, and female criminal violence. *Feminist Criminology,* 2(2), 100–116.

Mangum, G., Weathers, S., Kasten-Bell, J., and Lazerus, S. (1998). *On being poor in Utah.* Salt Lake City: University of Utah Press.

Mann, C. (1993). *Unequal justice: A question of color.* Bloomington: Indiana University Press.

Manning, P. (1997). *Police work: The social organization of policing.* Prospect Heights, IL: Waveland Press.

Marchetti, E. (2008). Intersectional race and gender analyses: Why legal processes just don't get it. *Social Legal Studies,* 17(2), 155–74.

Martin, D. (1981). *Battered wives.* Volcano, CA: Volcano Press.

Martin, M. E. (1997). Double your trouble: Dual arrest in family violence. *Journal of Family Violence,* 12(2), 139–57.

Martin, R. (2009, March 4, 2009). Black women get beat by the police too. Retrieved from http://www.racialicious.com/2009/03/04/black-women-get-beat-by-the-police-too/.

Martin, S., and Jurik, N. (1996). *Doing justice, doing gender: Women in the law and criminal justice occupations.* Thousand Oaks, CA: Sage.

Martinez, J. (2007). Lesbian wolf pack guilty. *New York Daily News.* Retrieved from http://www.nydailynews.com/news/ny_crime/2007/04/19/2007-04-19_lesbian_wolf_pack_guilty.html

Mastro, D., and Robinson, A. (2000). Cops and crooks: Images of minorities on prime time television. *Journal of Criminal Justice, 28*(5), 385–96.

Mastro, D., and Stern, S. R. (2003). Representations of race in television commercials: A content analysis of prime-time advertising. *Journal of Broadcasting and Electronic Media, 47*(4), 638–47.

Mastro, D., and Tropp, L. R. (2004). The effects of interracial contact, attitudes, and stereotypical portrayals on evaluations of Black television sitcom characters. *Communication Research Reports, 21*(2), 119–29.

Matthews, N. (1994). *Confronting rape: The feminist anti-rape movement and the state.* (International Library of Sociology, 1st ed.). New York: Routledge.

Mauer, M. (2006). *Race to incarcerate* (revised and updated ed.). New York: New Press.

Mauer, M., and Chesney-Lind, M. (eds.). (2002). *Invisible punishment: The collateral consequences of mass imprisonment.* New York: New Press.

Mauer, M., and Huling, T. (1995). Young black Americans and the criminal justice system: Five years later. Washington, DC: The Sentencing Project.

McArdle, A., and Erzen, T. (eds.). (2001). *Zero tolerance: quality of life and the new police brutality in New York.* New York: NYU Press.

McClennen, J. C., and Gunther, J. J. (eds.). (1999). *A professional guide to understanding gay and lesbian domestic violence.* Lewiston, NY: Edwin Mellen Press.

McDaniels-Wilson, C., and Belknap, J. (2008). The extensive sexual violation and sexual abuse histories of incarcerated women. *Violence Against Women, 14*(10), 1090–1127.

McMahon, M., and Pence, E. (2003). Making social change: Reflections on individual and institutional advocacy with women arrested for domestic violence. *Violence Against Women, 9*(1), 47–74.

McMillen, S. (2008). *Seneca Falls and the origins of the women's rights movement.* New York: Oxford University Press.

Mead, L. M., and Beem, C. (eds.). (2005). *Welfare reform and political theory.* New York: Russell Sage Foundation.

Melloy, K. (2008). SF women rally to support incarcerated NJ lesbians of color. *EDGE.* Retrieved from http://www.edgeboston.com/index.php?ch=news&sc=glbt&sc3=&id=79603&pf=1.

Memmott, M. (2005). Spotlight skips cases of missing minorities. *USA Today.* Retrieved from http://www.usatoday.com/news/nation/2005-06-15-missing-minorities_x.htm.

Merrill, L. L., Newell, C. E., Thomsen, C. J., Gold, S. R., Milner, J. S., Koss, M. P., and Rosswork, S. G. (1999). Childhood abuse and sexual revictimization in a female navy recruit sample. *Journal of Traumatic Stress, 12*(2), 211–25.

Messner, M. A., and Sabo, D. F. (eds.). (1990). *Sport, men, and the gender order: Critical feminist perspectives.* Champaign, IL: Human Kinetics Books.

———. (1994). *Sex, violence, and power in sports: Rethinking masculinity.* Freedom, CA: Crossing Press.

Meyer, C., and Oberman, M. (2001). *Mothers who kill their children: Understanding the acts of moms from Susan Smith to the "prom mom."* New York: NYU Press.

Meyer, D. R., and Cancian, M. (1996). Life after welfare. *Public Welfare, 54*(4), 25–30.

Meyer, E. (2011). Unusual trial ready to begin in student residency dispute. *Akron Beacon Journal.* Retrieved from Ohio.com website: http://www.ohio.com/news/112920979.html.

Meyers M. (1997). *News coverage of violence against women.* Thousand Oaks, CA: Sage.

Mignon, S. I., and Holmes, W. (1995). Police response to mandatory arrest laws. *Crime and Delinquency, 41*(4), 430–42.

Miller, J. (2011). Schwarzenegger issues pardon, commutation in Inland cases. *The Press-Enterprise.* Retrieved from The Press-Enterprise website: http://www.pe.com/localnews/politics/stories/PE_News_Local_D_women03.c897d6.html.

Miller, J. G. (1996). *Search and destroy: African-American males in the criminal justice system.* New York: Cambridge University Press.

———. (2008). *Getting played: African American girls, urban inequality, and gendered violence.* New York: NYU Press.

Miller, N. (1997). Domestic violence legislation affecting police and prosecutor responsibilities in the United States: Inferences from a 50-state review of state statutory codes. Alexandria, VA: Institute for Law and Justice.

Miller, S. L. (1994). Expanding the boundaries: Toward a more inclusive and integrated study of intimate violence. *Violence and Victims, 9*(2), 183–94.

———. (ed.). (1998). *Crime control and women: Feminist implications of criminal justice policy.* Thousand Oaks, CA: Sage.

———. (2001). The paradox of women arrested for domestic violence. *Violence Against Women, 7*(12), 1339–76.

———. (2005). *Victims as offenders: The paradox of women's violence in relationships.* New Brunswick, NJ: Rutgers University Press.

Miller, S. L., and Meloy, M. (2006). Women's use of force: voices of women arrested for domestic violence. *Violence Against Women, 12*(1), 89–115.

Miller-Young, M. (2010). Putting hypersexuality to work: Black women and illicit eroticism in pornography. *Sexualities, 13*(2), 219–35.

Mills, L. G. (1999). Killing her softly: Intimate abuse and the violence of state intervention. *Harvard Law Review, 113*(2), 550–613.

Mogul, J. L., Ritchie, A. J., and Whitlock, K. (2011). *Queer (In) justice: The criminalization of LGBT people in the United States.* Boston: Beacon Press.

Monahan, J. L., Shtrulis, I., and Givens, S. B. (2005). Priming welfare queens and other stereotypes: the transference of media images into interpersonal contexts. *Communication Research Reports, 22*(3), 199–205.

Monnat, S. M. (2010). Towards a critical understanding of gendered color-blind racism within the U.S. welfare institution. *Journal of Black Studies, 40*(4), 637–52.

Moraga, C., and Anzaldúa, G. (eds.). (1981). *This bridge called my back: Writings by radical women of color.* Watertown, MA: Persephone Press.

Morash, M., and Schram, P. (2002). *The prison experience: Special issues of women in prison.* Prospect Heights, IL: Waveland Press.

Morrison, T. (ed.). (1992). *Race-ing justice, en-gendering power: Essays on Anita Hill, Clarence Thomas, and the construction of social reality.* New York: Pantheon Books.

Morton, P. (1991). *Disfigured images: The historical assault on Afro-American women.* New York: Praeger.

Moss, V. A., Pitula, C. R., Campbell, J. C., and Halstead, L. (1997). The experience of terminating an abusive relationship from an Anglo and African American perspective: A qualitative descriptive study. *Issues in Mental Health Nursing, 18*(5), 433–54.

Ms. Foundation for Women. (2003). Safety and justice for all: Examining the relationship between the women's anti-violence movement and the criminal legal system. New York: Ms. Foundation for Women.

Muhammad, M. (2009). *Scared Silent: The Mildred Muhammad Story.* Largo, MD: Strebor Books.

Mullins, L. (1997). *On our own terms: Race, class, and gender in the lives of African American women.* New York: Routledge.

Mumola, C. J. (1999). Substance abuse and treatment, state and federal prisoners (Bureau of Justice. Statistics, Trans.). Washington, DC: U.S. Department of Justice.

Municipality of Anchorage. (2000). Analysis of police action and characteristics of reported domestic violence in Anchorage, Alaska ten year study, 1989–1998. Anchorage.

Mutua, A. D. (ed.). (2006). *Progressive black masculinities.* New York: Routledge.

Nash, S. T. (2005). Through black eyes: African American women's constructions of their experiences with intimate male partner violence. *Violence Against Women, 11*(11), 1420–40.

National Center for Injury Prevention and Control. (1997). Data elements for emergency department systems, release 1.0. Atlanta, GA: Centers for Disease Control and Prevention.

National Clearinghouse for the Defense of Battered Women. (2001). *The impact of arrests and convictions on battered women.* Philadelphia. Retrieved from http://www.biscmi.org/wshh/NCDBW_%20Impact_of_Arrest.pdf.

National Coalition of Anti-violence Programs. (2004). Anti-lesbian, gay, bisexual and transgender violence in 2003 (2004 print ed.). New York: National Coalition of Anti-Violence Programs.

———. (2010). Hate violence against the lesbian, gay, bisexual, transgender and queer communities in the United States in 2009 (2010 release ed.). New York: National Coalition of Anti-violence Programs.

National Victim Center, and the Crime Victims Research and Treatment Center. (1992). Rape in America: A report to the nation. Arlington, VA.

Neubeck, K. J., and Cazenave, N. A. (2001). *Welfare racism: Playing the race card against America's poor.* New York: Routledge.

Neville, H. A., and Hamer, J. (2001). "We Make Freedom": An exploration of revolutionary black feminism. *Journal of Black Studies, 31*(4), 437–61.

Nicolaidis, C., Timmons, V., Thomas, M. J., Waters, A. S., Wahab, S., Mejia, A., and Mitchell, S. R. (2010). "You don't go telling white people nothing": African American women's perspectives on the influence of violence and race on depression and depression care. *African Journal of Public Health, 100*(8), 1470–76.

O'Brien, P. (2001). *Making it in the "free world": Women in transition from prison.* Albany: State University of New York Press.

O'Sullivan, E. A. (1978). What has happened to rape crisis centers? A look at their structure, members, and funding. *Victimology, 3*(1–2), 45–62.

O'Toole, L. L., Schiffman, J. R., and Edwards, M.L.K. (eds.). (2007). *Gender violence: Interdisciplinary perspectives* (2nd ed.). New York: NYU Press.

Oberman, M. (2003). Mothers who kill: Cross-cultural patterns in and perspectives on contemporary maternal filicide. *International Journal of Law and Psychiatry, 26*(5), 493–514.

Office of Family Support. (1996). Utah single parent employment demonstration program: It's about work. Salt Lake City Utah Department of Human Services.

Office on Violence Against Women. (2006). Safe Return Initiative: Phase I Report 2003–2005. Minnesota: Institute on Domestic Violence in the African American Community.

Oliver, K. (2010, May 19). Aiyana Jones police raid fallout: Lawyer says Detroit cops are trying to 'cover-up' child's killing. Retrieved from http://www.cbsnews.com/8301-504083_162-20005427-504083.html.

Oliver, W. (1994). *The violent social world of black men.* New York: Lexington Books.

———. (2000). Preventing domestic violence in the African American community: The rationale for popular culture interventions. *Violence Against Women, 6*(5), 533–49.

Olson, K., and Pavetti, L. (1996). Personal and family challenges to successful transition from welfare to work. Washington, DC: Urban Institute.

Oppenlander, N. (1982). Coping or copping out: police service delivery in domestic disputes. *Criminology, 20*(3–4), 449–466.

Owen, B. (1998). *In the mix: Struggle and survival in a women's prison.* Albany: State University of New York Press.

Parenti, C. (2000). *Lockdown America: Police and prisons in the age of crisis.* New York: Verso.

Parham, T. A. (2002). Understanding personality and how to measure it. In T. A. Parham (ed.), *Counseling persons of African descent: raising practitioner competence* (Multicultural Aspects of Counseling Series, Vol. 18) (38–55). Thousand Oaks, CA: Sage.

Pattillo, M. (2008). *Black on the block: the politics of race and class in the city.* Chicago: University of Chicago Press.

Pattillo-McCoy, M. (2000). *Black picket fences: privilege and peril among black middle class.* Chicago: University of Chicago Press.

Pavetti, L. (1996). *Time on welfare and welfare dependency,* House of Representatives, 104th Congress Sess.

———. (1997). Moving up, moving out or going nowhere? A study of the employment patterns of young women. Washington, DC: Urban Institute.

Pavetti, L., Olson, K., Pindus, N., and Pernas, M. (1996). Designing welfare to work programs for families facing personal or family challenges: Lessons from the field. Washington, DC: Urban Institute.

Peacock, T., George, L., Wilson, A., Bergstrom, A., and Pence, E. (2002). Community-based analysis of the U.S. legal system's interventions in domestic abuse cases involving indigenous women (National Institute of Justice, Trans.). Washington, DC: U.S. Department of Justice.

Peng, Y., and Mitchell, D. C. (2001). Dual arrest among intimate partners for family violence offenses in Connecticut. Middletown: Connecticut State Police, Crime Analysis Unit.

Petchesky, R., and Judd, K. (eds.). (1998). *Negotiating reproductive rights: women's perspectives across countries and cultures.* New York: Zed Books.

Petersilia, J. (2003). *When prisoners come home: Parole and prisoner reentry.* New York: Oxford University Press.

Peterson, C. D. (1995). Female-headed families on AFDC: who leaves welfare quickly and who doesn't. *Journal of Economic Issues, 29*(2), 619–29.

Pettiway, L. (1997). *Workin' it: Women living through drugs and crime.* Philadelphia: Temple University Press.

Pierce-Baker, C. (1998). *Surviving in silence: Black women's stories of rape.* New York: W.W. Norton.

Piven, F. F., Acker, J., Hallock, M., and Morgen, S. (eds.). (2002). *Work, welfare, and politics: Confronting poverty in the wake reform.* Eugene: University of Oregon Press.

Piven, F. F., and Cloward, R. A. (1979). *Poor people's movements: Why they succeed, how they fail.* New York: Vintage Books.

Pollack-Byrne, J. (1990). *Women, prison, and crime.* Belmont, CA: Wadsworth Publishing.

———. (2002). *Women, prison, and crime* (2nd ed.). Belmont, CA: Wadsworth Thompson Learning.

Popkin, S., Gwiasada, V., Olson, L., Rosenbaum, D., and Buro, L. (2000). *The hidden war: Crime and the tragedy of public housing in Chicago.* New Brunswick, NJ: Rutgers University Press.

Porta, D., and Diani, M. (2006). *Social movements: An introduction.* Malden, MA: Blackwell Publishing.

Portillo, E. (2010). Tiffany Wright's killing still unsolved a year later. *Charlotte Observer.* Retrieved from CharlotteObserver.com website: http://www.charlotteobserver.com/2010/09/14/1693258/tiffany-wrights-killing-still.html.

Potter, H. (2006). An argument for black feminist criminology: Understanding African American women's experience with intimate partner abuse using an integrated approach. *Feminist Criminology, 1*(2), 106–24.

———. (2007). Battered women's use of religious services and spirituality for assistance in leaving abusive relationships. *Violence Against Women, 13*(3), 262–84.

Pradia, K. S. (2010). My life saved by reprieve of 24-year sentence for crack. *CNN.* Retrieved from cnn.com website: http://www.cnn.com/2010/OPINION/12/22/pradia.sentencing.drug.reform/index.html?hpt=C2.

Radloff, L. S. (1977). The CES-D scale: A self-report depression scale for research in the general population. *Applied Psychological Measurement, 1*(3), 385–401.

Rafter, N. (1992). *Partial justice: Women, prison, and social control* (2nd ed.). New Brunswick, NJ: Transaction Publishers.

Ransby, B. (2003). *Ella Baker and the black freedom movement: A radical democratic vision.* Chapel Hill: University of North Carolina Press.

Rand M. (1997). *Violence-related injuries treated in hospital emergency departments.* Washington, DC: Office of Justice Programs.

———. (2009). *Criminal Victimization, 2008.* Washington, DC: Office of Justice Programs.

Raphael, J. (1996). *Prisoners of abuse: Domestic violence and welfare receipt.* Chicago: Taylor Institute.

Raphael, J. (2001). Domestic violence as a welfare-to-work barrier: Research and theoretical issues. In C. M. Renzetti, J. L. Edleson, and R. K. Bergen (eds.), *Sourcebook on violence against women* (443–56). Thousand Oaks, CA: Sage.

Raphael, J., and Ashley, J. (2008). Domestic sex trafficking of Chicago women and girls. Chicago: Illinois Criminal Justice Information Authority.

Raphael, J., and Shapiro, D. L. (2004). Violence in indoor and outdoor prostitution venues. *Violence Against Women, 10*(2), 126–39.

Ratner, P. A. (1993). The incidence of wife abuse and mental health status in abused wives in Edmonton, Alberta. *Canadian Journal of Public Health, 84*(4), 246–49.

Reiman, J. (1996). . . . *And the poor get prison: Economic bias in American criminal justice.* Boston: Allyn and Bacon.

Rennison, C. M., and Welchans, S. (2000). Criminal victimization 1999: Changes 1998–99 with trends 1993–99 (Bureau of Justice Statistics, Trans.). Washington, DC: U.S. Department of Justice.

Renzetti, C. M. (1992). *Violent betrayal: Partner abuse in lesbian relationships.* Newbury Park: Sage.

———. (1998). Connecting the dots: Women, public policy, and social control. In S. Miller (ed.), *Crime control and women: Feminist implications of criminal justice policy.* Thousand Oaks, CA: Sage.

———. (2001). "One strike and you're out": implications of a federal crime control policy for battered women. *Violence Against Women, 7*(6), 685–98.

Renzetti, C. M., Edleson, J. L., and Bergen, R. K. (eds.). (2001). *Sourcebook on violence against women.* Thousand Oaks, CA: Sage.

Renzetti, C. M., and Miley, C. H. (1996). *Violence in gay and lesbian domestic partnerships.* New York: Haworth Press.

Richie, B. E. (1985). Battered black women: A challenge for the Black community. *Black Scholar, 16*(2), 40–44.

———. (1996). *Compelled to crime: the gender entrapment of black battered women.* New York: Routledge.

———. (2000). A black feminist reflection on the anti-violence movement. *Signs, 25*(4), 1133–37.

———. (2003). Gender entrapment and African American women: An analysis of race, ethnicity, gender and intimate violence. In D. F. Hawkins (ed.), *Violent crime: assessing race and ethnic differences* (198–201). Cambridge, UK: Cambridge University Press.

———. (2005). A black feminist reflection on the antiviolence movement. In N. Sokoloff (ed.). *Domestic violence at the margins: Readings on race, class, gender, and culture.* Piscataway, NJ: Rutgers University Press.

———. (2006). Women and drug use: The case for a justice analysis. *Women & Criminal Justice, 17*(2/3), 137–43.

Riger, S. (1984). Vehicles for empowerment: the case of feminist movement organizations. *Prevention in Human Services, 3*(2–3), 99–117.

Riger, S., Bennett, L. W., Wasco, S. M., Schewe, P. A., Frohmann, L., Camacho, J. M., and Campbell, R. (2002). *Evaluating services for survivors of domestic violence and sexual assault* (1st ed.). Thousand Oaks, CA: Sage.

Riger, S., and Krieglstein, M. (2000). The impact of welfare reform on men's violence against women. *American Journal of Community Psychology, 28*(5), 631–47.

Riger, S., Raja, S., and Camacho, J. M. (2002). The radiating impact of intimate partner violence on women's lives. *Journal of Interpersonal Violence, 17*(2), 184–205.

Ritchie, A. J. (2006). Law enforcement violence against women of color. In INCITE!: Women of Color Against Violence (ed.), *Color of violence: The INCITE! anthology*. Cambridge, MA: South End Press.

Rivera, J. (1997). Domestic violence against Latinas by Latino males: An analysis of race, national origin, and gender differentials. In A. K. Wing (ed.), *Critical race feminism: A reader*. New York: NYU Press.

Roberts, D. (1998). *Killing the black body: Race, reproduction, and the meaning of liberty*. London: Vintage.

———. (2002). *Shattered bonds: the color of child welfare*. New York: Basic Books.

———. (2006). Feminism, race, and adoption policy. In INCITE!: Women of Color Against Violence (ed.), *Color of violence: The INCITE! anthology*. Cambridge, MA: South End Press.

Robinson, A. (2002). "There's a stranger in this house": African American lesbians and domestic violence. *Women and Therapy, 25*(3–4), 125–32.

Robinson, A. L., and Chandek, M. S. (2000a). The domestic violence arrest decision: Examining demographic, attitudinal, and situational variables. *Crime and Delinquency, 46*(1), 18–37.

———. (2000b). Differential police response to black battered women. *Women— Criminal Justice, 12*(2–3), 29–62.

Robinson, L. (2003). *I will survive: the African American guide to healing from sexual assault and abuse*. Emeryville: Seal.

Robinson, L., and Boyd, J. (2003). *I will survive: The African American guide to healing from sexual assault and abuse*. Emeryville, CA: Seal Press.

Robinson, T. L. (2000). Making the hurt go away: Psychological and spiritual healing for African American women survivors of childhood incest. *Journal of Multicultural Counseling and Development, 28*(3), 160–76.

Robnett, B. (2000). *How long? How long?: African American women in the struggle for civil rights*. New York: Oxford University Press.

Rodríguez, D. (2006). *Forced passages: Imprisoned radical intellectuals and the U.S. prison regime*. Minneapolis: University of Minnesota Press.

Rodriguez, M. (2008). CHA plan for transformation pose challenge for Bronzeville. *Medill Reports*. Retrieved from Medill Reports Chicago website: http://news. medill.northwestern.edu/chicago/news.aspx?id=84621.

Rodriguez, M., Valentine, J. M., Son, J. B., and Muhammad, M. (2009). Intimate partner violence and barriers to mental health care for ethnically diverse populations of women. *Trauma, Violence, and Abuse, 10*(4), 358–74.

Romano, R. C., and Raiford, L. (eds.). (2006). *The civil rights movement in American memory*. Athens: University of Georgia Press.

Römkens, R. (2006). Protecting prosecution: exploring the powers of law in an intervention program for domestic violence. *Violence Against Women, 12*(2), 160–86.

Rosen, C. J. (1986). The excuse of self-defense: correcting a historical accident on behalf of battered women who kill. *American University Law Review, 36*(1), 11–56.

Ross, L. (1998). *Inventing the savage: the social construction of Native American criminality*. Austin: University of Texas Press.

Rothenberg, P. (1998). *Race, class, and gender in the United States: An integrated study* (4th ed.). New York: Worth Publishers.

Russell, D.E.H. (1990). *Rape in marriage*. Indianapolis: Indiana University Press.

———. (ed.). (1993). *Making violence sexy: Feminist views on pornography*. New York: Teachers College Press.

Russo, A. (2002). If not now, when? Contemporary feminist movements to end violence against women. In A. Russo (ed.), *Taking back our lives: A call to action for the feminist movement* (3–30). New York: Routledge.

Russo, N. F., Denious, J. E., Keita, G. P., and Koss, M. P. (1997). Intimate violence and black women's health. *Women's Health, 3*(3–4), 315–48.

Ryan, C., and Gamson, W. A. (2006). The art of reframing political debates. *Contexts, 5*(1), 13–18.

Sallmann, J. (2010). Living with stigma: Women's experiences of prostitution and substance abuse. *Affilia, 25*(2), 146–59.

Sasson, T. (1995). *Crime talk: how citizens construct a social problem*. Hawthorne, NY: Aldine De Gruyter.

Saunders, D. G. (1986). When battered women use violence: Husband abuse or self defense. *Violence and Victims, 1*(1), 47–60.

———. (1995). The tendency to arrest victims of domestic violence: A preliminary analysis of officer characteristics. *Journal of Interpersonal Violence, 10*(2), 147–58.

———. (1998). Wife abuse, husband abuse, or mutual combat? In K. Yllö and M. Bograd (eds.), *Feminist perspectives on wife abuse* (90–113). Beverly Hills, CA: Sage.

Schechter, S. (1982). *Women and male violence: the visions and struggles of the battered women's movement*. Boston: South End Press.

———. (1988). Building bridges between activists, professionals, and research. In K. Yllö and M. Bograd (eds.), *Feminist perspectives on wife abuse* (299–312). Thousand Oaks, CA: Sage.

———. (1998). *Race, class, women, and the state*. Buffalo, NY: Black Rose Books.

Schmitt, B. (2010). Fieger: New autopsy suggests cover-up, shows Aiyana shot in head. *Detroit Free Press*. Retrieved from Detroit Free Press website: http://www.freep.com/article/20100602/NEWS01/6020302/Fieger-New-autopsy-suggests-cover-up-shows-Aiyana-shot-head.

Schneider, E. M. (2002). *Battered woman and feminist lawmaking*. New Haven, CT: Yale University Press.

Schornstein, S. L. (1997). *Domestic violence and health care: What every professional needs to know*. Thousand Oaks, CA: Sage.

Schram, P., and Koons-Witt, B. (eds.). (2004). *Gendered (in)justice: Theory and practice in feminist criminology*. Long Grove, IL: Waveland Press.

Schram, S. F. (1995). *Words of welfare: The poverty of social science and the social science of poverty*. Minneapolis: University of Minnesota Press.

Schram, S. F., Soss, J., and Fording, R. C. (eds.). (2003). *Race and the politics of welfare reform*. Ann Arbor: University of Michigan Press.

Schur, E. (1984). *Labeling women deviant: gender, stigma, and social control*. Philadelphia: Temple University Press.

Scott, K. Y. (1991). *The habit of surviving: Black women's strategies for life*. New Brunswick, NJ: Rutgers University Press.

Seccombe, K., James, D., and Battle Walters, K. (1998). "They think you ain't much of nothing": The social construction of the welfare mother. *Journal of Marriage and Family, 60*(4), 849–65.

Sekaquaptewa, D., and Thompson, M. (2003). Solo status, stereotype threat, and performance expectancies: Their effects on women's performance. *Journal of Experimental Social Psychology, 39*(1), 68–74.

Sens, R. (1999). Between a rock and a hard place: domestic violence in communities of color. *Colorlines, 2*(1).

Sharma, A. (2001). Healing the wounds of domestic abuse: Improving the effectiveness of feminist therapeutic interventions with immigrant and racially visible women who have been abused. *Violence Against Women, 7*(12), 1405–28.

Shaylor, C. (2003). "It's like living in a black hole": Women of color and solitary confinement in the prison industrial complex. In N. E. Dowd and M. S. Jacobs (eds.), *Feminist legal theory: An anti-essentialist reader* (316–25). New York: NYU Press.

Sherman, L. W., and Berk, R. A. (1984a). The Minneapolis domestic violence experiment. *Police Foundation Reports* (Vol. 1, pp. 1–8). Washington, DC: Police Foundation.

———. (1984b). The specific deterrent effects of arrest for domestic violence. *American Sociological Review, 49*(2), 261–72.

Sherman, L. W., and Cohn, E. G. (1989). The impact of research on legal policy: the Minneapolis domestic violence experiment. *Law and Society Review, 23*(1), 117–44.

Shichor, D. (1995). *Punishment for profit: Private prisons/public concerns.* Thousand Oaks, CA: Sage.

Shichor, D., and Sechrest, D. (eds.). (1996). *Three strikes and you're out: Vengeance as public policy.* Thousand Oaks, CA: Sage.

Short, J. (1997). *Poverty, ethnicity, and violent crime.* Boulder, CO: Westview Press.

Silliman, J., and Bhattacharjee, A. (eds.). (2002). *Policing the national body: Sex, race, and criminalization.* Cambridge, MA: South End Press.

Silliman, J., Fried, M., Ross, L., and Gutierrez, E. (2004). *Undivided rights: Women of color organize for reproductive justice.* Cambridge, MA: South End Press.

Sklar, K. K. (2000). *Women's rights emerges within the anti-slavery movement, 1830–1870: A short history with documents (The Bedford Series in History and Culture).* New York: Bedford/St. Martin's.

Slote, K. Y., Cuthbert, C., Mesh, C. J., Driggers, M. G., Bancroft, L., and Silverman, J. G. (2005). Battered women speak out: participatory human rights documentation as a model for research and activism in the United States. *Violence Against Women, 11*(11), 1367–95.

Smart, C. (1995). *Law, crime, and sexuality: Essays in feminism.* Thousand Oaks, CA: Sage.

Smith, A. M. (2007). *Welfare reform and sexual regulation.* New York: Cambridge University Press.

Smith, B. (1989). A press of our own kitchen table: Women of color press. *Frontiers: A Journal of Women's Studies, 10*(3), 11–13.

Smith, B., and Stone, L. H. (1989). Rags, riches, and bootstraps: beliefs about the causes of wealth and poverty. *Sociological Quarterly, 30*(1), 93–107.

Smith, K. (2011). *Poster Child: The Kemba Smith Story.* Kemba Smith. www.kembasmith.com

Social Justice Editors. (2000). "Overview: Critical Resistance to the Prison-Industrial Complex." *Social Justice, 27*(3), 1–17.

Sokoloff, N. J. (ed.). (2005). *Domestic violence at the margins: Readings on race, class, gender, and culture.* Piscataway, NJ: Rutgers University Press.

Sokoloff, N. J., and Dupont, I. (2005). Domestic violence at the intersections of race, class, and gender: Challenges and contributions to understanding violence against marginalized women in diverse communities. *Violence Against Women, 11*(1), 38–64.

Sommerville, D. M. (2005). Rape. In D. Hine (ed.), *Black women in America: An historical encyclopedia* (Vol. 3 set, pp. 21–28). New York: Oxford University Press.

Spalter-Roth, R., Burr, B., Hartmann, H., and Shaw, L. (1995). Welfare that works: The working lives of AFDC recipients. Washington, DC: Institute for Women's Policy Research.

Spector, J. (ed.). (2006). *Prostitution and pornography: Philosophical debate around the sex industry.* Stanford, CA: Stanford University Press.

Springer, K. (1999). *Still lifting, still climbing: African American women's activism.* New York: NYU Press.

———. (2002). Third wave black feminism? *Signs, 27*(4), 1059–82.

———. (2005). *Living for the revolution: Black feminist organization 1968–1980.* Durham, NC: Duke University Press.

Stabile, C. A. (2006). *White victims, black villains: Gender, race, and crime news in US culture.* New York: Routledge.

Staples, R. (1999). Domestic violence in black American families: The role of stress. In R. Staples (ed.), *The black family: Essays and studies* (259–63). Belmont, CA: Wadsworth.

Stark, E. (1995). Re-presenting woman battering: From battered woman syndrome to coercive control. *Albany Law Review, 58*(4), 973–1026.

———. (2007). *Coercive control: How men entrap women in personal life.* New York: Oxford University Press.

Stark, E., and Flitcraft, A. (1988). Violence among intimates: An epidemiological review. In V.B.V. Hasselt, R. L. Morrison, A. S. Bellack, and M. Hersen (eds.), *Handbook of family violence.* New York: Plenum.

Stark, E., and Flitcraft, A. (1996). *Women at risk: domestic violence and women's health.* Thousand Oaks, CA: Sage.

Steele, C. M. (1997). A threat in the air: How stereotypes shape intellectual identity and performance. *American Psychologist, 52*(6), 613–29.

Steele, C. M., and Aronson, J. (1995). Stereotype threat and the intellectual test performance of African Americans. *Journal of Personality and Social Psychology, 69*(5), 797–811.

Steffans, K. (2010). Open Letter: Karrine Steffens speaks out about recent physical abuse. *VIBE.* Retrieved from Vibe.com website: http://www.vibe.com/posts/open-letter-karrine-steffans-confesses-recent-physical-abuse.

Stein, N. (1999). *Classrooms and courtrooms: Facing sexual harassment in K-12 schools.* New York: Teachers College Press.

Stephens, T. (2010). Black woman beaten with hammer, dragged behind truck in Texas by White Man. *Rolling Out.* Retrieved from Rollingout.com website: http://rollingout.com/news-politics/black-woman-beaten-with-hammer-dragged-behind-truck-in-texas-by-white-man/

Stets, J. E., and Straus, M. A. (1990). Gender differences in reporting marital violence and its medical and psychological consequences. In M. A. Straus and R. J. Gelles (eds.), *Physical violence in American families: Risk factors and adaptations to violence in 8,145 families* (151–66). New Brunswick, NJ: Transaction.

Stone, R. (2004). *No secret no lies: How black families can heal from sexual abuse.* New York: Harlem Moon.

Strang, H., and Braithwaite, J. (eds.). (2002). *Restorative justice and family violence.* Cambridge, UK: Cambridge University Press.

Struckman-Johnson, C., and Struckman-Johnson, D. (2006). A comparison of sexual coercion experiences reported by men and women in prison. *Journal of Interpersonal Violence, 21*(12), 1591–1615.

Sudbury, J. (1998). *'Other kinds of dreams': Black women's organisations and the politics of transformation.* New York: Routledge.

———. (2002). Celling black bodies: Black women in the global prison industrial complex. *Feminist Review, 70,* 57–74.

———. (ed.). (2005). *Global lockdown: Race, gender, and the prison-industrial complex.* New York: Routledge.

Sudbury, J., and Okazawa-Rey, M. (eds.). (2009). *Activist scholarship: antiracism, feminism, and social change.* Boulder, CO: Paradigm Publishers.

Sullivan, C. M., and Rumptz, M. H. (1994). Adjustment and needs of African-American women who utilized a domestic violence shelter. *Violence and Victims, 9*(3), 275–86.

Sutherland, C. A., Sullivan, C. M., and Bybee, D. K. (2001). Effects of intimate partner violence versus poverty on women's health. *Violence Against Women, 7*(10), 1122–43.

Swan, S. C., and Snow, D. L. (2002). A typology of women's use of violence in intimate relationships. *Violence Against Women, 8*(3), 286–319.

———. (2006). The development of a theory of women's use of violence in intimate relationships. *Violence Against Women, 12*(11), 1026–45.

Swartz, J. A., O'Brien, P., and Lurigio, A. J. (eds.). (2006). *Drugs, women, and justice: Roles of the criminal justice system for drug-affected women.* New York: Haworth Press.

Swartz, K. (2009). Army reservist beaten in front of child. *Atlanta Journal-Constitution.* Retrieved from AJC.com website: http://www.ajc.com/news/clayton/army-reservist-beaten-in-138917.html,

Swickard, J., and Damron, G. (2011). Aiyana Stanley Jones: 1 year later, questions linger in deaths of 2 kids. *Detroit Free Press.* Retrieved from Detroit Free Press website: http://www.freep.com/article/20110501/NEWS01/105010525/Aiyana-Stanley-Jones-1-year-later-questions-linger-deaths-2-kids?odyssey=tab%7Ctopne ws%7Ctext%7CFRONTPAGE.

Taft, C. T., O'Farrell, T. J, Torres, S. E., Panuzio, J., Monson, C. M., Murphy, M., and Murphy, C. M. (2006). Examining the correlates of psychological aggression among a community sample of couples. *Journal of Family Psychology, 20*(4), 581–88.

Taylor, J. Y. (2000). Sisters of the yam: African American women's healing and self recovery from intimate male partner violence. *Issues in Mental Health Nursing*, 21(5), 515–31.

———. (2005). No resting place: African American women at the crossroads of violence. *Violence Against Women*, 11(12), 1473–89.

Terry, D. (2011). Eavesdropping laws mean that turning on an audio recorder could send you to prison. *New York Times*. Retrieved from *New York Times* website: http://www.nytimes.com/2011/01/23/us/23cnceavesdropping.html?_r=2.

Tester, G. (2008). An intersectional analysis of sexual harassment in housing. *Gender and Society*, 22(3), 349–66.

The Allstate Foundation Domestic Violence Program, and National Network to End Domestic Violence Fund. (2006). Allstate Foundation's National Poll on Domestic Violence Executive Summary.

The Black Girls (ed.). (1995). *Black girl talk*. Ontario, Canada: Sister Vision.

The Sentencing Project. (2006). Featured stories: Kemba Smith, from http://www.sentencingproject.org/detail/feature.cfm?feature_id=1&id=135.

Thomas, A. J., Witherspoon, K. M., and Speight, S. L. (2004). Toward the development of the stereotypic roles for black women scale. *Journal of Black Psychology*, 30(3), 426–42.

Thompson, A. C. (2008). *Releasing prisoners, redeeming communities: Reentry, race, and politics*. New York: New York University Press.

Thompson, B. (2002). Multiracial feminism: recasting the chronology of second wave feminism. *Feminist Studies*, 28(2), 337–60.

Tjaden, P., and Thoennes, N. (1998). Prevalence, incidence, and consequences of violence against women: Findings from the national violence against women survey, Research in brief (National Institute of Justice, Trans.). Washington, DC: U.S Department of Justice.

———. (2000a). Extent, nature, and consequences of intimate partner violence: Findings from the national violence against women survey. Washington, DC: National Institute of Justice and The Centers for Disease Control and Prevention.

———. (2000b). Full report on the prevalence, incidence and consequences of intimate partner violence against women: Findings from the national violence against women survey. Washington, DC: National Institute of Justice and The Centers for Disease Control and Prevention.

———. (2006). Extent, nature, and consequences of rape victimization: Findings from the national violence against women survey. Washington, DC: National Institute of Justice and the Centers for Disease Control and Prevention.

Tolman, R. M., and Rosen, D. (2001). Domestic violence in the lives of women receiving welfare. *Violence Against Women*, 7(2), 141–58.

Tonry, M. (1994a). Racial politics, racial disparities, and the war on crime. *Crime and Delinquency, 40*(4), 475–94.

————. (1994b). *Sentencing matters: studies in crime and public policy.* New York: Oxford University Press.

Touraine, A. (2004). On the frontier of social movements. *Current Sociology, 52*(4), 717–25.

Townsend Gilkes, C. (2001). *If it wasn't for the women . . . : Black women's experience and womanist culture in church and community.* Maryknoll, NY: Orbis.

Travis, J. (2005). *But they all come back: Facing the challenges of prisoner reentry.* Washington, DC: Urban Institute Press.

Travis, J., and Waul, M. (2003). *Prisoners once removed: The impact of incarceration and reentry on children, families, and communities.* Washington, DC: Urban Institute Press.

Troup-Leasure, K., and Snyder, H. (2005). Statutory rape known to law enforcement (Office of Juvenile Justice and Delinquency Prevention, Trans.). Washington, DC: U.S. Department of Justice.

Truman, J. L. (2011). *Criminal Victimization, 2010.* Washington, DC: Office of Justice Programs.

Truman, J. L., and Rand, M. (2010). *Criminal Victimization, 2009.* Washington, DC: Office of Justice Programs.

Twine, F., and Warren, J. (eds.). (2000). *Racing research, researching race: Methodological dilemmas in critical race studies.* New York: NYU Press.

U.S. Government Accountability Office. (2008a). *Military personnel: The DOD and Coast Guard Academies have taken steps to address incidents of sexual harassment and assault, but greater federal oversight is needed.* (GAO-08-296). Washington, DC.

————. (2008b). *Military personnel: Preliminary observations on DOD's and the Coast Guard's sexual assault prevention and response programs.* Washington, DC.

Venkatesh, S. (2000). *American project: The rise and fall of a modern ghetto.* Cambridge, MA: Harvard University Press.

Venkatesh, S., Celimli, I., Miller, D., Murphy, A., and Turner, B. (2004). Chicago public housing transformation: A research paper. New York: Center for Urban Research and Policy, Columbia University.

Violence and Victimization Division of the National Institute of Justice. (2001). Broadening our understanding of violence among racial, ethnic and cultural minorities: workshop summary, from http://www.nij.gov/topics/crime/violence-against-women/workshops/minorities.htm#111201.

Vivian, D., and Langhinrichsen-Rohling, J. (1994). Are bi-directional violent couples mutually victimized? A gender-sensitive comparison. *Violence* and *Victims, 9*(2), 107–24.

Walker, L. E. (1979). *The battered woman.* New York: Harper and Row.

Walker, S., Spohn, C., and DeLone, M. (2000). *The color of justice: Race, ethnicity, and crime in America*. Belmont, CA: Wadsworth/Thomson Learning.

Waltermaurer, E., Watson, C., and McNutt, L. (2006). Black women's health: The effects of perceived racism and intimate partner violence. *Violence Against Women, 12*(12), 1214–22.

Wanless, M. (1996). Mandatory arrest: A step towards eradicating domestic violence, but is it enough? *University of Illinois Law Review, 2*, 533–87.

Ward Doran, M. B., and Roberts, D. (2002). Welfare reform and families in the child welfare system. *University of Maryland Law Review, 61*, 386–89.

Warikoo, N., Meyer, Z., and Hunt, A. (2010). Police, family look for answers in girl's death in Detroit. *Detroit Free Press*. Retrieved from Detroit Free Press website: http://www.freep.com/article/20100517/NEWS05/5170350/Police-family-look-answers-girl-s-death-Detroit.

Warshaw, C. (1993). Limitations of the medical model in the care of battered women. In P. B. Bart and E. G. Moran (eds.), *Violence against women: The bloody footprints* (134–46). Thousand Oaks, CA: Sage.

Washington, P. A. (2001). Disclosure patterns of black female sexual assault survivors. *Violence Against Women, 7*(11), 1254–83.

Websdale, N. (2001). *Policing the poor: from slave plantation to public housing*. Boston, MA: Northeastern University Press.

Welch, K. (2007). Black criminal stereotypes and racial profiling. *Journal of Contemporary Criminal Justice, 23*(3), 276–88.

Weldon, S. L. (2002). *Protest, policy, and the problem of violence against women: A cross-national comparison*. Pittsburgh: University of Pittsburgh Press.

Wesley, J. K. (2006). Considering the context of women's violence: Gender, lived experiences, and cumulative victimization. *Feminist Criminology, 1*(4), 303–28.

West, C. M. (1998). Leaving a second closet: Outing partner violence in same-sex couples. In J. L. Jasinski and L. M. Williams (eds.), *Partner violence: A comprehensive review of 20 years of research* (163–183). Thousand Oaks, CA: Sage.

———. (ed.). (2002a). *Violence in the lives of black women: Battered, black, and blue.* Binghamton, NY: Haworth.

———. (2002b). Introduction. In C. M. West (ed.), *Violence in the lives of black women* (1–4). Binghamton, NY: Haworth.

———. (2003). "Feminism is a Black thing"? Feminist contributions to Black family life. In L. A. Daniels (ed.), *The state of Black America: The Black family building on its resilience* (13–27). New York: National Urban League.

———. (2004). Black women and intimate partner violence: New directions for research. *Journal of Interpersonal Violence, 19*(12), 1487–93.

———. (2006). Sexual violence in the lives of African American women: Risk, response, and resilience. Harrisburg, PA: National Resource Center on Domestic Violence and the National Online Resource Center on Violence Against Women.

West, C. M., and Rose, S. (2000). Dating aggression among low-income African American youth: An examination of gender differences and antagonistic beliefs. *Violence Against Women, 6*(5), 470–94.

West, T. (1999). *Wounds of the spirit: Black women, violence, and resistance ethics.* New York: NYU Press.

White, A. M. (1999). Talking feminist, talking black: Micromobilization process in a collective protest against rape. *Gender and Society, 13*(1), 77–100.

White, E. (ed.). (1990). *Black women's health book: Speaking for ourselves.* Seattle, WA: Seal Press.

———. (1995). *Chain, chain, change: For black women in abusive relationships* (2nd ed.). Seattle, WA: Seal Press.

———. (2001). *Dark continent of our bodies: Black feminism and the politics of respectability.* Philadelphia: Temple University Press.

Whyte, W. F. (1993). *Street corner society: the social structure of an Italian slum* (4th ed.). Chicago: University of Chicago Press.

Williams, O. J., and Tubbs, C. Y. (2002). Community insights on domestic violence among African Americans: Conversations about domestic violence and other issues affecting their community. St. Paul, MN: Institute on Domestic Violence in the African American Community.

Williams, R. Y. (2004). *The politics of public housing: Black women's struggles against urban inequality.* New York: Oxford University Press.

Wilson, K., Vercella, R., Brems, C., Benning, D., and Refro, D. (1992). Levels of learned helplessness in abused women. *Women and Therapy, 13*(4), 53–67.

Wilson, M. (1993). *Crossing the boundary: Black women survive incest.* Seattle, WA: Seal Press.

Wing, A. K. (ed.). (1997). *Critical race feminism: A reader.* New York: NYU Press.

Wolfer, T. A. (2000). Coping with chronic community violence: Varieties and implications of women's efforts. *Victims and Violence, 15*(3), 283–301.

Worcester, N. (2002). Women's use of force: Complexities and challenges of taking the issue seriously. *Violence Against Women, 8*(11), 1390–1415.

Worden, R. E., and Pollitz, A. A. (1984). Police arrests in domestic disturbances: A further look. *Law and Society Review, 18*(1), 105–19.

Worrall, A. (1990). *Offending women: Female lawbreakers and the criminal justice system.* New York: Routledge.

Wright, E. A. (2000). Not a black and white issue: For battered and abused Latinas and black women dialing 911 may be risky business. In N. Worcester and M. H. Whatley (eds.), *Women's health: Readings on social, economic, and political issues* (549–52). Dubuque, IA: Kendall/Hunt Publishing.

Wright, P. (2003). *Prison nation: The warehousing of America's poor.* New York: Routledge.

WSB-TV. (2009). Police: Man beat woman at Cracker Barrel. Retrieved from Wsbtv.com website: http://www.wsbtv.com/news/20926383/detail.html.

Wyatt, G. E. (1992). The sociocultural context of African American and white American women's rape. *Journal of Social Issues, 48*(1), 77–91.

———. (1997). *Stolen women: Reclaiming our sexuality. Taking back our lives.* New York: Wiley.

Wyatt, G. E., Axelrod, J., Chin, D., Carmona, J. V., and Loeb, T. B. (2000). Examining patterns of vulnerability to domestic violence among African American women. *Violence Against Women, 6*(5), 495–514.

Yllö, K. (1988). Political and methodological debates in wife abuse research. In K. Yllö amd M. Bograd (eds.), *Feminist perspectives on wife abuse.* Thousand Oaks, CA: Sage.

Zerai, A., and Zakia, S. (2006). A black feminist analysis of responses to war, racism, and repression. *Critical Sociology 32*(2–3), 503–26.

Zierler, S., Cummingham, W. E., Andersen, R., Shapiro, M. F., Nakazono, T., Morton, S., . . . Bozzette, S. A. (2000). Violence victimization after HIV infection in a US probability sample of adult patients in primary care. *American Journal of Public Health, 90*(2), 208–15.

Zorza, J., and Woods, L. (1994). *Mandatory arrest: problems and possibilities.* New York: National Center on Women and Family Law.

Zweig, J. M., and Burt, M. R. (2006). Predicting case outcomes and women's perceptions of the legal system's response to domestic violence and sexual assault: Does interaction between community agencies matter? *Criminal Justice Policy Review, 17*(2), 202–33.

Index

Welfare policy, 56–58; coercion
through, 113–14; male violence
related to, 115
Welfare Reform and Sexual Regulation
(Smith, A. M.), 113
Welfare state, 103–4
Wesley, Jennifer, 60–61
West, C. M., 31
West, Traci, 154
White, Evelyn, 59, 152
*White Victims, Black Villains:
Gender, Race and Crime News
in US Culture* (Stabile),
62

White women: Black women compared
with, 125–26; intimate partner assault
homicides of, 26
Williams-Bolar, Kelley, 100–101
Wilson, Derrica, 126
Wilson, Melba, 153–54
Witnesses, 39, 41, 45
Woman of Color Institute, 1–2, 156
Women of Color Caucus, 149–50
Women's liberation movement, 68, 72;
everywoman analysis and, 110–11. *See
also* Black feminist activism
Wright, Mitchell, 30–31
Wright, Tiffany, 30–31

About the Author

BETH E. RICHIE is Director of the Institute for Research on Race and Public Policy, Professor of African American Studies and Criminology, Law, and Justice at the University of Illinois at Chicago, and author of *Compelled to Crime: The Gender Entrapment of Battered Black Women*.